THE
HISTORY OF
IRAN

THE HISTORY OF IRAN

Elton L. Daniel

The Greenwood Histories of the Modern Nations
Frank W. Thackeray and John E. Findling, Series Editors

Greenwood Press
Westport, Connecticut • London

Library of Congress Cataloging-in-Publication Data

Daniel, Elton L.
　　The history of Iran / Elton L. Daniel.
　　　　p.　cm.—(The Greenwood histories of the modern nations, ISSN 1096–2905)
　　　Includes bibliographical references and index.
　　　ISBN 0–313–30731–8 (alk. paper)
　　　　1. Iran—History.　2. Iran—History—20th century.　I. Title.　II. Series.
　　DS272.D36　2001
　　　955—dc21　　　　00–033132

British Library Cataloguing in Publication Data is available.

Library of Congress Catalog Card Number: 00–033132
ISBN: 0–313–30731–8
ISSN: 1096–2905

First published in 2001

Greenwood Press, 88 Post Road West, Westport, CT 06881
An imprint of Greenwood Publishing Group, Inc.
www.greenwood.com

Printed in the United States of America

The paper used in this book complies with the
Permanent Paper Standard issued by the National
Information Standards Organization (Z39.48–1984).

10 9 8 7 6 5 4 3 2 1

Contents

Series Foreword

The Greenwood Histories of the Modern Nations series is intended to provide students and interested laypeople with up-to-date, concise and analytical histories of many of the nations of the contemporary world. Not since the 1960s has there been a systematic attempt to publish a series of national histories, and, as series editors, we believe that this series will prove to be a valuable contribution to our understanding of other countries in our increasingly interdependent world.

Over thirty years ago, at the end of the 1960s, the Cold War was an accepted reality of global politics, the process of decolonization was still in progress, the idea of a unified Europe with a single currency was unheard of, the United States was mired in a war in Vietnam, and the economic boom of Asia was still years in the future. Richard Nixon was president of the United States, Mao Tse-tung (not yet Mao Zedong) ruled China, Leonid Brezhnev guided the Soviet Union and Harold Wilson was prime minister of the United Kingdom. Authoritarian dictators still ruled most of Latin America, the Middle East was reeling in the wake of the Six-Day War and Mohammad-Reza Shah Pahlavi was at the height of his power in Iran. Clearly, the past thirty years have been witness to a great deal of historical change, and it is to this change that this series is primarily addressed.

With the help of a distinguished advisory board, we have selected nations whose political, economic and social affairs mark them as among the most important in the waning years of the twentieth century, and for each nation we have found an author who is recognized as a specialist in the history of that nation. These authors have worked most cooperatively with us and with Greenwood Press to produce volumes that reflect current research on their nation and that are interesting and informative to their prospective readers.

The importance of a series such as this cannot be underestimated. As a superpower whose influence is felt all over the world, the United States can claim a "special" relationship with almost every other nation. Yet many Americans know very little about the histories of the nations with which the United States relates. How did they get to be the way they are? What kind of political systems have evolved there? What kind of influence do they have in their own region? What are the dominant political, religious and cultural forces that move their leaders? These and many other questions are answered in the volumes of this series.

The authors who have contributed to this series have written comprehensive histories of their nations, dating back to prehistoric time in some cases. Each of them, however, has devoted a significant portion of the book to events of the past thirty years, because the modern era has contributed the most to contemporary issues that have an impact on U.S. policy. Authors have made an effort to be as up-to-date as possible so that readers can benefit from the most recent scholarship and a narrative that includes very recent events.

In addition to the historical narrative, each volume in this series contains an introductory overview of the country's geography, political institutions, economic structure and cultural attributes. This is designed to give readers a picture of the nation as it exists in the contemporary world. Each volume also contains additional chapters that add interesting and useful detail to the historical narrative. One chapter is a thorough chronology of important historical events, making it easy for readers to follow the flow of a particular nation's history. Another chapter features biological sketches of the nation's most important figures in order to humanize some of the individuals who have contributed to the historical development of their nation. Each volume also contains a comprehensive bibliography, so that those readers whose interest has been sparked may find out more about the nation and its history. Finally, there is a carefully prepared topic and person index.

Readers of these volumes will find them fascinating to read and useful in understanding the contemporary world and the nations that comprise it. As series editors, it is our hope that this series will contribute to a heightened sense of global understanding as we enter a new century.

Frank W. Thackeray and John E. Findling
Indiana University Southeast

Preface

Iran has almost three thousand years of history, and it is home to one of the world's richest and most complex cultures. To attempt to treat such a subject adequately in one volume, or even many volumes, is not an easy task. Virtually all fields of Iranian history suffer from being under-researched. Most lack adequate primary source material, because it is either nonexistent or inaccessible. They are also marked by many controversies and academic debates. Each has special problems in the way names and technical terms are represented in English translation or transliteration. There are many uncertainties in terms of chronology and obtaining precise dates for events. In numerous cases, it is possible to say *what* happened but only to guess at *why* because there is so little concrete information about the motivation and intent of the actors.

That said, the purpose of this book is to provide general readers with a concise, readable, and up-to-date survey of the country's history based on the expertise of the contemporary historian. It is largely a political history, with a concentration on the modern period.

No attempt has been made to employ a rigorous and systematic transliteration of names and terms. When names and technical terms are transliterated, a simple scheme without any special diacritics is used; the letters *ayn, hamzeh,* etc., are not indicated. In deference to a common tendency among contemporary Iranians when representing names in Latin script, "ou" has been used for the long vowel "u"; no distinction is made between the short and long "a." Personal names are usually transliterated unless there is a well-established English equivalent (one exception: Mosaddeq instead of Mossadegh or one of the many other variations of this name). The convention of using the abbreviation "b." for "son of" in certain names from the Islamic period has been followed. Otherwise, names of religious sects, dynasties, geographical sites, and so on, are given in what is judged to be the most commonly recognized Anglicized form.

Readers should be aware that in some periods, especially the 19th century, individuals used honorific titles, which frequently changed, as well as personal names. Thus the famous reformer Amir Kabir might also be referred to as Mirza Taqi Khan, Amir Nezam, and so on. Such variations are sometimes mentioned here, but the best-known form is the one usually given. Days in the traditional Islamic calendar began at sunset; thus one could correspond to either of two Gregorian equivalents depending on the hour. Difficulties are also frequently encountered in determining the year some event occurred, or authorities may disagree on the most likely chronology—that applies even in the case of fairly recent events. It is typically a matter of personal choice as to which to use; unless there is some special and substantial significance to the date, variations or disputes about them are not mentioned.

It would never have been possible to write this book without drawing on the work of many other scholars; I could not cite them all, but they have my thanks. I have also benefited from the help, direct and indirect, of many friends and colleagues over the years. Foremost among them is the teacher who first introduced me to Iranian studies, Hafez Farmayan. I learned much of use in preparing this volume from working and conversing at various times with Ehsan Yarshater, Manouchehr Kasheff, Ahmad Ashraf, Mohsen Ashtiany, David Morgan, Julie Meisami, John Perry, and Parvaneh Pourshariati. They are not, however, to be blamed in any way for the blemishes of this book or the opinions it expresses; as the traditional saying has it, the responsibility for this story rests with the one who tells it.

Timeline of Historical Events

ca. 4000 B.C.	Bronze Age settlements (Sialk, Hasanlu, Hissar)
2700–1600 B.C.	Elamite Kingdom
ca. 728	Deioces founds Median Kingdom
ca. 550 B.C.	Cyrus defeats Astyages
522–486 B.C.	Darius the Great
331 B.C.	Alexander the Great defeats Darius III at Gaugamela
ca. 238 B.C.	Revolt of Arsaces, the Parthian king
A.D. 224	Ardashir defeats and kills Artabanus V
260	Shapur I captures Roman emperor Valerian
528	Khosrow I crushes the Mazdakites
ca. 570	Birth of the Prophet Mohammad
608–22	The "Great War" between Sasanians and Byzantium
637	Battle of Qadesiyya
642	Battle of Nehavand; Iran under Islamic rule
651	Murder of last Sasanian king

747	Abbasid Revolution in Khorasan
819–1005	Samanid dynasty in eastern Iran
945	Buyids occupy Baghdad
1040	Battle of Dandanqan
1055	Seljuks capture Baghdad
1092	Assassination of Nezam-al-Molk
1219	Beginning of Mongol invasion
1258	Hulegu sacks Baghdad; kills caliph
1295	Ghazan Khan converts to Islam
1380–93	Conquests of Timur (Tamerlane)
1501	Shah Esmail founds Safavid kingdom
1514	Ottomans defeat Safavids at Chaldiran
1587–1629	Shah Abbas the Great
1722	Afghan invasion and siege of Isfahan
1736–47	Nader Shah
1750–79	Karim Khan Zand
1797	Establishment of Qajar dynasty
1804–13	First Russo-Persian War
1826–28	Second Russo-Persian War
1813	Treaty of Golestan
1828	Treaty of Turkmanchai
1833	Death of Crown Prince Abbas Mirza
1848	Appointment of Amir Kabir as prime minister
1851	Dar-al-Fonoun college founded in Tehran
1852	Murder of Amir Kabir
1856–57	Anglo-Persian War
1872	The Reuter Concession; cancelled in 1873
1891	The Tobacco Protest
1896	Assassination of Naser-al-Din Shah

1901	D'Arcy Concession for petroleum and gas
1905	Beginning of Consitutional Revolution
1907	Anglo-Russian Convention on Iran
1908	Mohammad-Ali Shah declares martial law and suspends First Majles
1909	Formation of Anglo-Persian Oil Company
1911	Russian ultimatum and intervention; collapse of Second Majles
1919	Abortive Anglo-Persian Agreement
1921	Coup d'etat by Reza Khan and Zia-al-Din Tabatabai
1925	Constituent Assembly votes to establish monarchy under Reza Shah
1936	Veiling of women outlawed
1938	Completion of Trans-Iranian Railway
1941	Allied occupation; abdication of Reza Shah
1951	Mosaddeq becomes Prime Minister
1953	Mosaddeq overthrown in coup d'etat
1955	Iran joins Baghdad Pact
1959	Defense agreement with the United States
1962	Inauguration of the "White Revolution"
1963	Religious protests; Ayatollah Khomeini exiled
1967	Coronation of Mohammad-Reza Shah
1971	Celebration at Persepolis of 2,500 years of monarchy in Iran; Tehran agreement on oil prices
1973	Mohammad-Reza Shah announces steep increase in price of oil
1978	Riots and demonstrations lead to "Black Friday" massacre
1979	Mohammad-Reza Shah leaves Iran; Khomeini returns; beginning of hostage crisis; Constitution of the Islamic Republic of Iran adopted

1980	Bani Sadr elected president; beginning of Iran-Iraq War
1981	American Embassy hostages released; Khomeini removes Bani Sadr from office
1983	Tudeh (Communist) Party banned; consolidation of clerical power completed
1988	Khomeini accepts cease-fire in Iran-Iraq War
1989	Condemnation of Salman Rushdie; ouster of Ayatollah Montazari; death of Khomeini
1993	Re-election of Hashemi Rafsanjani as president
1997	Election of Mohammad Khatami as president
1999	Student demonstrations and mass protests in Tehran
2000	Elections for new Majles result in victory for "reformist" slate

1

The Land and People of Iran

To the average American, the name Iran probably conjures up an image of a remote and upstart country inhabited by a people whose religious fanaticism is matched only by the intensity of their disdain for the United States and its values, who speak an obscure tongue called Farsi, and whose precise ethnic identity is blurred and not clearly distinguished from that of their Arab neighbors. A mention of Persia, however, is more likely to evoke ideas of an ancient and exotic land with a rich historical and cultural tradition of fabled rulers, sumptuous carpets, luxuriant gardens, and mellifluous poetry. While Iran and Persia, and especially Iranian and Persian, are not synonyms, it is important to realize that the terms do in fact overlap and are commonly used to refer to the same land and people. Given the stereotypes associated with each term, and the fact that even experts disagree on precisely how they should be used, it is best to begin by trying to explain what is meant by Iran as the subject of this book.

The name Iran was used as early as the third century B.C. by a ruler who described his empire as Iranshahr and himself as "king of kings of Iran." The word itself was derived from even older terms that referred more to a people than a land—Arya and Airya, that is, the ethnonym of a people calling themselves the Aryans (the meaning is uncertain, but

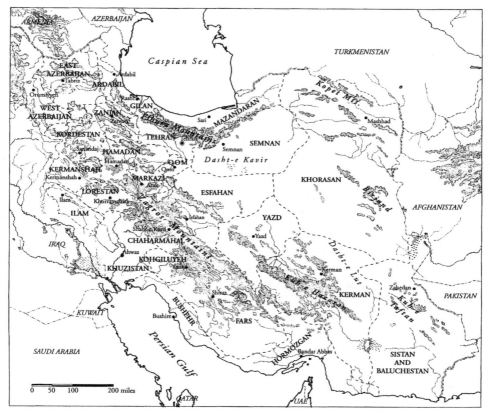

Modern Iran: Provinces and Provincial Capitals
(note that number and boundaries of provinces tend to change frequently)

perhaps something like the pure, the noble, or those of good birth). As will be discussed in detail in the following chapter, the Aryans were a branch of the Indo-European peoples who appeared around 2000 B.C. and gradually migrated into India and southwest Asia, in the latter case forming tribes speaking similar languages now classed as Iranian. In its original form, Iran could thus be understood to mean "the land of the Aryans," a nebulous and shifting domain ranging at times from the Tigris to the Oxus and beyond.

To further complicate matters, the most historically significant of the Irano-Aryan tribes appeared in a region of the Zagros Mountains which had been known to earlier Semitic peoples as Parahshe, perhaps meaning "the land of horses." The tribe probably took its name from this place. The classical Greeks knew these people as Persians and referred to both their homeland and the empire they built up as Persia. Persia remained the most common way for Europeans to refer to this country, and Persian to designate its people and the language they spoke, right down to the 20th century.

In 1935, however, the proudly nationalistic ruler of the country, Reza Shah Pahlavi, insisted that foreign governments use the name Iran instead of Persia, going so far as to order the post office not to deliver letters marked otherwise. Since then the name Iran has gained currency in English and other languages. In this sense, however, it is simply the name of a relatively young nation-state that has been dramatically transformed over the course of the last century and a half. Its direct historical roots go back, at most, to the 16th century. Its internationally recognized territorial boundaries were defined in various treaties of the 19th and early 20th centuries and are still disputed in some areas (notably the border with Iraq and certain islands in the Persian Gulf). The current character and government of this state were shaped barely twenty years ago as the result of its "Islamic Revolution."

In other words, Iran once had the broad meaning of "the land of the Aryans" but has come to be used in a more restricted sense for a specific nation-state and the geographic area it occupies. Persia, on the other hand, originally had a narrow meaning as the homeland of one Aryan tribal group, the Persians, but acquired a wider meaning as it has been applied to all the lands ruled by Persians or dominated by Persian culture. Both terms thus have historical, geographic, political, ethnic, and cultural implications, which vary considerably from one historical period to another, and readers must be aware of the precise context in which they are being used to understand them properly. A strong argument can be made that in English usage "Iran" and "Iranian" should be reserved for reference to the larger groups of Aryan lands and peoples, and Persia for the empire or country. For the modern nation, however, Iran has probably become too widely accepted to be discarded. It can also be a useful term in that it must be remembered that an "Iranian," that is, an inhabitant of that country, is not necessarily a Persian speaker. In a linguistic context, however, Iranian should always be used only to refer to the broad group of Indo-European languages in that category. Finally, for the name of the national language, Persian is certainly preferable to Farsi, a needlessly affected usage which is as out of place as insisting on Deutsch for German or Français for French.

For simplicity and convenience, then, Iran will be used in this book to indicate the modern nation-state, the various governments that preceded it, and the geographical area they have occupied. Iranian may apply either to citizens of this nation-state (Persian and non-Persian speaking) or to various ancient peoples who inhabited the same general area (although, again, many were not actually ethnic Iranians).

Some consideration may now be given to what is meant by geographic Iran and the ways in which geographic factors have influenced the development of human society there.

GEOGRAPHY

East of Mt. Ararat and south of the Aras River (i.e., about 45° E longitude and 38° N latitude), the great Alpine-Himalayan mountain belt stretching across Eurasia divides into a wedge of two mountain ranges. One of them, the Elburz, extends eastward for some 300 miles around the southern rim of the Caspian Sea. This range is continued considerably further east, toward the Hindu Kush Mountains, by a disconnected series of other chains, including the Kopet Dagh, Binalud, and Hazar Masjid. The Elburz Mountains rise dramatically, like a wall, from the Caspian depression, which is below sea level, to heights of 10,000 feet and more. The greatest of its peaks is the volcanic cone of Mt. Damavand (elev. 18,955 ft.), a mountain that figures about as prominently in the culture of Iran as Mt. Fuji does in that of Japan. The other range, the Zagros, consists of a broad swath of parallel mountain ridges and valleys running toward the southeast for at least 600 miles. With related chains, they extend from Lake Urmia in the northwest to the Straits of Hormuz in the southeast. From there, the Makran Mountains go on to the borders of Pakistan. A third, less well-defined, line of mountains, notably the

Kuh-e Sorkh, the Qaen and Birjand massifs, and the Kuh-e Taftan, more or less connects the eastern extremities of the Elburz and Zagros. These three lines of mountains thus make up a triangle measuring about 1,000 miles from west to east and north to south and about 1,500 miles from northwest to southeast. The mountains, which are a product of relatively recent and quite violent geological activity, are usually steep and jagged. It is not at all uncommon to see exposed layers of sedimentary rock that have been thrust almost vertical. The whole region remains very active seismologically, so that earthquakes are both common and destructive.

The territory encompassed by this triangle of mountains is generally known as the Iranian plateau, a vast upland region having a mean elevation of over 3,000 feet. At its core are two great desert basins, the Dasht-e Kavir and the Dasht-e Lut, the desiccated remains of what were once lakebeds. The northernmost of these deserts, the Dasht-e Kavir, is elongated in an east-west direction. Its terrain is varied, but the most distinctive feature, for which it is named, is the *kavir* or "salt desert." A kavir is marked by a brittle and highly saline crust over a layer of viscous mud, probably formed by the salt leaching what little moisture there is from the already arid atmosphere. The largest kavir is about 200 miles in length and 40 miles in width. Absolutely nothing lives in the kavirs. The extremely hot, windy Dasht-e Lut, which extends toward the southeast, is drier and sandier than the Dasht-e Kavir, but it also has a large, shallow salt lake (about 100 by 15 miles in extent) at its floor. These two deserts form some of the most inhospitable real estate on earth; as the famous Russian traveler Nikolai Khanykov once observed, the Gobi Desert seems fertile by comparison.

In addition to these great mountain ranges and desert basins, two adjacent plains fall within the boundaries of contemporary Iran. One is the coastal strip between the Elburz Mountains and the Caspian, an area that has abundant rainfall caught by the northern slopes of the Elburz. Due to the low elevation of these coastal plains, the climate is also quite mild, even subtropical in some places. The other, in the extreme southwest, is Khuzistan, essentially an extension of the Mesopotamian plains between the Zagros and the headwaters of the Persian Gulf. Relatively well watered, it has one major river, the Karun.

Two-thirds of Iran consists of little more than wasteland. Difficulties such as rugged terrain, shallow soil, or inadequate drainage contribute to this, but the most significant limiting factor is the lack of water. A desert area can be defined as one that receives less than six inches (150 mm) of precipitation annually; land that receives less than four inches

(100 mm) cannot support plant life and is essentially sterile. The import of this for Iran is abundantly clear when one considers that half the country receives less than the required minimum of four inches of precipitation, and only one-third receives more than eight inches (200 mm). Moreover, much of the precipitation falls in the wrong season (as snow in winter) or in inaccessible mountainous areas. It is also concentrated in the northern and western portions of the country.

Despite this lack of water, there is a remarkable diversity of flora and fauna in Iran thanks to the wide variations in climate, altitude, soil conditions, terrain, and hydrography. Over 10,000 species of plant life have been identified, a good many of them unique to the country. They range from various kinds of grasses, borage, thorn cushions, and ferns to oaks, elms, juniper, and tamarisk. Recent descriptions of animal species in Iran have catalogued 125 mammals, 491 birds, 155 freshwater fish, and well over 100 reptiles and amphibians; the number of insect species is unknown but thought to be quite large. People are often surprised to learn that animals such as lions, tigers, panthers, wild boar, and even crocodiles and flamingos are all indigenous to Iran.

Harsh in other ways, nature has been relatively kind to Iran in terms of mineral resources. There are significant deposits of iron, copper, lead, zinc, and other metals, some of which have been exploited since ancient times. Most important for contemporary Iran, of course, are its large reserves of petroleum, natural gas, and coal, resources that have provided the means for the country's dramatic economic transformation in the 20th century. The exact amount of these resources available today is uncertain, with the government claiming recoverable reserves of over 90 billion barrels of oil and almost 14 trillion cubic meters of natural gas. Exploitation of these resources is not only a major component of the current gross national product, it also accounts for more than 80 percent of the country's exports and most of the government's revenues.

REGIONS AND CITIES

To a visitor, one of the most striking impressions of Iran is the sheer size of the country, a feeling enhanced by the ruggedness of the land and the difficulties of transportation. In its contemporary political borders, Iran has an area of 628,000 square miles (1,648,000 sq. km), making it the sixteenth largest country in the world. This is an area larger than France, Spain, Germany, and Italy combined; larger than Alaska, Iran would occupy much of the United States east of the Mississippi.

The Zagros and Elburz have relatively few passes, and those are typically at high altitudes, so that they present formidable barriers to human movement. The desert regions are not only largely uninhabited, they have been virtually impassable until modern times. Unwary travelers in the kavirs can actually break through the salt crust to be swept away and drown in the briny slime below. Transportation by water is impractical, since there is only one navigable river in the entire country, the Karun, and that only for about one hundred miles. By traditional means, in the days before mechanized transport, it would take almost two months to travel from northern Iran to the Persian Gulf and as much as six months to cross the plateau from east to west. Technical, economic, and political as well as geographic factors retarded the development of transportation systems, and even after extensive recent improvements, access to many areas is not easy. Although Spain, another plateau country, is one-third the size of Iran, it has twice as many kilometers of rails and roads (three times as many paved roads). France has a rail system approximately five times bigger and a road system ten times as large. A good impression of the difficulty involved in traveling even today in many parts of Iran can be gleaned through films such as Abbas Kiarostami's *Life and Nothing More*, which depicts the travails of a man trying to go by car from Tehran to one of the Caspian provincial towns.

Under such conditions, political unity, centralized authority, and cultural homogeneity have historically been very difficult to sustain in Iran. Regionalism has been a very pronounced factor in the history of the area. Perhaps the most significant and persistent division has been between the western areas, which have tended to interact in complex ways with the civilizations of Mesopotamia, and those of the northeast, which face Central Asia and constitute the main frontier areas. Apart from the development of related but different West Iranian and East Iranian traditions, a number of distinct subregional or provincial areas have appeared, in addition to the Caspian and Mesopotamian areas mentioned above.

At the northwest corner of the Iranian triangle is the province of Azerbaijan (contiguous with, but not to be confused with, the new Republic of Azerbaijan to the north). Relatively fertile, and marked by many large plains and valleys, it has been both one of the main means of access to the plateau area and fairly densely populated. This area has a particularly strong sense of regional identity and has often produced separatist movements or demands for autonomous government.

The Caspian provinces of Gilan, Mazandaran, and Gorgan are quite different from the rest of the country. There are many dense forests in the Elburz, and along the coast it is possible to grow a variety of crops including rice, tea, citrus fruits, and cotton. The Caspian is also a rich source of fish and caviar. Until quite recently, these areas were remote, with only one difficult mountain pass giving access to or from the plateau. Not surprisingly, these areas are densely populated and differ from the plateau areas in virtually every respect, from dialect to housing styles.

Khorasan, in the northeast, has numerous streams and oases, which made it a major agricultural center. The mountain ranges there, though sometimes quite high, are widely separated and easy to traverse. It was thus one of the main avenues for the influx of new peoples into Iran, and the center of its defense against such incursions. Both literally and figuratively it represents the Iranian frontier.

Fars (Persia proper), in the southwest, was the home of the ancient Persians and the center of their empire. It has perhaps the most pleasant climate and attractive scenery in Iran. Although its political and economic importance receded over the centuries, it has remained a particularly strong center of Persian culture and tradition.

The southeastern areas, Kerman, Sistan, Makran, and Baluchistan, tend to be the remotest, poorest, least developed, and most sparsely populated areas. In earlier centuries, however, Sistan was the center of a significant regional culture. Extremely hot and subject to infamous hurricane-force summer winds, it has an important river, the Helmand, which makes agriculture possible, as well as its marshy, freshwater lake, Hamun.

Khuzistan, an extension of the Mesopotamian plains, was the site of some of the oldest cultures in the area. It has an ethnically diverse population, including substantial numbers of Arabs. It is, of course, an extremely important region today because of its vast petroleum reserves.

The configuration of urban areas in Iran has changed constantly according to political and economic circumstances. Whatever city happens to become the seat of government tends to be the dominant metropolis. Tehran, once little more than a village, became the capital at the end of the 18th century and has since grown into the largest city by far, with an estimated population in 1997 of over 8 million. Tabriz, a former capital and center of the province of Azerbaijan, has often been second only to Tehran in importance. Historically, most of the significant cities have flourished in the belt of territory surrounding the central deserts and astride either the main east-west or north-south corridors of trade. These include the architectural jewels of Isfahan and Yazd in central Iran; the fabled city of nightingales and poets, Shiraz, in Fars; Kerman in the southeast; Mashhad, famous for its religious shrine, in Khorasan; and Hamadan in the central Zagros. Two other remote but important provincial centers are Rasht, in Gilan, and Ahvaz, in Khuzistan.

ECONOMY

Geographical constraints have also had important consequences for the economy and society of Iran. Where rainfall is adequate or marginal in Iran, there are many fertile valleys and grasslands suitable for grazing animals. Since the natural vegetation tends to be sparse, however, it is difficult for such animals to remain in one place for any length of time. Thus nomadic pastoralism was one of the first and most persistent human economic activities to flourish in this area. This has often been of the "vertical" variety, with people and animals moving from lowlands in wintertime to highlands in summer. The animals raised by the pastoralists have provided not only food but material for crafts such as the making of carpets, felt, and tents. The pastoralists have typically been organized into large tribal confederations capable of controlling the vast territories needed for maintaining their herds.

The tribes have been a powerful social and political factor throughout Iranian history. The skills necessary for herding animals, hunting and chasing off predators, directing migrations, disciplining tribesmen, and protecting lands and animals from rivals can easily be adapted and directed toward military purposes as well. It has typically been the tribes which produced the soldiers and rulers of the country and which provided the power base for most of its dynasties. They also resisted payment of taxes and disrupted security in many parts of the country. Even at the beginning of the 20th century, Turkoman tribes were known to abduct Iranian peasants to sell as slaves, and other tribesmen would waylay travelers and strip them of their possessions. Among the most prominent tribal groups of recent times have been the various Turkoman tribes in the north (Afshar, Qajar, Yomut, Goklen, etc.), the Bakhtiari, Mamasani, and Qashqai tribes in Fars, and the various Kurds, Lurs, and Baluchis in other areas.

Once established, governments have needed to continue to cultivate the support of friendly tribal groups and have tried to control hostile tribes by combat, deportation, or forcible settlement. At the beginning of the 20th century, approximately one-fourth of the population were tribal peoples, and they were a potent force in Iranian affairs. With the advent of mechanized armies in the 1930s, however, there were systematic efforts to break the power of the tribes and to coerce the tribal population into a sedentary way of life. These have been largely successful, and the tribes are no longer so significant a force in either the Iranian economy or society. Less than 5 percent of the population now consists of nomadic pastoralists.

The aridity of the Iranian plateau retarded its agricultural development in comparison to adjacent regions such as Mesopotamia, which had great rivers to draw upon for a supply of water. Eventually, at some uncertain date, there was a technological breakthrough that made it possible to farm crops outside the few oases, streams, and other places with sufficient rainfall for agriculture. This was the development of underground canals known as *qanat*s. The qanat system took advantage of the natural slope of the plateau basins. A well would be dug in the foothills to reach a water source, perhaps fed by runoff from snow melting and seeping underground. Then a sequence of wells connected by underground channels would be constructed to lead to a distribution system in an area suitable for cultivation, where it could support the needs of one or more villages. The slope, of course, had to be controlled carefully to prevent erosion, and the wells and shafts needed to be lined and kept under constant maintenance to prevent them from collapsing. This ingenious system had many advantages in addition to increasing the amount of arable land: Since the channels were underground, loss from evaporation was minimized. Gravity provided the means of moving the water, so no additional mechanical energy was required. The numerous well shafts along the way kept the length of the tricky underground canal short and facilitated repairs of each segment. (This also gives the qanats their distinctive appearance—from the air the wells and excavated dirt around them resemble lines of small lunar craters.) Built up over the centuries, the qanat system eventually became immense. It has been estimated that the total length of the qanat system today, counting both shafts and canals, is in excess of 300 million meters (about the distance from the earth to the moon!), which gives some idea of the tremendous investment in money and manpower it represents.

The type of agriculture that developed around the qanat system had many distinctive features, which have been the subject of a classic study by the historian A. K. S. Lambton. The agricultural enterprise required five components: land, water, seed, animal labor for plowing, and human labor. Ownership of each element entitled one to a corresponding share of the harvest. Absentee landlords of the ruling and urban classes owned vast estates of land. They similarly tended to finance and own the qanats that supplied the water and might provide the seed for crops as well. The land was usually worked in small, disconnected plots, each of which had relatively modest yields. The multitude of peasants required to farm these plots rarely owned any land themselves; neither did they usually own the draft animals, which were hired from others. The social consequences of this system were brutal. Peasants received only a small share of the already modest yield of the few plots they worked, while the bulk of the production of large numbers of plots was concentrated in the hands of the landlords, the socioeconomic elite often referred to as the "thousand families" who literally owned and controlled the country.

Life for the Iranian peasants, who made up the vast majority of the population, has thus been incredibly harsh and virtually unchanged for centuries. They were scattered in numerous remote and often isolated small villages, usually numbering between 500 and 1,000 inhabitants. Illiterate, living barely above subsistence level, they had to endure severities of climate, natural disasters, vermin and insects, wild animals, problems with the water supply, nomadic predators, avaricious landlords, and ruthless tax collectors. The peasants have eked out their meager existence, almost invisible to history, but it should not be forgotten that their efforts were absolutely essential to life and civilization on the Iranian plateau.

In contemporary Iran, the importance of agriculture and the peasantry has been steadily eroding, though not so dramatically as that of the pastoralists. The new Republican government has made agricultural revival one of the pillars of its economic policy, partly out of necessity and partly because rural society is more conducive to the traditional social values it prefers (and probably also because religious leaders have been major landowners). Almost half the Iranian population still lives in rural areas, and living conditions for villagers have generally improved. At the same time, much progress has been made both in terms of land reform and in modernizing and mechanizing farming techniques. The amount of land under cultivation is near its practical limit (25 percent is arable, with about 15 percent able to be used at any one time). Agriculture makes up at least 25 percent of the gross national product, and Iran is among the world's leading producers of crops such as pistachios, apricots, dates, raisins, citrus crops (limes, oranges, tangerines), and other fruits.

There are, however, some ominous aspects to this facet of contemporary Iranian life. Agricultural development is not keeping pace with the overall population growth. The country is today able to meet only 75 percent of its domestic food needs. The qanat system has also been increasingly neglected in recent years, and there are fewer and fewer people with the technical knowledge of how to build and maintain the qanats. This is because abundant energy and mechanical devices have made it feasible to sink wells to tap the deep water table and pump water for large-scale irrigation. The long-term environmental consequences of this will almost certainly be adverse.

Finally, some consideration must be given to the role of cities and urban life in Iran. Although undeniably important, this is easily exaggerated, particularly for premodern periods. Indeed, as recently as 1940, barely 20 percent of the population lived in cities (places with a population over 5,000, of which there were less than 200). In many ways, the development of cities was even more affected by geography than was rural society, since cities not only need a substantial agricultural hinterland to support them, but also require their own large and reliable sources of water. In the case of Iran, this means that they must be concentrated in narrow zones along the eastern and western sides of the Zagros or the northern and southern sides of the Elburz. This also made it difficult to take advantage of the terrain for defensive purposes; cities usually had to be located in open areas and were vulnerable to attack. In older times, they were thus usually walled in and the gates shut at night, giving them the character of a fortress.

Much has been made of Iran's strategic position as a geographic link between the Near East, China, and India, and thus of its potential for trade and commerce. In fact, it has usually been easier to go around the Iranian plateau than over it. Isolation from, not integration into, routes of world trade has been a frequent historical reality for Iran. Thus, long-distance trade has been of limited and sporadic importance as an economic base for Iranian cities. Rather, most of its cities were really little more than large villages that served as regional markets and centers for local craft industries. Truly large cities have usually developed because they were political capitals or military and administrative centers. This, in addition to their geographic vulnerability, made them inherently unstable—few Iranian cities have had long, continuous periods of importance.

Over the last fifty years, the nature of the urban economy and society in Iran has changed dramatically. The majority of the population now lives in cities; there are many more large cities; and the urban population is younger, more literate, and more affluent than ever before. The industrial and service segments of the economy have now eclipsed the agricultural sector. All of these changes are primarily due to one factor of overwhelming importance, the development of petroleum resources and the wealth it has produced.

DEMOGRAPHY

In Iran today, language and religion as well as nationality and other factors are important aspects of identity. While the inhabitants of the country may be called Iranians in the sense of being political citizens of Iran, they are by no means all *ethnically* Iranian. In terms of language, there are three major groupings: Iranian, Turkic, and Semitic.

Linguistic Iranians are those who speak one of the languages or dialects belonging to that branch of the Indo-European languages. The most important of these is Persian, understood by most of the population today and the mother tongue of just over half of the people. It is a grammatically simple but beautiful literary language, rich in nuance and meaning. Modern Persian developed in Central Asia in the 10th century, mixing Arabic vocabulary and script with elements of Pahlavi or Middle Persian, itself a derivative of Old Persian, the language of the first imperial dynasty in Iran. The various dialects of Kurdish make up a second and very important component of this language group. The Kurds, concentrated in the central Zagros region and comprising slightly under 10 percent of the population, have a very strong sense of ethnic identity and have often struggled for autonomy. Baluchi is the most widespread language in southwestern Iran; Luri is spoken by several tribal groups in southern Iran. As another Indo-European speaking people, the small Armenian population in Iran might also be included in this category. It should be noted that there are numerous minor dialects to be found in parts of Iran, as well as distinctive differences in speech patterns between rural and urban populations, and so on.

Turkic peoples began arriving on the borders of the Iranian plateau by the 6th century and entering Iran in significant numbers by the 10th century. Large numbers moved there before and during the period of the Mongol invasions. Mostly nomadic tribesmen, they were attracted to pasturelands in northern Iran, especially Azerbaijan; one powerful tribe, the Qashqais, nomadized in Fars. At least 27 percent of the population speaks some variety of Turkish.

Although Arabs conquered Iran in the 7th century and supposedly settled in large numbers in parts of western Iran, Khorasan, and Central Asia, relatively few native Arabic speakers are now found there. Most are concentrated in the province of Khuzistan, and number about half a million. A few Assyrians also live in Iran, notably in the area around Lake Urmia.

The religious configuration of the population is also complex. At first glance it appears quite homogeneous, with 99 percent of the people being Muslims. However, they are split between two major, and at times hostile, sects of Islam, the "Twelver" Shi'ites (about 89 percent) and the Sunnites (10 percent). The remaining tiny minority is divided into Zoroastrians, Christians, Jews, and Bahais (the first and last being particularly interesting as religions that actually developed in Iran rather than emanating from abroad). There is little predictable correspondence between the religious and linguistic elements of identity: A Persian speaker might well be a Jew or Zoroastrian rather than a Muslim; a Kurd might be a Shi'ite or a Sunni. At times, an individual's religious affiliation might be more important than language; at others, the linguistic identity predominates. A recurrent challenge for rulers and governments in Iran has been the problem of submerging these diverse and multiple sources of identity into a larger sense of common nationality.

As indicated earlier, population trends in Iran have shifted in unprecedented ways. At the beginning of the 19th century, the population was barely 6 million. In earlier times, in periods of exceptional political circumstances, it was undoubtedly higher, but 10 or 11 million was probably the practical limit. The population was overwhelmingly rural, with less than 20 percent of the people living in cities and the rest concentrated in the villages or among the nomadic tribes. Illiteracy and poverty were widespread. By 1976, the population had grown to over 33 million, with about half the people living in cities. In just the last twenty years, that population has almost doubled, to well over 60 million, and is now concentrated in the cities (about 60 percent of the total). At the same time, it has become younger (almost half the people are under fifteen years of age) and much more literate (from 15 percent in 1956 to 72 percent in 1991). The consequences of such dramatic change are difficult to anticipate. Among other things, it is likely that the population has now outstripped the capacity of the land to feed it, even if maximum production were attained. A great challenge of the coming century will thus undoubtedly be the problem of providing for this population, particularly as the assets of a petroleum economy are depleted.

POLITICAL SYSTEM

For over 2,000 years, monarchy and dynastic rule were the norm of political life in Iran. By one count, there have been forty-six such dynasties and over 400 kings. These included, of course, rulers who were good and bad, strong and weak, famous and obscure. Some were of non-Iranian origin or came in as foreign conquerors. They have been known by many titles—shah, *shahanshah, padishah, malek,* amir, or sultan. Still, they were all monarchs, and they all adhered to (or were judged against) a sophisticated theory of kingship and just rule that drew on a deeply ingrained sense of obedience and deference to authority.

That long monarchical tradition was interrupted, and quite probably ended, in 1979 with the proclamation of an "Islamic Republic" and the drafting of a new constitution. As much a statement of ideology as a framework for government, the constitution ballooned into a long and complicated document dealing with everything from foreign policy to the calendar. In general, it sought to completely Islamize the state in accordance with the ideas of the architect of the revolution, the Ayatollah Rouhollah Khomeini. Apart from incorporating his idea of a supreme religious leader, it created multiple and ill-defined centers of power. It preserved an elected parliament, the Majles, which had been established under an earlier constitution, and it provided for the popular election of a president who would appoint a prime minister and cabinet to be approved by the Majles. However, it also established a "Council of Guardians" comprised of twelve appointees, six religious scholars and six lawyers, with the power to certify all candidates for election, interpret the constitution, and veto any legislation by the Majles deemed not to be in conformity with Islam. It further stated that "absolute sovereignty belongs to God" and sought to abolish all distinctions between religious and secular life. Practically speaking, ultimate authority was vested in the Faqih, a supreme religious jurist, who would be "courageous, resourceful, capable, and recognized and accepted as leader by the majority of the people," and/or a "Leadership Council" of three to five high-ranking religious authorities. The Faqih would command the military and appoint the highest judicial officials, and could confirm or dismiss a president. Technically, the Faqih and the Leadership Council were to be elected by an "Assembly of Experts"; the office, of course, immediately went to Khomeini himself.

At first, it thus appeared, as the sociologist Said Amir Arjomand put it, that this new political order merely substituted "the turban for the crown," with a religious autocrat, the Ayatollah Khomeini, in place of a king. In time, however, the various institutions envisaged by the constitution began to take on lives of their own, and the ambiguities of the constitution virtually guaranteed conflicts between them. After Khomeini's death in 1989, the Assembly of Experts somewhat hesitantly elected a former president, but not very eminent jurist, Ali Khamenei, as the new Faqih. Shortly thereafter the constitution was amended to abolish the office of prime minister and transfer his powers to the president, thus in theory strengthening that office. Finally, yet another center of power, the Expediency Council, was established to try to mediate the conflicts that were constantly cropping up among the Majles, the president, and the Council of Guardians.

Since Khomeini's death, a new political dynamic has been evolving between the Faqih, who lays claim to Khomeini's authority but lacks his charisma, and a president with increased powers and the mantle of popular support. The tension has been palpable since the elections of 1997, in which the clear candidate of the religious establishment for the presidency was rejected in favor of a perceived moderate and outsider, Ayatollah Mohammad Khatami. Although the formal introduction of political parties was long delayed, opposing political groups and factions clearly abound and are currently locked in struggle with each other in the Majles, the offices of government, and the streets. The outcome of this process is far from clear but intriguing to contemplate. The controversies have undeniably reinvigorated political life in Iran and at least created the potential for transforming an autocratic or oligarchic theocracy into a viable if eccentric form of democracy.

CULTURAL CHARACTERISTICS

Generalizations about "national characteristics" tend to be of limited value or even dangerously misleading. This is particularly true in the case of a culture as subtle and complex as that of Iran, which has for centuries left outside observers feeling, often simultaneously, attracted and repelled, dazzled and disappointed, impressed and annoyed. Travelers to Iran in the 19th century, for example, frequently remarked that the people there were remarkably hospitable, courteous, kind, talkative, intelligent, and agreeable, and yet went on to assert that they were also vain, insincere, condescending, deceitful, corrupt, self-absorbed, and primarily interested in personal gain. Frederick Shoberl, for example, in 1822 praised the Iranians as "polite, complimentary, and obliging" but complained about their "voluptuousness" and "odious" moral character. How could the same culture inspire such contradictory reactions?

As often as not, simple misunderstanding contributed to opinions about both the virtues and faults of Iranians. One of the most perceptive observers of the country, the English scholar Edward G. Browne, gave a classic example of such an error. A Belgian mining engineer told him that the Iranians did not have "a single admirable characteristic," for "when they desire to support an assertion with an oath they say, 'Bi-jan-i-'aziz-i khudat,' 'By thy precious life,' or 'Bi-marg-i-shuma,' 'By your death,' that is, May *you* die if I speak untruly." As Browne realized, this was not the point; it was a common rhetorical expression really based on the self-deprecating assumption that one's own life was of little consequence compared to that of a friend or associate.[1]

Some basic understanding of the Iranian cultural context is thus necessary for comprehending much of its history. There are several such aspects of Iranian culture that have been so widely and persistently noted by historians and anthropologists that they do deserve some comment here. Perhaps the most succinct and convincing statement of the seemingly contradictory elements at work in the Iranian national character was given by a professor of Persian at the University of Edinburgh, L. P. Elwell-Sutton:

> An extreme individualism contrasts with a readiness to accept authority. A tendency to zealotry and fanaticism, especially in religious matters, struggles with negativism and passivity, with acceptance of fate and concealment of one's real feelings. Iranians have an intense interest in the new and exotic, coupled with a marked capacity for learning and absorbing; but they are also sceptics, with a strong sense of humor and a distrust of pretension and pomposity. They are famed for their politeness, hospitality, and *ta'arof* (courtly phrases); they can also be obstinate, sensitive to criticism, and touchy where their dignity is concerned. They can be hard-working and efficient when they choose, and their readiness to delay and procrastinate is proverbial. There is a deep, underlying patriotism coupled with a suspicion of alien influences, but this does not prevent some from succumbing to the blandishments of foreign interests.[2]

To the extent that these observations are true, some would seem to have very deep historical roots, while others are of more recent vintage.

First of all, Iran, like many traditional societies around the world, has tended to operate on the basis of personal relationships among individuals, not on the basis of impersonal and impartial institutions. The primary building block of such relations, and one of fundamental importance in Iranian life, is the family. In the 5th century B.C., that always shrewd Greek cultural historian Herodotus noted that Iranians had several wives and numerous concubines and that "next to prowess in arms, it is regarded as the greatest proof of manly excellence to be the father of many sons." At least among elite families, that sentiment—as well as what it implies about the authority of fathers and the place of women in society—has remained remarkably constant. Thanks to the practice of polygamy and multiple marriages, powerful families were usually large families, and large families were often powerful ones. Probably the best known example of the extremes to which this could reach is the case of the early 19th century ruler Fath-Ali Shah, who had about a thousand wives or concubines and no less than 260 children.

But the Iranian family need not be just a father, his many wives, and numerous children. It can also include household servants and retainers, near and distant blood relatives, and, through judicious marriage alliances with other families, various in-laws. Beyond that there would be, of course, numerous contacts and relations with friends and associates (the *dowreh* or "circle" with whom one regularly meets). As much as possible, Iranians have preferred to move within this network of personal acquaintances rather than deal with strangers. Even today, it would not be unusual, for example, for an Iranian to hire a relative or personal acquaintance for a job, even though he could easily employ a better and cheaper, but unknown, competitor. Such social networking, which Iranians call *partibazi*, is regarded as essential for obtaining services, getting into choice schools, finding a job, and so on. Such family and personal ties may not be as easy to detect in political and historical affairs but are certainly important factors. To give an example, one might note the recent case of the great nationalist prime minister of the early 1950s, Mohammad Mosaddeq, who will figure prominently in these pages. His father was a member of a large, powerful, and affluent family of bureaucrats, the Ashtianis, who produced several other important officials and political figures. His mother was the sister of one of the richest and most influential princes of the royal family that ruled Iran in the 19th and early 20th centuries. He himself married into the family of a prominent religious leader in Tehran. The political position Mosaddeq attained certainly owed much to his own talent and ability, but the significance of his family connections in securing it should not be under-estimated.

Herodotus further asserted that the relative rank of two Iranians meeting in the street could be determined simply by observing the greetings they exchanged. Although the specific customs may have changed, that principle has remained largely true right down to the present day. In a society so strongly influenced by personal relations, social status is of tremendous importance. A whole range of behavior and discourse in Iran is in fact guided by considerations of the relative social positions of individuals in any interaction. Consequently, determining status and acting accordingly is a matter of great concern: This helps explain why the Victorian traveler Ella Sykes felt that an "ordinary Persian's idea of conversation was to inquire about the price of one's possessions and one's private matters like income, age, social position, etc.," or why, today, one might be startled by a taxi driver's blunt questions about what one does for a living and how much one makes. The term most often used to describe the type of interaction that is expected to take place between individuals of equal or unequal status is *taarof*, literally, politeness or knowing what to do in a given situation. It may involve anything from elaborate exchanges of greetings and inquiries about one's health to extravagant offers of presents (which may or may not be intended to be taken at face value). Iranians are acutely aware of the subtext of such interactions; foreigners usually are not and often blunder into such infamous indiscretions as admiring a carpet during a visit to the home of an acquaintance—and accepting it when the host immediately offers it as a "gift" (and adding insult to injury by not offering something of equal value in exchange). The ritualized exchange of gifts, incidentally, has been one of the most typical ways of cementing ties between social superiors and subordinates.

Herodotus also claimed that no nation so readily adopted foreign customs as Persia, and that Persians thought nothing more disgraceful than telling a lie. There was certainly something to these observations in his time, but they would probably be suspect today. Iranians have indeed shown a remarkable ability to assimilate aspects of foreign cultures, and "fighting the lie" was a key component of their ancient religion. Historical experience, however, has had its impact on these sentiments. As individuals, communities, and a nation, Iranians may well feel beleaguered. In addition to the difficulties of wresting a living from a harsh environment and dealing with socioeconomic exploitation and abuse, Iranians have also been subjected to repeated outside attacks and invasions over the centuries. All of this has reinforced a feeling of being under siege by hostile forces and a corresponding need to insulate oneself from them. The social life is structured accordingly, and many observers have tended to emphasize Iranian suspicion of and resistance to outside forces as well as the layers of obfuscation that Iranians routinely employ to disguise their intentions. As many sociologists, anthropologists, and linguists have noted, the traditional Iranian home is divided into an *anderun*, an inner area where family members (or at least the patriarch) may be at ease and unguarded in behavior, and a *birun*, or outer area where interactions with others take place and are governed by expectations of behavior such as *taarof*. This corresponds to a more general division of actions into their secret, innermost intentions, which are kept concealed (the *baten*), and their external aspects (the *zaher*), which may not mean at all what they seem. Various techniques are used to protect one's self and to advance one's goals, notably *taqiyya* (dissimulation, originally the practice of concealing one's true religious beliefs in order to avoid persecution) and *zerangi* (cleverness, the art of disguising one's intent in order to obtain what is wanted). Given such attitudes, it is not surprising that a fondness for conspiracy theories has become entrenched in Iranian life or that casual visitors have sometimes found Iranians "superficial" or "hypocritical" or "devious" or "xenophobic."

One final point that must be made concerns the deep affection Iranians have for the country in which they live. This is true first of all in the sense of a physical attachment to the land, however desolate and barren it may seem to others. The feeling is manifested in ancient religious texts and an epic tradition that celebrated Iran as the most favored clime, poems that praise the natural beauty of the country, literature cataloguing and describing the areas and features of the towns and provinces, and the eagerness with which Iranians relax and picnic outdoors. It is also true in a patriotic sense, whether in the monumental inscriptions of ancient kings or in more recent political sentiments. The effort of Iranians to assert their identity and preserve their independence will constitute a major theme of the following pages.

NOTES

1. E. G. Browne. *A Year Amongst the Persians* (Cambridge: Cambridge University Press, 3rd ed., 1950), p. 25.

2. L. P. Elwell-Sutton, "Reza Shah the Great: Founder of the Pahlavi Dynasty," in George Lenczowski, ed., *Iran under the Pahlavis* (Stanford: Hoover Institution Press, 1978), p. 35.

2

Ancient Iran

The land of Iran was home to human cultures long before the arrival of the Iranian peoples who gave the country its name. The development in Iran from simple hunting and gathering societies to complex civilizations followed the same fundamental pattern that can be found in many other parts of the world, but with various particular features determined by the area's special geographical characteristics and historical circumstances.

PREHISTORIC IRAN

During the Upper Palaeolithic period and before the end of the last ice age (approximately 100,000 to 15,000 years ago), the climate of Iran was radically different from what it is today. Abundant rainfall produced numerous streams, and the interior of the plateau would have held a huge lake. Other areas that are relatively marginal today, such as the Neyriz and Maharlu lakes in the southern province of Fars, were much richer then. No doubt game and fish were abundant, and the many caves and rock shelters to be found in the mountainous areas provided attractive habitats for the Stone Age hunters and gatherers of that era. Archaeological explorations have identified many such sites in northwestern, southern, and northeastern Iran, yielding bones of both

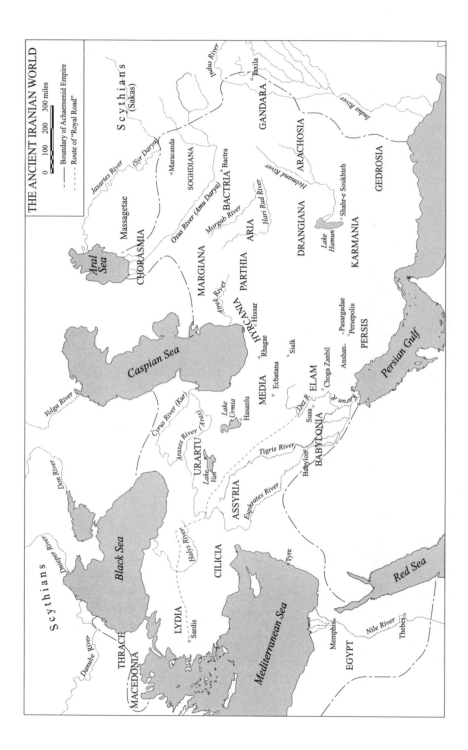

THE ANCIENT IRANIAN WORLD

0   100   200   300 miles

— · — Boundary of Achaemenid Empire
- - - - Route of "Royal Road"

Scythians

Scythians (Sakas)

Aral Sea

CHORASMIA

Massagetae

Jaxartes River (Syr Darya)

Maracanda

SOGHDIANA

Oxus River (Amu Darya)

Bactra

BACTRIA

MARGIANA

Morgab River

Atrek River

PARTHIA

ARIA

Hari Rud River

Indus River

Taxila

GANDARA

ARACHOSIA

Helmand River

Indus River

GEDROSIA

HYRCANIA

Hissar

DRANGIANA

Lake Hamun

Shahr-e Soukhteh

KARMANIA

Caspian Sea

Rhagae

Sialk

Volga River

Cyrus River (Kur)

MEDIA

Ecbatana

Dez R.

Susa

Anshan

Choga Zambil

Karun R.

Pasargadae

Persepolis

PERSIS

Persian Gulf

Arazes River (Aras)

URARTU

Lake Urmia

Hasanlu

ELAM

Lake Van

ASSYRIA

Tigris River

Euphrates River

Babylon

BABYLONIA

Don River

Dnieper River

Black Sea

Halys River

LYDIA

CILICIA

Sardis

Tyre

Mediterranean Sea

Red Sea

THRACE

MACEDONIA

Danube River

Memphis

EGYPT

Nile River

Thebes

Neanderthal and Modern man as well as numerous flint cores, blades, and other artifacts.

As the climate became warmer and drier, conditions in Iran more closely approximated what they are today. Diminishing supplies of water and other resources must have made it increasingly difficult to sustain earlier population levels. At that point, however, another factor of critical importance came into play. The interior valleys and flanks of the Zagros Mountains at that time were ideally suited for the natural growth of various cereal grains that could be used to supplement the food supply. Pollen deposits found in core samples taken from the bed of Lake Urmia indicate that as early as 13,000–12,000 B.C. efforts were under way by hunting and gathering communities to increase the production of these grains through such ecological interventions as cutting down trees or burning off forested areas. By 7000 B.C., some cereal grains had been domesticated, and these early attempts at cultivation had been replaced by the more sophisticated methods of true agriculture. The food-producing revolution of the Neolithic period (7000–5000 B.C. in this area) made possible the establishment of more or less permanent settlements. These appear to have been more heavily concentrated on the western slopes of the Zagros, but some also developed on the plateau side, one of the oldest in Iran being that at Sialk near the modern city of Kashan in the east-central Zagros. These settlements tended to be quite small (.5 hectare or less) and located near a reliable source of water (a stream or spring), often in quite isolated areas. Because agriculture was still a precarious enterprise, subject to the whims of nature and other hazards, these communities typically combined farming with some hunting or herding of animals. The number of small, simple, agrarian settlements continued to increase until around 4000 B.C., in what is known as the Chalcolithic period (ca. 5000–3300 B.C.). The archaeological evidence indicates that the number of settlements then began to drop, and in many places agriculture was actually abandoned in favor of nomadic pastoralism. Settlements that endured, however, increased dramatically in size (by a factor of three to as much as six times) and tended to be located strategically near natural transportation corridors. The reason for this is not clear. Some scholars have suggested that there was a change in the climate that adversely affected crops and made it necessary to supplement them with animal products. Others point to experiments at irrigation that went awry and caused previously fertile land to go out of production. However, the most important factor was probably related to the changes taking place in Mesopotamia, where the foundations of the urban revolution were being laid. The greatly increased agricultural production there may have attracted people from the Iranian plateau, and the corresponding demand in Mesopotamia for resources not available locally, such as metals and stones, created opportunities for the development of regional trade limited only by the difficulties of transport at the time.

Although the environment in Iran was poorly suited for the kind of agricultural revolution that had occurred in Mesopotamia, it was much better endowed in terms of mineral resources. The usefulness of metals had been known at least as early as 9000 B.C., but copper metallurgy became common only after 5000 B.C. At that point, copper began to replace bones and flints for things such as pins, needles, arrowheads, weapons, ceremonial objects, agricultural implements, and other tools. The Iranian plateau was rich in copper deposits, and evidence of their exploitation has been found at important mines located near Kerman (Tell-e Eblis), Qazvin, and Isfahan (Anarak). Use of other minerals, some of them ancillary to copper production, also began to develop: lead, gold, silver, and stone. A number of settlements were involved in the exploitation of these resources, one of the most impressive being Shahr-e Soukhteh in Sistan, which has been thoroughly studied by a team of Italian archaeologists. Probably founded ca. 4000 B.C., it flourished from 3200 to 1800 B.C. Situated near the Helmand River and Lake Hamun, it had abundant supplies of water, fish, and game, which made possible a rich and varied diet for its inhabitants. The people were also able to build up a regional trade in pottery, shells, turquoise, and lapis lazuli. With a peak size of over 100 hectares and a population of at least 8,000, it was the largest settlement by far in eastern Iran. Its pattern of socioeconomic organization—with the fundamental unit being a large urbanized center surrounded and supported by numerous outlying villages—was an enduring one throughout the region.

The growth of commodity exchange stimulated the formation of a number of regional cultures in Iran. In the east, as at Shahr-e Soukhteh, these are rather obscure and known primarily on the basis of ceramic patterns and the names of archaeological sites. In western Iran, however, several of these cultures were in contact with the complex societies of Mesopotamia and were eventually mentioned in their historical texts. They include the Quti, Lullubi, Urartians, Kassites, and Mannai (who produced the magnificent gold objects discovered near the village of Ziwiye). None of these peoples, in the east or west, seem to have ever made the revolutionary transition to the kind of literate, fully urban, state-structured societies that had appeared in Sumeria or the Indus. In all of Iran during the Bronze Age, that type of development was confined to one area, Khuzistan, and one people, the Elamites, who created what can be called the first true civilization in Iran.

THE ELAMITES

Khuzistan is the modern name for the alluvial plains formed by the Karun and Karkha Rivers at the head of the Persian Gulf. Unpleasantly hot and humid, the land was nonetheless extremely productive for agriculture and thus attractive for human settlement. Its proximity to the foothills of the Zagros Mountains also gave it access to convenient resources of wood, stone, metal, and livestock. Geographically and culturally, it should be regarded as an extension of the great Mesopotamian flood plains and their civilizations, but economically and politically it was also inevitably linked to the Iranian plateau. It soon became home to such great cities as Susa and Choga Mish, and its enterprising inhabitants made it a vital commercial link between Mesopotamia and the plateau regions as well as a breadbasket of the ancient world.

The people who came to dominate this area were the Elamites. They were, so far as can be determined, among the aboriginal inhabitants of the southern portions of the Iranian plateau. They attained literacy quite early, and many examples of their writings have been found (although its earliest form, proto-Elamite, remains undeciphered). Like the language of their contemporary neighbors, the Sumerians, Elamite is unique and has no discernable connection with any other language group.

In the early Bronze Age, the Elamites created a vibrant regional civilization that spread its influence across much of the Iranian plateau. The original center of Elamite power, and always one of its most important cities, was Anshan, now positively identified as having been located at the site of Tepe Malyan in central Fars. Evidence of proto-Elamite presence by 3100 B.C., however, has been found not only at Anshan, but also at Sialk and Godin Tepe in the central Zagros; Hissar in northeastern Iran; and Shahr-e Soukhteh and Tepe Yahya (near Kerman in southeastern Iran). This apparently represented the evolution of a vast regional trading network under proto-Elamite auspices, which certainly helped transport materials such as the lapis of Shahr-e Soukhteh and copper from the mines of Tepe Yahya to Mesopotamia and perhaps even the Indus.

Elam had become a full-fledged kingdom by 2700 B.C. After that date it is mentioned frequently in Akkadian and Babylonian texts, as the rulers of Elam contested with those empires for control of the Khuzistan plains, the city of Susa, and access to the economic resources of the plateau. Little more is known, however, of the history of the three dynasties of the Old Elamite period (2400–1600 B.C.) than the names of the rulers and that the culture fell increasingly under the influence of the Semitic civilizations of Mesopotamia. This was followed by a vigorous Elamite cultural revival during the Middle Elamite period (1500–1100 B.C.), when a major Elamite religious center was constructed at Choga Zunbil. The zenith of Elamite power came around 1175 B.C. when one of its kings sacked Babylon and carried off many of its treasures to Susa (including the famous stone pillar inscribed with the law code of Hammurabi). Thereafter Elamite power declined steadily; the Assyrian king Ashurbanipal thoroughly defeated the Elamites and seized Susa in 636. By then, however, the Elamites had already been eclipsed by a new people arriving from the north and east, the ethnic Iranians.

The Elamites can thus be regarded as the founders of the first "Iranian" empire in the geographic sense. Their development, with an emphasis on the importance of long-distance trade and the complex, symbiotic relationship between Mesopotamia and the plateau, illustrates factors of constant importance in Iranian history. It is furthermore likely that Elamite culture had a powerful influence in shaping that of their successors, the Persians, but this is difficult to trace and at present imperfectly understood.

THE ADVENT OF THE IRANIANS

Probably by the end of the third millenium B.C., the Indo-Europeans had split into several branches, moving on the one hand into western Europe and on the other into the Balkans, Central Asia, and south and southwest Asia. Like the Greeks, the Anatolians (such as the Hittites), and the Tocharians, the Indo-Iranians constituted a major division of the Indo-Europeans in the east. Many, if not all, of these Indo-Iranians called themselves Aryans and shared a number of cultural characteristics, which are clearly reflected in the languages they and their descendants spoke, including the breeding of cattle and horses, bronze metallurgy, the veneration of certain anthropomorphized deities (*daevas* such as Mithra, Indra, and Varuna), and ritual practices (purification, marriage restrictions, a chanted liturgy, and the use of a sacred drink called variously *soma* or *haoma*). It is really impossible to link the Indo-Iranians with the artifacts of a specific material culture, but it seems likely that a significant component of them corresponded to either or both of the cultures known to archaeologists as the Andronovo and Srubnaya (or Kurgan). The peoples of those cultures occupied a broad swath of territory from the steppes north of the Black Sea to the Pamir Mountains; and their bronze metallurgy, stockbreeding, and other practices correspond fairly closely to what would be expected of the Indo-Iranians at that stage of their development.

Between 2000 and 1500 B.C. a number of older cultures and civilizations in the area from the Mediterranean to the Indus collapsed. The reasons for this are uncertain and much debated, but it is generally agreed that it was not due to invasion by conquering hordes of Aryan warriors. Rather, the collapse of the ancient societies seems to have created a vacuum into which various Indo-European peoples, including the Indo-Iranians, began to be drawn, gradually absorbing or replacing the earlier cultures. The earliest known example of such an Indo-Iranian people was the Mitanni, who were established in northern Syria in the 14th century B.C., apparently as a small elite group ruling over a larger, indigenous, non-Aryan culture. Not long after, the Indo-Aryans separated from the larger group of Indo-Iranians and began to infiltrate the Indus and Ganges plains. The main body of the remaining Indo-Iranians was probably spread across the Pontic-Caspian steppe lands and into Central Asia between the Oxus and Jaxartes Rivers as far as the Pamirs. Eventually, these Indo-Iranians entered history as the nomadic Alans, Scythians, and Sarmatians in the west and the Sakas and Massagetae in the east; or the sedentary, urbanized Chorasmians and Sogdians in Central Asia.

Against this background, the first groups of Iranians also began to appear on the Iranian plateau, although the problem of exactly when and how this occurred is the subject of considerable debate. At least in terms of the languages they are known to have spoken, these ancient Iranians can be divided into two main categories, those who spoke or eventually used Old Persian and those who spoke or used the language known as Avestan. These two language groups also appear to be associated with two different geographic areas, to the west and east of the central plateau. Thanks to mention in the historical records of surrounding cultures as well as archaeological remains, much is known about the history of the Iranians in the west, who eventually produced the Median and Persian (Achaemenid) empires, but the history of those in the east is much more obscure. Although the two groups certainly shared a common Aryan heritage and may well have interacted with each other or been related in some way, their cultural and historical development was also quite different in several respects.

THE AVESTAN PEOPLE

Avesta is the name given to the books that comprise the sacred scriptures of the Zoroastrian religion, a mixed collection of hymns, prayers, anti-demonic incantations, laws, and other material. Some of the texts are in the "Old Avestan" dialect, notably the hymns (Gathas) of the Prophet Zoroaster, while other supplementary or explanatory texts which make up the "Younger Avesta" are in a different and later dialect. The compositions that make up Avesta were at first transmitted only in oral form. Although not written down until many centuries had passed, they nonetheless preserved much of their original form, and they constitute an invaluable guide to the culture of the people who originally produced them.

Other than Aryan, it is not known what these Iranians may have called themselves; hence, they are best described simply as "the Avestan people." According to the Avestan tradition, the Aryans in general inhabited a vast region called Airyo-shayana (the Abode of the Aryans), "where the high mountains, rich in pastures and waters, yield plenty to the cattle; where the deep lakes, with salt waters, stand; where wide-flowing rivers swell and hurry towards Ishkata and Pouruta, Mouru and Haroyu, the Gava-Sughdha and Hvairizem" (*Mehr Yasht*, 14). This corresponds to the area between the Oxus and Jaxartes and from the Aral Sea to the Helmand basin and the Punjab. The homeland of the Avestan people proper, however, would seem to be Aiyranem Vaejah, which is described as both a fabulous place—the first and most desirable of all lands created, the center of the world, site of the sacred mountain Hara, birthplace of the first man and the first king—and an actual realm, dwelling place of the Prophet Zoroaster and the ruler who protected him. It is depicted as a land of great mountains and intense cold with the river of "Religious Law" flowing through it to a salt sea. These ambiguous geographic features could be located in any number of places, but some area in the vicinity of the Pamir Mountains, either Chorasmia or Sistan, seems the most likely locale, although Azerbaijan has also been proposed as a possibility.

The society of the Avestan people was in many respects a simple one, but it changed considerably in the period from Old Avestan to Young

Avestan times. There is no indication that urban life or trade and commerce were of any importance in the Old Avestan period. The economy was based primarily on the herding of livestock; the people were pastoralists, cattle served as the basic unit of economic exchange, and the cow was venerated as sacred. By Younger Avestan times, limited agriculture, the extension of which was seen as an act of great piety, was also practiced, and some villages or farming settlements had been established. In the relatively tranquil Old Avestan period, social organization centered on the family and the clan and was probably classless; in the more disturbed and warlike Younger Avestan times, there were three classes: herdsmen, priests, and warriors. At all times, the promotion of patriarchal family life was of paramount concern; marriage and the production of children, especially sons, were strongly encouraged.

Living in a difficult and perilous world, the Avestan people were already manifesting the sentiment, so common throughout subsequent Iranian cultural development, of being besieged by hostile forces, both demonic and human. The human "enemies" in this case are by Younger Avestan times vividly depicted as nomadic raiders who came on "swift horses" to pillage, kill, and steal cattle. Interestingly, many of the customs of the Avestan people seem to have been almost deliberately designed to reinforce a sense of identity as a people apart from non-Aryans and even other Aryans (notably their veneration of the dog and celebration of incestuous marriages between close blood relations, both of which were in stark contrast to the practices of the otherwise closely related culture of the Indo-Aryans).

ZOROASTER AND AVESTAN RELIGION

The greatest cultural contribution of the Avestan people was their religious thought, thanks to the great prophet who appeared among them, Zoroaster (Zarathushtra, from a word thought to mean "possessor of camels"). Traditional biographical accounts hold that Zoroaster was born in a place called Ragha, which has been identified with Rayy (a site near modern Tehran). He later left his home because of the hostility of its people to his religious teachings and traveled widely before being welcomed, at the age of forty, by Kavi (King) Vishtaspa, who also adopted his faith. Zoroaster remained in Vishtaspa's realm until his death at the age of seventy-seven.

The conversion of Kavi Vishtaspa is supposed to have occurred 258 years before Alexander's conquest of Iran, and this has been interpreted to mean that Zoroaster therefore lived ca. 628–551 B.C. Vishtaspa also happens to have been the name of the father of the famous Persian king Darius I (discussed below), which would fit with this dating. All of this has led many scholars to believe that Zoroaster must therefore have been active in northwestern Iran not long before the rise of the Persian Empire; even the great authority on ancient Iran, A. T. Olmstead, indulged in speculation about the conversations that must have gone on at Vishtaspa's court between Zoroaster and the young Darius. Recent research, however, has cast considerable doubt on this dating and geographical setting. The traditional dating is rooted in cosmology, not history, and no contemporary records confirm it. The similarity of the language and metrical system of the Gathas to those of the Vedas, the simplicity of the society depicted throughout the Avesta, and the lack of awareness of great cities, historical rulers, or empires all suggest a different time frame. The geographical references also apply better to Sistan, the Helmand River, and the Lake Hamun basin than to northwestern Iran. All in all, it seems likely that Zoroaster and the Avestan people flourished in eastern Iran at a much earlier date (anywhere from 1500 to 900 B.C.) than once thought.

The ancient Iranians originally believed in a number of gods and goddesses who personified forces of nature (wind, rain, water, vegetation, etc.) and astronomical entities such as the sun, moon, planets, and conspicuous stars like Sirius or the Pleiades. Some were known as *ahuras* and others as *daevas*. Worship of these deities was probably communal in nature, without need of temples or priests, but eventually there were cult rituals presided over by officials known as *karapans* or *usijs*, more like sorcerers than priests. Zoroaster, who describes himself also as a priest-poet (*zaotar*) of the old religion, reacted strongly against such beliefs and laid the foundations of a remarkable religious system that emphasized instead the worship of one supreme, transcendant, yet nonetheless personal god; uncompromising ethical conduct; and the celebration of life and the good things of the world.

The Gathas reveal that Zoroaster was troubled by the violence of his times, the concept of the *daevas*, and the cult practices of the *karapans*: "Have the *daevas* ever exercised good dominion? And I ask of those who see how, for the *daevas* sake, the *karapan* and the *usij* give cattle to violence, and how the *kavi* [kinglets] made them continually to mourn, instead of taking care that they make the pastures prosper through Right" (*Yasna* 44.20). While at one level it was a reflection on the suffering of sacrificial cattle, the stealing of cattle by raiders, and the disruption of

agricultural life that disturbed Zoroaster, the spiritual crisis that this provoked led him also to seek answers to questions of the most profound
religious and philosophical significance: "This do I ask Thee, oh Lord,
tell me truly; Who is the creator, the first father of righteousness; Who
laid down the path of the sun and stars? Who is it through whom the
moon now waxes, now wanes? All this and more do I wish to know"
(*Yasna* 44.3).

As a result of his religious visions and insights, Zoroaster came to feel
that there was a god who spoke to him and to whom and on whose
behalf he spoke in turn. He addressed this deity variously as Ahura,
Mazda, or a combination of the two (Ahura Mazda, Mazda Ahura), the
"Wise God" who was the creator of light and the earth and all good
things. In the intense poetry of the Gathas, he communicated directly
and intimately with this god, complaining to him about the persecution
he was suffering and the poverty to which he had been reduced: "To
what land shall I go to flee, whither to flee? From nobles and from my
peers they sever me, nor are the people pleased with me [. . .], nor the
Liar rulers of the land. How am I to please thee, Mazda Ahura? I know
wherefore, O Mazda, I have been unable (to achieve) anything. Only a
few herds are mine (and therefore it is so) and because I have got but
few people. I cry unto thee, see thou to it, O Ahura, granting me support
a friend gives to friend. Teach me through the Right what the acquisition
of Good Thought is" (*Yasna* 46.1–2).

In Zoroaster's cosmology, Ahura Mazda was a great creator-god, a
deity, light, truth, and all forms of righteousness. He had made cattle,
the waters, wholesome plants, stars, the earth, and everything good; he
had established Righteousness (*asha*). But there was also another "primal
spirit," a "twin" eventually known as Angra Mainyu (Ahriman), who
was the absolute negation of Ahura Mazda, the embodiment of the "Lie"
(*druj*), darkness, and evil. At the beginning of time, these twin spirits
had created "life and not-life," with the one who "followed the lie"
choosing to do and create "the worst things," and the other, "the holiest
Spirit," choosing to do Right.

So, too, created beings, especially man, had to make the same free
choice between Good Thought and the Right or Worst Thought and the
Lie. The *daevas* "chose not aright, for infatuation came upon them as they
took counsel together, so that they chose the Worst Thought; then they
rushed together to violence, that they might enfeeble the world of men"
(*Yasna* 30.6). They were thus to be cursed and rejected as demons. Likewise, those who were "beloved of the *daevas*," the *karapans*, the bad *kavis*,

had chosen wrongly: they did not "obey the statutes and ordinances concerning husbandry"; they would "destroy the life of the Ox with shouts of joy"; and they "accustomed mankind to evil actions, so as to destroy Life." The followers of the Mazda-worshipping (Mazdayasnian) religion, however, struggled to uphold the Right and be a foe to the Lie: They venerated the sacred elements of earth, water, and fire (the symbol of Ahura Mazda); praised the sun, whose rays were pleasing to Ahura; practiced good husbandry; extended agriculture; renounced the stealing and needless harm of cattle or the plundering of settlements; and celebrated through festivals the good gifts of Ahura Mazda.

Finally, there was a profound redemptive and messianic aspect to Zoroaster's belief. He offered reassurance that following the Mazdayasnian religion would, with the aid of "deliverers" (saoshyants), ultimately bring "long punishment for the follower of the Druj, and blessings for the followers of the Right." In one sense, this might be the defeat of the enemies of the Mazdayasnians and the gift of cattle and material prosperity. Yet it also had a cosmological significance through a belief in the ultimate and inevitable triumph of good over evil, when the adherents of each would receive what they were due: "Then truly on the Lie shall come the destruction of delight; but they who get themselves good name shall be partakers in the promised reward in the fair abode of Good Thought, of Mazda, and of Right" (Yasna 30.10). Thus the evil would be punished or destroyed forever, while "the righteous man . . . shall be hereafter in the pasture of Right and Good Thought"; Ahura Mazda would "give continued life to their bodies and indestructibility" so that they might "gain the prize over the others."

The religion of Zoroaster obviously developed in the context of an older religion which it sought to transform radically, and it also continued to develop in the context of a larger religious system in which it was but one element. Not every idea of Zoroaster was followed rigidly; most notably his absolute rejection of the daevas and his insistence on the veneration only of Ahura Mazda were modified to accommodate the worship of other divinities: Sraosha, "Obedience"; Ardvi Suri Anahita, goddess of the waters; Mithra, the sun and war god; the "wives" of Ahura and his personified attributes (the Bounteous Immortals); the spirits of heroes and rulers (fravashis). Nonetheless, Zoroaster's powerful conceptions of Ahura, the cosmic struggle of good and evil, man's free will and ability to choose his actions, and the ultimate reward of the virtuous who persevere in the face of adversity nonetheless exerted a powerful and lasting influence on Iranian religion and culture as well as that of other cultures that came into contact with it. For his followers, as confirmed in the catechism recited when tying on the cord (*kusti*) that marked one out as a Zoroastrian, it was "of all religions that exist or shall be . . . the greatest, the best, and the most beautiful."

THE EPIC TRADITION

In addition to their religious thought, the Avestan people also contributed to another enduring aspect of Iranian culture, the epic tradition. This was built in part on the foundation of older Aryan mythology but also on accounts of the heroic exploits of various kings (recognizably the *kavis* mentioned in connection with Zoroaster) and other local champions. These stories, arranged in accordance with a cyclical view of history, probably began with accounts of the creation of the world, the first man (Yima, later called Jamshid), the first king (Hushang), the first dynasty (the Pishdadians), and the evil usurper Dahaka (Zahhak). They also included tales of the Kayanian kings, culminating in the reign of Kavi Vishtaspa (Goshtasp) and the warfare between the Iranians and their natural enemies, the Turanians (probably nomadic peoples to the north of Iran, later identified with the Turks). Although this epic tradition grew and changed over the centuries and did not attain a true literary form until much later, above all in the "Book of Kings" (*Shahnameh*) genre, its stories were so rich, detailed, coherent, and meaningful that they came to be accepted as records of actual events—so much so that they almost totally supplanted in collective memory the genuine history of ancient Iran. In that sense, they are every bit as important for understanding Iranian culture as the study of what "really" happened.

THE MEDES

Compared to the history of the Avestan people, who apparently had no literate neighbors to record their activities, much more is known about the Iranians in the west, the great tribes of the Medes and the Persians in particular, who appeared on the periphery of the relatively advanced and highly literate civilizations in Mesopotamia around the 9th century B.C. It is hotly debated whether these tribes moved down from the Caucasus into the valleys of the Zagros or arrived from the east by skirting the central desert. Without getting into all the technical arguments and their implications, the latter possibility seems more likely.

In any case, the people known as the Medes were established by 900

B.C. along the interior (southern) slopes of the Elburz and the western fringes of the plateau basin. For some time they were divided into several tribes and numerous small, autonomous settlements. One of these, the site known as Tepe Nush-e Jan, has been excavated and gives many insights into their life and cultural development. One important group or caste in Median society was the Magi, described by Herodotus as one of six "tribes." They reportedly exercised a monopoly over Median religion, but their exact beliefs and practices are open to question; they appear to have been regarded as powerful sorcerers as much as priests.

The Medes, like some of their counterparts in the east, might have remained at this diffuse, tribal, semi-sedentary stage for some time, but the process of what can be called their national consolidation and state formation was accelerated because they almost immediately came into contact with the aggressive and expansionist Assyrian Empire. The Assyrian war machine, the very foundation of its civilization, had an insatiable need for horses and iron, and the highlands of northwestern Iran represented a prime source of supply for both. The Assyrians penetrated deep into the area in 881 B.C. and for the next three centuries were locked in a struggle to control it. Iranians were early and frequent targets of these campaigns: in 843 B.C., Shalmaneser III extracted tribute from "twenty-seven kings of Parsuash"; in 820 the Medes were soundly defeated; and from 809 to 788 B.C. Queen Semiramis and King Adadnerari III routed the Medes and occupied much Median territory, leaving a deep, almost legendary, fear of Assyrian tyranny among the Medes.

Eventually the Medes, like many of the other small cultures in the area, realized that only a united effort could resist Assyrian incursions. They were drawn into various anti-Assyrian coalitions, became more unified themselves, and finally took the leadership role in a counterattack. In the somewhat fictionalized account of Herodotus, it was a clever and ambitious man named Deioces, famed for his administration of justice, who persuaded the Medes to accept him as a king, to establish the rituals surrounding the institution of monarchy, and to build a fortified capital city (Ecbatana, modern Hamadan). He ruled for fifty-three years (ca. 727–675 B.C.), during which time he united the people of Media and resisted the Assyrians. Deioces almost certainly corresponds to a chieftain mentioned in Assyrian records as Daiaukku, who rebelled along with the people of Urartu against Sargon II and was sent into exile in Syria. Although he was eventually defeated, Daiaukku had demonstrated that the Assyrians were vulnerable. There was then a general revolt of the Medes, with assistance from Scythian nomads, around 674 B.C. under the leadership of a ruler named Khshathrita (mistakenly called Phraortes, son of Deioces, by Herodotus), who managed to defeat several Assyrian armies but was killed attacking one of their strongholds, supposedly Nineveh itself. The zenith of Median power was reached under Uvakhshtra, the king known to Herodotus as Cyaxares. He came to power in 625 B.C., defeating the Scythians who had occupied Media, and thus restoring Median independence. According to Herodotus, Cyaxares effected a general reorganization of the Median army, abandoning tribal units in favor of functional ones (cavalry, archers, infantry) and using principles and tactics learned from both the Assyrians and the Scythians. He also brought other Iranians, notably the Persians, into his confederation and forged an alliance with Babylonia, the great rival of Assyria in Mesopotamia. His efforts (614–609) resulted in the overwhelming defeat of the Assyrians and the partition of their territory with his Babylonian allies. Cyaxares went on to start building up an empire of his own, attempting to expand into Anatolia. His battle with the Lydians was one of the most famous in antiquity: It ended with a negotiated settlement after both sides were cowed by an eclipse of the sun (which makes it possible to date this event with precision to 28 May 585). Even so, this was the end of the kingdom of Urartu, which was taken over by the Medes, and the Babylonians began to seek ways to protect themselves from the power of their erstwhile ally. Cyaxares may also have extended Median power well to the east. He died not long after concluding peace with the Lydians and was succeeded by his son Astyages (584–549).

The first years of Astyages' reign are obscure and were probably spent in campaigns across the Araxes into Armenia and Georgia. They also seem to have been troubled by internal discord, with the king, the Magian priests, and peasants aligned against the aristocratic great families. In any case, there are many indications that Astyages was not a particularly popular ruler, and that disaffection with him among aristocratic circles contributed to his fall and the ascendancy of the Persians.

THE PERSIAN EMPIRE

The Persians were settled in Fars (Assyrian Parsumash, Greek Persis) in the southern Zagros by 700 B.C. Perhaps led by the semi-legendary founder-hero Achaemenes, they were concentrated around the great Marvdasht plain between the Kur and Polvar Rivers north of modern Shiraz, an area they must have regarded as their homeland and where they later built their greatest monuments. According to Herodotus, they were divided into numerous tribes, some nomadic herdsmen and others sedentary agriculturalists. In 670, the Persians allied with the Elamites against the powerful Assyrian king Sennacherib. In the time of the Persian king Teispes (675–640), they were forced to recognize the authority of the Median king Khshathrita. After the Medes were themselves defeated by Scythians, the Persians were able to recover their autonomy and make a key breakthrough in their historical development—the conquest of Anshan, the old Elamite capital. Rule over this area may have been divided between Teispes' two sons, Ariaramnes and Cyrus I, with the latter acting as "king" of Anshan. As noted earlier, the rule of Cyrus over this area around 640 is definitely attested in Assyrian historical records. He had acknowledged Assyrian suzerainty and sent a son, Arukku, as a hostage to the court of Ashurbanipal. Although its authenticity has been questioned, there is also an inscription purportedly in the name of Ariaramnes in which he boasts of his consolidation of these lands: "This land of the Persians which I possess, provided with fine horses and good men, it is the great god Ahuramazda who has given it to me. I am king of this land."

In time, Persia became a vassal state of the Median kingdom, albeit an important one. The need to strengthen their relations perhaps explains how it was that Cyrus' son Cambyses I (600–559), another king of Anshan, came to marry Mandane, the daughter of the Median king Astyages. Mandane gave birth to a son who, as Cyrus II the Great, would become one of the most celebrated figures in all of Iranian history and indeed one of the most remarkable in the history of the world.

Numerous stories were told about the youth of Cyrus, all of them stamped with elements of legend or propaganda or both. One account, for example, probably emanated from Medes who disliked Cyrus and resented Persian power. It claimed that Cyrus was not of royal birth at all, but the son of a tribal bandit and a woman who was a goat-herder (and who had a dream foretelling that her son would be the founder of an empire). He served as a cupbearer for Astyages, who entrusted him with the suppression of a revolt only to have Cyrus himself rebel and usurp the throne. Herodotus, on the other hand, says that Astyages was disturbed by a dream implying that his grandson Cyrus would steal his throne. He therefore ordered his steward Harpagus to kill the child. Instead, Harpagus gave the baby to a shepherd who substituted it for his own stillborn infant. Ten years later, as a result of playing a game in which Cyrus was pretending to be "king" of some boys, Astyages recognized his grandson. Reassured by the Magi that this harmless game was what had been foretold by the dream, Astyages returned Cyrus to his parents in Anshan. Harpagus, however, he punished by treacherously butchering Harpagus' own teenage son and serving the flesh to him at a banquet. Bent on revenge, Harpagus encouraged Cyrus to oppose Astyages and persuaded other Median nobles who were unhappy with Astyages to support Cyrus. The symbolic dreams of future greatness, the foundling child, the servant who becomes ruler are all typical folklore motifs which have been woven into stories about great Middle Eastern monarchs since the time of Sargon of Akkad. Although they can only be regarded as stories, they do serve to illustrate the fascination Cyrus held for his contemporaries.

Cyrus became king of Anshan in 559 or 558. By then, with the Assyrian Empire destroyed, the Babylonians were concerned about the power of their former allies, the Medes, and cultivated Cyrus as a counterweight to them. It is also possible, as suggested by Herodotus, that some Median nobles who were disaffected with Astyages began to cooperate with Cyrus. Cyrus did in fact revolt against Astyages, probably around 550 B.C.; Astyages set out with an army to crush Cyrus and capture Anshan; but the larger Median army was somehow defeated (there are indications that a substantial component of Astyages' army defected to Cyrus). Cyrus took Astyages captive, captured Ecbatana, and carried off its treasure to Anshan. He thus joined the kingdoms of Media and Persia and assumed the Median title of "great king, king of kings, king of the lands." Thereafter, he treated the Medes well and sought to bolster the unity of the Median and Persian people. The legitimacy of his rule, however, was most solidly based, not on his maternal connection to the Median royal house, but on his descent from the semi-legendary Persian hero Achaemenes and the kings of Anshan: In his inscriptions, he proclaimed himself "Cyrus the king, an Achaemenid" and "son of Cambyses, the great king, king of Anshan, grandson of Cyrus, the great king, king of Anshan." It should be noted that the idea of descent from a line of kings was always a critical element in the Iranian conception of monarchy; this is perhaps what is meant by the customary title "king of kings" (rather than, as often thought, the notion of being a king over other kings).

From his base of power in western Iran, Cyrus set out on a course of spectacular and unprecedented empire-building. He first turned his attention to the east and the assertion of his authority over the Iranian peoples in Parthia and Hyrcania (ca. 549). His first serious challenge, however, came from the west. King Croesus of Lydia, seeing an opportunity to take advantage of the collapse of Median power (and famously misled by the oracle of Delphi), invaded Cappadocia in central Anatolia. After one major battle, Croesus withdrew to his capital, Sardis, and appealed for help from other nations imperiled by the rise of Persian power: Egypt, Babylonia, and the Spartan Greeks. Cyrus quickly besieged and captured Sardis, probably in 547. Some reports claim that Croesus was executed (or committed suicide), others that Cyrus took pity on him, spared his life, and treated him magnanimously. As the new master of Lydia, Cyrus also inherited the Lydian claim to suzerainty over the Greek city-states of Ionia and other territories in eastern Anatolia. One major city, Miletus, accepted Persian rule; others were forced to submit by Cyrus' generals.

After perhaps fighting a few more desultory campaigns in eastern Iran and Central Asia, Cyrus was ready to take advantage of political chaos in Babylonia to enlarge his empire with yet another rich prize. The current ruler of Babylonia, Nabonidus (Nabu-naid), was extremely unpopular, especially with the powerful priests of the Babylonian god Marduk. As reports arrived of the approach of Cyrus' army in 539 B.C., a revolt broke out and Nabonidus was forced to flee. According to Herodotus, the people of Babylon still resisted Cyrus and were prepared for a long siege, but Cyrus diverted the Euphrates so that his troops could enter the city via the riverbed undetected by the people, who were engaged in a religious celebration, and was thus able to capture it. In documents issued in his own name, however, Cyrus (or the Babylonian priests who wrote them for him) insisted that his troops had entered Babylon peacefully and that he was welcomed by its inhabitants. Conversely, the fall of Nabonidus was explained to the Babylonian populace as the result of his iniquity and the anger of Marduk against him.

Just as Cyrus' conquest of Lydia had brought him control over the former Lydian dependencies, so he also acquired the vast territories that had made up the Babylonian Empire all the way to the Mediterranean and the borders of Egypt. The Babylonians had been in the habit of symbolizing their control over these territories by suppressing their religions, destroying the local temples, or carrying off their sacred religious objects to emphasize their subordination to the Babylonian god Marduk. Cyrus affirmed his rule by doing exactly the opposite, returning the provincial gods to their "homes" and allowing the free exercise of their cults. There are examples to be found throughout his dominions, but the most famous instance by far was his return of the Jews held captive in Babylon and his granting permission for the rebuilding of the temple in Jerusalem. For this, the prophet Isaiah sang his praises, calling him the "anointed of the Lord." Not much is known about the last decade of Cyrus' rule. It was probably spent mostly in consolidating and governing his huge empire and in building palaces and other monuments, notably those at Pasargadae, in the area where the Persian tribes had settled. He died fighting the nomadic Massagetae along the Oxus River ca. 530, at the age of seventy, and was buried in a simple but impressive tomb at Pasargadae.

The personality and exploits of Cyrus have exerted a fascination upon writers down to the present day. Many of them, usually monarchists or apologists for one type of autocracy or another, have held him up as a paragon of the ideal ruler. Much recent scholarship has likewise emphasized, rather anachronistically and just as tendentiously, his supposed "tolerance" of other cultures and his concern for "human rights." In reality, for every story about the virtue and justice of Cyrus, there is usually a contrary version that is much less flattering. It would be quite easy to paint a picture of Cyrus as the stereotypically "bad" Iranian king: an opportunistic adventurer willing to fight even his own grandfather; a man who usurped a kingdom, seized other countries by force, killed his vanquished enemies, was dominated by women in his harem, left the kingdom to an undeserving son, and ruled so laxly that the entire empire erupted with revolts not long after his death. Little is ultimately known of how Cyrus actually acquired and governed his empire, much less about his intentions and sentiments, so the way is always open to different interpretations. The favors he granted he probably bestowed to secure political tranquility, not out of any philosophical purity. The praise given him by Isaiah perhaps says as much about Jewish messianic expectations of deliverance from Babylonian oppression as about Cyrus. The gracious words of the "Cyrus Cylinder" are formulaic repetitions of sentiments expressed by priests on behalf of Mesopotamian rulers at least as far back as the time of Hammurabi; they reflect not so much his convictions as the degree to which Cyrus was awed by Babylonian antiquity and deferred to the norms of a culture he felt manifestly grander than his own. In sum, Cyrus was primarily a conqueror who dazzled his contemporaries and stirred their imagination with his rise from relative obscurity to mastery of an empire of unprecedented dimensions— but one with an enviable ability to do so without making unnecessary enemies and to come away with a remarkably unscathed historical reputation.

Events after the death of Cyrus are as fascinating as the murkiest detective novel. Put as simply as possible, Cyrus was succeeded by Cambyses II (530–522), his son by his favorite wife, Cassandane. As crown prince, Cambyses seems to have acted, briefly and not very well, as governor of Babylon. A few years after becoming king, Cambyses attacked and occupied Egypt (525), where he again reportedly disgraced himself by conduct so violent and disrespectful as to be considered insane. Some of the accusations against him, however, can definitely be proven to be false (the inscriptions on the tombs of the sacred Apis bulls in Egypt, for example, reveal no basis for believing Herodotus' story that Cambyses had mocked and abused the cult). His long absence in Egypt, however, certainly created ample opportunity for the seeds of sedition to be planted back in Persia. Cambyses set out from Egypt around 522 to deal with disturbances or some threat to his rule but died on the way, by accident, suicide, or worse depending on which story is believed.

The troubles that broke out in the Persian Empire upon the death of Cambyses are related in two wonderful but often contradictory and equally suspect sources: the entertaining reports of Herodotus and the *res gestae* inscription and relief at Behistun, carved on a sheer cliff face some sixty meters above ground level, at the command of the eventual master of the situation, King Darius I. About the time Cambyses was departing Egypt, a man claiming to be Bardiya (called Smerdis by Herodotus), the full brother of Cambyses, laid claim to the throne. Cambyses, however, had supposedly murdered the real Bardiya and kept the death a secret; the imposter was a certain Magian priest named Gaumata who had learned of Bardiya's murder and happened to resemble him in appearance so closely that even the prince's mother and sisters were tricked. Joined by other rebellious people, he managed to become ruler of Persia and Media. After Cambyses' death, according to Herodotus, a cabal of seven Persian aristocrats became suspicious of Bardiya and conspired to determine his true identity and eventually to kill him and make one of their own number, Darius, the new king. This was followed by a general slaughter of Magians throughout the realm. Herodotus claims that most subjects mourned the loss of Bardiya and that only the Persians had reason to celebrate his fall. Darius, on the other hand, says in his inscription that people everywhere were afraid of Gaumata, the pseudo-Bardiya, until he alone rose up to challenge him and, with the help of Ahura Mazda and "a few men" (whose names he lists), killed him and took the kingdom from him. Darius then restored order, overturned the sanctuaries Gaumata had built, and returned property he had appropriated to its rightful owners. The meaning of this incident has been the subject of endless speculation. It has been interpreted as evidence of a struggle between Persians and Medes, Zoroastrians and Magians, or aristocrats and the populace. The idea of a hoax such as that supposedly perpetrated by Gaumata strains credulity, so there are suspicions that he really was Bardiya, the son of Cyrus, and that it was Darius who was the true usurper. The figure of a radical priest who seizes power and attempts to ameliorate the lot of ordinary people, on the other hand, is a familiar one in Iranian history. Ultimately, all that can be said for sure is that Darius emerged as the chief beneficiary of all this confusion.

Darius ruled for over thirty years (522–486 B.C.). Despite the inauspicious beginnings of his reign, he, like Cyrus, has been styled "the Great," and just as deservedly. In virtually every respect save extent of territory he was the real architect of the Persian Empire. Cyrus conquered an empire, but Darius put it in order and perfected the institutions to maintain it, which may be an even greater accomplishment.

After the death of Bardiya/Gaumata, Darius still had to surmount enormous obstacles before stabilizing his rule. Sensing weakness, many provincial leaders, from Bactria and Margiana in the distant east to Babylon, Egypt, Elam, Media, and even Persis, attempted to mount insurrections. Darius, who was a remarkable soldier as well as a politician, crushed them all. In the Behistun inscription, Darius says he suppressed eleven revolts in nineteen battles and defeated each of the rebel kings (nine at first, later amended to include a tenth, who are depicted on the relief bound and submissive before the towering figure of Darius). He also conducted additional campaigns, such as those against Skunkha, the king of the "Pointed-Hat" Scythian nomads in the north, Libya, Thrace, and India, which either added new territories or firmed up Persian authority over areas previously held only loosely.

Darius thus ruled an empire stretching from Libya to the Crimea, from Central Asia to the Persian Gulf, and from the Aegean Sea to the Indus River, with a population estimated at 50 million people. The empire-wide revolts had demonstrated the ineffectiveness of Cyrus' policy of ruling such a vast territory through compliant local vassals and officials; the small, apparently exclusively Persian, support on which Darius could rely to restore order also indicated the need for institutional change. Darius was able to perfect a suitable administrative system for this vast realm, quite different from the rather loose government of Cyrus and Cambyses. Darius arranged the territories into twenty provinces. With the exception of Persis, the home province, which was under the direct rule of the king and exempt from taxation, each paid taxes and tribute to the central government and was under the jurisdiction of an official known as a satrap. The satrap was usually a Persian and a member of either the royal family or one of the great aristocratic families. The satrap, however, worked with various other provincial officials and inspectors, the "eyes and ears" of the king, to ensure that he governed justly and did not grow overpowerful or too independent. There was no capital city per se for the empire, since the court followed the physical presence of the king, but there were fixed chancery offices and treasuries in important cities. Four sites were of particular importance (each perhaps serving as the royal residence during one of the four seasons): Susa (the former Elamite capital, which now served as the winter residence); Babylon, Ecbatana (the former Median capital, now a summer residence), and Persepolis (primarily a palace and ceremonial center for the spring New Year festivities). Just as the administration was centralized and Persianized, the military was also made more professional and Persian. In the Behistun inscription, Darius explicitly noted that all the men who supported him in his rise to power were Persians, and he probably saw that Persians constituted the most reliable base of power for his rule. While not excluding the use of other military units, he made Persians the core of his new professional army, forming an elite guard known as the Ten Thousand Immortals (since any vacancy in the ranks was immediately filled).

Darius also recognized the importance of law, logistics, and economics for the well-being of an empire. He took pride in drawing up a new code of law for the empire as a whole, the "Ordinance of Good Regulations," and he standardized existing legal codes in provinces such as Egypt. Judges who took bribes or were otherwise corrupt were very severely punished. Transportation was important for both security and promoting trade and commerce. Darius therefore extended or repaired a system of roads, including the great "Royal Road" stretching 2,600 kilometers from Sardis to Susa, and set up stations at which official travelers could rest and draw rations. Roads were well guarded and policed, and a postal service carried messages with exemplary speed to their destinations. Given its presence in the eastern Mediterranean as well as the Persian Gulf, Darius' empire was a maritime as well as a land power (a rare occurrence in Iranian history). To bolster this, Darius ordered the digging of a canal linking the Nile River with the Red Sea; it was officially opened in 497. Economic measures included the standardization of weights and measures and, most important, the establishment of a new monetary system that used gold and silver coins of specific weights.

Monarchy was the essential element holding together the Persian

Empire, and Darius took great pains to associate his rule with the requirements of an incipient Iranian theory and ceremonial of kingship. Whether truthfully or by propaganda, he emphasized the legitimacy of his rule in terms of this theory, which drew on both the Iranian tribal tradition (emphasizing genealogy and prowess in war) and that of the Near Eastern empires (divine right and implementation of the law). First, at the very beginning of the great Behistun inscription, Darius proclaimed his royal descent, not from Cyrus but from Achaemenes, said to be Cyrus' ancestor (and the man for whom the dynasty is named): Darius was thus not a usurper but the representative of the ninth generation of a line of kings in a royal family. Second, he ruled by the grace of god: "By the favor of Ahuramazda I am king; Ahuramazda bestowed the kingdom upon me." Third, he ruled by virtue of his bravery and bold action: He had taken the initiative against Gaumata the Magian; he beat back the revolts that threatened the empire. Finally, he proclaimed his implacable opposition to oppression and injustice: "I was not a Lie-follower, I was not a doer of wrong. . . . According to righteousness I conducted myself; neither to the weak nor to the powerful did I do wrong." Royal ancestry, divine favor, valor in combat, zealous pursuit of justice: These constitute a virtual catalogue of the essential ideals of Iranian kingship. To emphasize the grandeur and sanctity of kingship, there was a formal investiture ceremony; special titles, forms of address, and insignia were used; and the king was held to be surrounded by a "divine splendor," a firelike aura or charisma, and could only be approached through an elaborate ritual protocol.

Darius can also be credited with asserting a new, confident cultural identity. One senses that both Cyrus, who relied on Babylonian bureaucrats and used the titulature of Babylonian kings in his documents, and Cambyses, who emulated the style of an Egyptian pharaoh, were somewhat awed by and deferential to the older civilizations they had conquered. Darius not only Persianized the administration and military, he promoted a specifically Persian culture. He is thought to have created, or at least perfected, a system for writing the Old Persian language that was used for important ceremonial inscriptions. At the same time, he was quite aware that the Persians were part of a larger Iranian world (his father had been a governor in eastern Iran, and Darius himself had campaigned extensively in areas inhabited by Iranian peoples). In his major inscriptions, he is both Persian and Iranian in his conception of self-identity: The inscription on his tomb proclaims him "Great king, king of kings, king of countries containing all kinds of men, king in this great earth far and wide, son of Hystaspes, an Achaemenid, a Persian, son of a Persian, an Aryan, of Aryan lineage."

Darius' extensive building activities, which were conducted through-out the empire, reflect much of his cultural outlook and interests. The great palace he built at Susa was a testament to the strength, wealth, and diversity of his kingdom. In an inscription describing its construction, he recorded how solid foundations were prepared for it and that it was made with bricks from Babylon; cedar from Lebanon; special timber from the borders of India; gold from Lydia and Bactria; turquoise, lapis lazuli, and carnelian from Central Asia; silver and ebony from Egypt; and stone for columns from Elam; craftsmen from the various provinces worked on it. At the same time, he was concerned to give Persis, the Persian homeland, monuments worthy of its new imperial stature. Cyrus and Cambyses had already built parks, gardens, palaces, and altars at the site of Pasargadae (thought to be derived from a word meaning "Camp of the Persians"). These buildings tended to be rather eclectic in character; Cyrus' tomb, for example, while dignified and appropriate, was heavily influenced by Lydian models. Darius shifted the building program from Pasargadae to another ceremonial center at the nearby site of Persepolis, where a huge walled terrace was prepared for a grand complex of buildings including a treasury, audience hall, banqueting hall, and private palace. They were not finished during his lifetime, but his successors completed or extended them. One of the inscriptions sums up the pride and confidence felt by Darius in his homeland: "This land Parsa, which Ahuramazda has granted me, which is beautiful, possessing good horses and good men, by the favor of Ahuramazda and of me, Darius the king, it has no fear of an enemy."

Matters pertaining to society and religion under Darius and the later Achaemenids are difficult to describe. It is obvious that an empire as large and sophisticated as that of the Persians must have included people of many different professions—warriors, priests, merchants, herdsmen, peasants, artisans, and so on—but it appears that kinship and ethnicity were much more important than class in structuring society. In many ways, the system followed by Cyrus and institutionalized by Darius was modeled on that of a tribal confederation rather than a sedentary state. In his inscriptions, Darius had identified himself as an individual, a member of a clan (Achaemenid), a people (Persian), and a nation (Ar-yan), as well as the overlord of other nations that were his by right of conquest and that paid tribute to him. In the apportioning of military and administrative authority, he relied first and foremost on his family and friends, then on the Persian people, and finally on kindred Iranians and other vassals. The many stories in Greek sources about Persian kings turning down good advice from foreign advisors in favor of bad advice from their own ministers may reflect the importance of these concentric circles of prestige in determining the king's policy. The closer one could approach the physical presence of the king, the higher one's social stature; closeness in kinship and service to him might confer exemption from taxation, gifts of honor, and other privileges.

The importance of kinship and lineage may also be the key to understanding the role of women in Achaemenid society. Little is known, of course, about the lives of ordinary women, but documents from the Persepolis Fortification Tablets suggest that at least some women could work outside the house and received wages accordingly. They also indicate that free-born women in Persis were encouraged to have children, receiving a special stipend on giving birth (twice the amount for a boy as for a girl, probably because of the need to build up the military forces). Greek sources report that rulers and nobles maintained harems of several consorts, numerous concubines (Artaxerxes II, for example, reportedly had 360), and female slaves. Most were supposedly kept strictly secluded in the harem. At least within the royal family, however, women of noble birth could be quite powerful and influential, even if they did not participate directly in public life. Marriages (i.e., the taking of a consort) were particularly important in conferring political legitimacy, building up family alliances, and determining the line of succession. Cyrus the Great, for example, had standing among the Medes since he was the son of the Median princess Mandane; he is also said to have married Amytis, daughter of Astyages and widow of a nobleman killed by Cyrus, to bolster his authority in Media. (The fact that she would technically have been his aunt was of no concern, since marriages to nieces, sisters, and even daughters were regarded as perfectly acceptable and desirable.) Cyrus' favorite wife, however, was Cassandane, sister of an important Persian nobleman and mother of four of his children (including his successor, Cambyses). When she died in 538, he ordered the whole empire to mourn for her. Atossa, probably Cyrus' daughter by Cassandane, was married first to her brother Cambyses, then added to the harem of Gaumata, and finally married by Darius, no doubt to add the legitimacy of Cyrus' line to his own (he also married Artystone, another of Cyrus' daughters). Someone like Atossa, however, was not just a trinket to augment kingly prestige; she was highly regarded for her intelligence and is reported to have been instrumental in planning policy toward the

Greeks and promoting the career of her son Xerxes as successor to Darius. It was not at all uncommon for the daughter of a king to be given in marriage to an important general or official as a sign of special royal favor. There were also women who were wealthy and independent to the point of being subjects of gossip about their scandalous behavior. Amytis, daughter of Xerxes, was reputed to be beautiful, extremely licentious, and involved in political intrigues. Perhaps the most notorious was Parysatis, half-sister and wife of Darius II, depicted as a vicious schemer who did great harm to the Persian state in her vindictive but unsuccessful drive to promote her favorite son, Cyrus, to the throne. Some of these stories may have been concocted by political philosophers hostile to the influence of women and the harem on government, but there is no doubt about the capabilities of noble women in this period: Documents from Persepolis have proven that they could travel, own property, govern their estates, run businesses and supervise employees, and receive food and other provisions from state depositories.

There is much in the religion of the Persians, particularly after Darius, that is similar to that of Zoroaster and the Avestan people. It has been suggested that Darius made Zoroastrianism a kind of official religion at the expense of the Magians (who may have been non-Iranian in origin); his successor Xerxes explicitly stated that he had destroyed places where *daeva*s were worshipped and instituted worship of Ahura Mazda and Righteousness (*arta*). On the other hand, it has been pointed out that there is no indication of awareness of Zoroaster before the time of Artaxerxes II (ca. 405–359), and many Achaemenid religious practices were at variance with the teachings of Zoroastrianism: the kings had royal tombs and were presumably buried there instead of having their bodies exposed, and they often invoked other gods who were technically *daevas*, such as Mithra and Anahita, as well as Ahura Mazda. The problem is clarified somewhat if one assumes that "Zoroastrianism" at that time was an amalgam of Iranian religions that included some of the Gathic ideas and disregarded others, and that Achaemenid religion was also influenced by the old Near Eastern religions. Thus one may find vestiges of agrarian fertility religions (as in cults involving the deities of earth and water), pastoral religions (as in veneration of a warrior sun god and other astronomical deities), and kingly religion (worship of Ahura Mazda as a supreme god of justice). Moreover, Achaemenid rulers continued to respect and even participate in the religions of the subject peoples. Darius, for example, honored Cyrus' promise to fund rebuilding of the Jewish temple in Jerusalem, venerated the Apis bull in Egypt, and so on.

IRAN AND THE GREEKS

From the reign of Darius onward, accounts of Achaemenid history (by both ancient and modern authors) tend to be dominated by the events related to the Greek and Persian wars. With the defeat of Lydia, the Greeks of Ionia and some of the Aegean Islands came under Persian rule, and Iran became a Mediterranean power. On the whole, Darius was quite well disposed toward the Greeks and readily employed them as advisors, mercenaries, and craftsmen. In both the subject territories and mainland Greece, the rise of Persian power polarized Greek opinion. Some Greeks welcomed the prospect of Persian rule since being part of the cosmopolitan Persian Empire offered economic opportunities, access to non-Greek learning and cultural traditions (which in fact greatly enriched Greek thought and helped stimulate the "Ionian Enlightenment"), or support for one local political faction against another. Other Greeks saw Persia as a threat to their political position, independence, cultural autonomy, strategic interests, or economy. To them, even something such as Darius' campaign against the Scythians could be interpreted as a threat to vital supplies of grain from the Greek colonies in the Black Sea area. Sparta took the lead in anti-Persian activities and was joined, after a coup, by Athens. Athens depended heavily on access to sea routes and ports for the export of its wine and olives, and it felt cultural affinities to the other Ionian Greeks. It sent its pro-Persian statesmen into exile and gave active support to Aristagoras, the tyrant of Miletus, when he attempted to lead a revolt of the Ionian cities. Darius suppressed the revolt and, in 490 B.C., struck back by attacking Eretria and landing a small expeditionary force at Marathon, perhaps in expectation of a pro-Persian coup in Athens. Instead, the Persian force was cut off and destroyed by the Athenian general Miltiades. Not long after, Egypt revolted against the Persians, and Darius was unable to take any further action against the Greeks. Xerxes I (486–465) tried conscientiously to carry on and complete many of his father's projects, including the subjugation or intimidation of the Greeks (although in this he was, ironically, encouraged just as much by dissident Greeks who had sought refuge in Persia). He slowly and meticulously brought the resources of the empire to bear on the Greeks with a major invasion involving both land and naval forces, bridging the Bosphorus and digging a canal across the Athos peninsula to facilitate safe passage. The small Spartan force blocking the pass at Thermopylae was annihilated, and the Persian army advanced to enter a lightly defended Athens and burn the Acropolis (480). The Athenians, led by the able general Themistocles, had decided to rely on their naval coalition and lured the Persian fleet into a trap at the straits of Salamis, where it was badly mauled. Xerxes compounded the disaster by accusing his allies of cowardice; alienated, they simply went home. Xerxes himself retired to Sardis, leaving the conduct of the war in the hands of a distinguished general, Mardonius, who had been one of its main proponents (and who could take the blame for its now inevitable outcome). In 479, Mardonius was killed and his army routed during the Battle of Plataea, and the Persian navy was finished off at the Battle of Mycale the same year.

Given the manifest discrepancy in the size and resources of the two combatants, the significance of the Greek and Persian wars for the history of Europe and Western civilization is incontestable, but its meaning for Iran is ambiguous. It was certainly never a simple case of Greek versus Persian or "East versus West"—even Themistocles wound up in exile serving the Persian king—so debates about a rich and powerful "Oriental despotism" trying unsuccessfully to snuff out the independence of small but liberty-loving states can be relegated to the realm of political philosophy. A more difficult problem is whether the Persian offensive was a major undertaking whose failure marked the beginning of the end for the Persian Empire or nothing more than an unimportant and inconsequential border skirmish. Certainly, Herodotus' claim that Xerxes descended on Greece with a force of over 5 million men can be dismissed, yet it would be equally rash to reduce the Persian perception of the Greek threat to that of an elephant being stung by a bee. In the ancient world, where logistics placed severe constraints on the size and mobility of armies, even a small force, when disciplined and determined, could pose a serious threat. Persian rulers themselves recognized that Greek soldiers were among the best in the world and sought them as mercenaries. They also had good reason to fear that the Greek example of interference in Persian affairs and encouragement of insurrection might prove contagious, as indeed it did. Finally, the danger Greek navies represented to Persian maritime interests could not be ignored.

All in all, it seems reasonable to assume that the Persians took the Greek problem very seriously, and the failure of a major campaign against the Greeks had repercussions in Iran itself. The financial strains of the war interrupted construction at Persepolis, in which Xerxes had been particularly interested; Xerxes himself turned his attention from foreign policy to religious matters (he appears to have been something of a fanatic) and was caught up in palace intrigues. He was assassinated at Persepolis in 465. Most of his successors were weak and ineffective and seldom took the field in military campaigns; harsh taxation and ruthless suppression of revolts made the Persians hated in many of their provinces. Corruption and in-fighting at court continued; Artaxerxes II barely escaped assassination by his brother Cyrus during his coronation ceremony in 404! Incredibly, Artaxerxes pardoned Cyrus, who repaid the gesture by hiring an army of Greek mercenaries to try to seize the throne in the disastrous enterprise described by Xenophon in the *Anabasis*. Fear of succession disputes and bloodletting at court reached terrible proportions; Artaxerxes III Ochus (ca. 359–337) found it expedient to kill all possible rivals, including eighty brothers murdered in one day. The bonds of trust between the Persian kings and their generals also seem to have dissipated; Artaxerxes III would only confirm his commander-in-chief after receiving his family as hostages for his good behavior. That is not to say that the struggle against the Greeks was entirely abandoned; it merely shifted to a new policy which emphasized diplomacy and bribery over military action. By fanning the flames of the Peloponnesian War and chipping away at Athenian naval power, the Persians gradually restored much of their position. They were also able to use fear of the rising power of Macedonia to make friends out of old enemies like Sparta and Athens. In 338 B.C., however, Philip of Macedon completed his unification of Greece, and Artaxerxes III died after having been poisoned by his own doctor as part of a plot by a court eunuch. By then, so many members of the Achaemenid house had been murdered that the succession had to go to Darius III, a grand-nephew of Artaxerxes II. After a brief respite following the assassination of Philip in 336, Darius was confronted by Alexander the Great, who completed the destruction of the Persian Empire in three famous battles: Granicus (334), which "freed" the Ionian Greeks and opened up Asia Minor; Issus (333), which made possible the capture of the Mediterranean ports and Egypt; and Gaugamela (331), after which Alexander could take Babylon and invade the Persian plateau. The Persian treasury at Susa was looted, and the majestic palace-complex at Persepolis was burned down. Darius fled to the east where, defeated and deserted, he was finally imprisoned and murdered by one of his own satraps in 330. Alexander penetrated deep into eastern Iran and Central Asia, leaving a trail of Greek colonies in his wake.

THE LEGACY OF ANCIENT IRAN

With the death of Darius III and the establishment of Greek rule, the first major chapter in Iranian history was over. The ancient Iranian religious and cultural heritage would remain influential for centuries to come. The example of the Persian Empire deeply influenced and affected cultures from the Mediterranean to India. The Greek and Persian wars left an indelible impression on the character and outlook of European civilization. Yet, ironically, recollection of the genuine history of this period in Iran itself dimmed rapidly. While the memory of rulers like Cyrus and Darius remained vivid outside Iran, they were almost completely forgotten in their own country, superceded by the myths and heroic legends of eastern Iran.

What then is the real significance of ancient Iranian history for an understanding of the later history of Iran? For one thing, the themes and issues of the history of the ancient period are often illustrative of problems that recur throughout the country's history, even though the precedents may not have always been remembered. Moreover, the recovery of the history of the ancient period in the 19th and 20th centuries, and the justifiable pride Iranians could take in the magnificent accomplishments of their ancestors, provided new sources of inspiration for political and intellectual leaders as well as alternative models for the construction of national identity in modern times.

3

From the Parthians to the Mongols

The middle or "medieval" period of Iran's history extends from the fall of the Achaemenids in the 4th century B.C. to the rise of the Safavids in the 16th century A.D. During this time, the boundaries of the Iranian world were more or less defined by the Euphrates, the Caucasus, the Oxus, and the Indus. The region was Iranian at its core but ethnically quite diverse on its periphery. The first half of its history began with a flurry of urbanization and long-distance trade and the close integration of Mesopotamia and the Iranian plateau, while the latter half was marked by the steady decline of both urban life and commerce as well as the decreasing importance of Mesopotamia in Iranian affairs; the whole period was punctuated by foreign invasions and periodic fluctuations between regionalism and centralization. Throughout, basic socioeconomic patterns were remarkably consistent, with an overwhelmingly agrarian economy and a society dominated by a numerically small elite of warriors, bureaucrats, and religious officials. Of course, over the span of these two millennia there were numerous political and cultural changes, which serve to mark out four major subperiods: the loosely organized, culturally diverse era of the Parthians (3rd century B.C. to the 3rd century A.D.; the centralized, imperial era of the Sasanians (3rd to 7th centuries); the era of the formation of the Perso-Islamic states (7th to

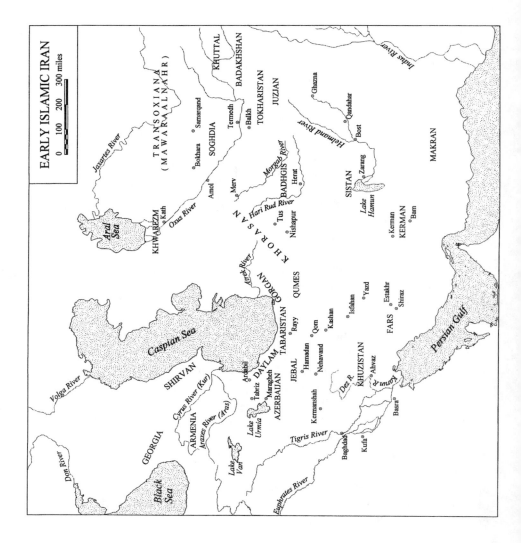

EARLY ISLAMIC IRAN

0 100 200 300 miles

end of the 10th centuries); and, finally, the era of Turko-Mongol domination (11th to 15th centuries). In the context of this work, it is possible to give only a brief overview of this rich and fascinating history.

THE PARTHIANS

The Parthians, a confederation of tribes, probably of Scythian origin, inhabiting the area between the Hari Rud River and the Caspian Sea (with a center near modern Ashkhabad), united under a king named Arsaces and rebelled against Greek rule around 238 B.C. Arsacid kings would hold various parts of Iran for some 400 years, but they constitute the most obscure period in all of Iran's history. No Parthian historical records, if they bothered to keep any, have survived, and the dynasty that replaced them had little interest in recording their accomplishments. Consequently, most information about them comes from classical sources, which give a distorted view in that they deal almost exclusively with the wars between the Parthians and the Greeks and Romans.

Parthian rule was mostly confined to eastern Iran until the decline of the Seleucids, under increasing pressure from the Romans, following the death of Antiochus IV Epiphanes. About 155 B.C., an Arsacid king, Mithridates I, moved into western Iran and, in 141, captured the most important city in Mesopotamia, Seleucia on the Tigris. A crushing defeat of the Roman army led by Crassus at the Battle of Carrhae in 53 B.C. confirmed the position of the Parthians as a major power in southwest Asia and the chief rival of Rome. Roman armies had great difficulty dealing with the Parthian use of light and heavy cavalry as well as their tactics of feigned retreat and massive volleys of arrows launched from horseback. Marc Antony continued to skirmish with the Parthians; Augustus negotiated a peace and the return of the legionary standards captured at Carrhae. Subsequent campaigns against the Parthians took place under Nero (55–63), Trajan (115–117), Marcus Aurelius (163–165), and Septimius Severus (194–198). Much less is known about Parthian relations with their neighbors to the east, but contacts with the Han Chinese and the Kushans seem to have been extensive and generally amicable.

Politically and culturally, the Parthian Empire was remarkably decentralized and diverse. Discrete areas were under the direct rule of the king, but most of the territory was controlled on his behalf by aristocratic warrior families, vassal kings, relatives, and local governors. According to traditional accounts, there were, as in the Achaemenid period, seven of the great feudal families (*vazorgan*). They held large provinces and maintained their own armies of freemen (*azadan*), which provided service to the Arsacid monarch as necessary. Among the most famous of these families were the Suren of Sistan, the Mehran of the central Elburz, and the Karen of Media.

Classical authors emphasize the pride Parthian rulers took in being regarded as philhellenes, and they do seem to have been quite comfortable with Greek culture. Up to the middle of the 1st century A.D., they used Greek and Greek characters for their inscriptions and coinage; they did, however, have their own language and script, and it eventually appeared on coins, ostraca, and other material. Insofar as there was a Parthian literature, it was largely if not completely oral. Parthian bards and minstrels were responsible for preserving the cycles of stories about epic heroes so important in the east Iranian tradition. In much later centuries, these were written down in the Iranian national epic immortalized by the poet Ferdowsi and in popular romances such as the story of the star-crossed lovers *Vis and Ramin*.

The Parthians certainly tolerated various religions: the mystery cults, Christianity, and Buddhism all had adherents in the Parthian Empire. The Parthians themselves may have blended elements of Hellenistic religion with Iranian ones. In general, however, they must have followed some form of Zoroastrianism since they maintained fire temples and practiced exposure of the dead; they are also credited in later tradition with having started a compilation of the Avesta.

SASANIAN IMPERIALISM

By the beginning of the 3rd century A.D., the Parthian Empire was under considerable strain. Although the last of its periodic wars with Rome had ended with an advantageous peace treaty in 218, the years of fighting had clearly sapped its strength and depleted its resources. Its territory in the east had been eroded by the Sakas and Kushans. Precious metals for coinage were in short supply, and outbreaks of plague and disease took their toll. The loose assembly of noble families and regional rulers over which the Arsacids presided was particularly vulnerable to disruption by a revolt aimed at the king himself.

Just such a revolt broke out around 205 in the province of Fars (Persis), which had long been a collection of virtually autonomous principalities with its own "kings" (governors formerly known as the *frataraka*) and written language (Middle Persian or Pahlavi). The origins and exact nature of the upheaval there are not at all clear, but it seems to have been inspired and directed by a commander of a local military garrison named Ardashir. During the period when the last Parthian kings were distracted by war with the Romans, Ardashir became ruler of Fars and was able to annex several districts on the fringes of the province from their pro-Parthian vassals. It was not long before Ardashir's tactical successes and increasing popularity enabled him to confront Artabanus V, the Parthian king, directly. The decisive battle was fought in 224 and resulted in the defeat and death of Artabanus. Ardashir moved immediately after his victory to secure the submission or defeat of the other noble families and local rulers and to establish his control over the whole of what had been the Parthian Empire. By 226, he had captured the capital city, Ctesiphon, in Mesopotamia, and was crowned there as the new king of kings. He is also thought to have taken Khorasan and Sistan and perhaps advanced as far as the Oxus and Indus territories.

The dynasty founded by Ardashir, the Sasanians, took its eponym from a certain Sasan, but the reason for that is a bit of a mystery. Ardashir was known as "son of Papak," and his relation to Sasan is uncertain. The Byzantine historian Agathias, who claimed to have had access to information from the Sasanian royal archives, said that Ardashir was the illegitimate child of Sasan by Papak's wife. A later inscription indicates that Ardashir was the son of Papak "the king," and that there was some unspecified relationship to Sasan "the lord," perhaps implying that Sasan was related to Papak's mother. In any case, the references to both Papak and Sasan must have been intended to establish the legitimacy of the dynasty through some kind of link to previous rulers.

Ardashir was a provincial strongman who had risen to be king of Iran, but his successor, Shapur I (240–271), had much grander ambitions. Like Darius, he has left a great inscription recording his ancestry, his accomplishments, and his religious zeal; in it, he explicitly referred to himself as king of kings of Iran and "non-Iran." His claims to empire extended from Arabia and Anatolia to the Caucasus and deep into Central Asia.

The chief foreign power in Shapur's way was Rome. He attacked the Romans in 241, advancing as far as Antioch in Syria. It is not clear whether this (or any subsequent campaign) was just an opportunistic raid or an effort to establish a permanent link to the Mediterranean. In any case, Shapur was driven back to the Euphrates by the emperor Gordian; and the two sides made a peace treaty in 244, after Gordian had been murdered by his own troops. In the last phase of the conflict, between 258 and 260, Shapur again advanced to Antioch and central Anatolia. It was there that he not only defeated but captured the emperor Valerian, whose abject humiliation was depicted in magnificent rock carvings on the cliff at Nakhsh-e Rostam in Fars and elsewhere. Roman prisoners captured in the battle were settled in various parts of Iran. The struggle between these two great imperial powers would continue to dominate the history of late antiquity. The Sasanians and the Romans (the Byzantines in later periods) fought at least ten major wars and numerous minor skirmishes without either side ever achieving a decisive victory.

Armenia was one area where Sasanian and Roman strategic interests were constantly in conflict. The Sasanians could not ignore it for several reasons. For one thing, it was at first ruled by members of the Arsacid family, who naturally tended to be hostile to the Sasanians. The Sasanians also feared that Armenia could be used by the Romans to menace Mesopotamia. In 252, Shapur I invaded Armenia and installed his own son as its king. The Sasanians retained direct control over Armenia down to about 279, when the Romans secured the restoration of an Arsacid king. The Sasanians continued to try to expand their influence over Armenia, if not by direct attack then through methods such as plotting the murder of its ruler or encouraging the conversion of the population to the Zoroastrian religion. In response, the kingdom of Armenia officially converted to Christianity in 301. In 364, Shapur II killed the Armenian king, devastated the countryside, and incorporated Armenia into his empire. Shapur III and the Byzantine emperor Theodosius decided in 387 to partition Armenia into two vassal states under Arsacid kings, one aligned with Rome and the other with Persia. In 428, the Sasanians, at the urging of some of the Armenian nobility, took direct control of their area. Yazdegerd II (440–457) tried to impose Zoroastrianism on the population and increased taxes. Dissident noblemen, church leaders, and peasants, joining forces with other peoples of the Caucasus, revolted against the Sasanians in 450, but they were crushed at the Battle of Avarayr in 451. Another revolt in 481–483 was also suppressed but led to some improvements such as freedom of religion for the Armenians. There was a third partition of Armenia in 591, followed by attempts to deport many of the inhabitants or otherwise depopulate the region.

By the time of Shapur I, the Sasanians had probably subjugated the Kushan principalities in Bactria and the Punjab. Shapur II also campaigned extensively in the east between 350 and 357, defeating the Chionites (Huns), some of whom were incorporated into his army. His successors faced a more formidable adversary in the Hephthalites (White

Huns), who were a thorn in the side of the Sasanians for quite some time. Bahram Gor (420–440) crossed the Oxus, defeated them, and forced them to agree to a peace treaty. They soon returned, however, defeating Persian armies and sometimes forcing the payment of tribute during the reigns of Yazdegerd II (440–457), Peroz (459–483), and Balash (483–485). They even began to play a role in Sasanian internal affairs as they helped put Peroz on the throne and twice assisted Kavad (485–498 and 501–531) in his efforts to become king. They were finally defeated in 554 by Khosrow I, who acted in concert with a new power in Central Asia, the Turks.

SASANIAN STATE AND SOCIETY

The most striking difference between the Parthian and Sasanian periods was the renewed emphasis on charismatic kingship and centralized government. In Sasanian theory, the ideal society was one which could maintain stability and justice, and the necessary instrument for this was a strong monarchy. According to the "Letter of Tansar," supposedly written by the chief Zoroastrian priest under Ardashir, society consisted of four classes—priests, soldiers, scholars, and artisans. Membership in a class was based on birth, although it was possible for an exceptional individual to move to another class on the basis of merit. The function of the king was to ensure that each class remained within its proper boundaries, so that the strong did not oppress the weak, nor the weak the strong. To maintain this social equilibrium was the essence of royal justice, and its effective functioning depended on the glorification of the monarchy above all other classes.

The exaltation of kingship was reflected in the attribution to rulers of illustrious ancestry going back to ancient kings and divinities, the use of magnificent crowns and regalia and grandiose titles, the introduction of elaborate court ceremonies and protocol, and the construction of grand palaces and monumental carvings. For example, Shapur I proclaimed himself "the Mazda worshipper, the god Shapur, king of kings of Iran and non-Iran, of the race of gods, son of the Mazda worshipper, of the god Ardashir, king of kings of the Iranians, of the race of gods, grandson of Papak, king; of the empire of Iran, I am the sovereign." In a famous letter to the Roman emperor quoted by Ammianus Marcellinus, Shapur II styled himself "king of kings, partner of the stars, brother of the sun and moon." The same sentiments were revealed in the rock carvings that depicted Sasanian kings in the presence of their divine ancestors, receiving the emblem of royalty from Ohrmazd (Ahura Mazda) himself, and on the imperial crowns which bore symbols of the sun and moon. Special fire temples in honor of the Sasanian house were established, and kings were venerated as deities after their death. The sacred nature of kingship was further emphasized by the belief that the king was endowed with a visible aura of royal glory (called *farr*).

The Sasanian monarchs employed many other methods besides royal propaganda to strengthen their hold on the empire. Many took concrete steps to win the loyalty and obedience of their subjects by attending to their material and social needs. They were very active in undertaking new irrigation works that would make more land available for agricultural production. They also sought to expand the urban life of the empire through the foundation of new cities. Ardashir alone is supposed to have founded eight cities, and Shapur I also established cities which he populated with prisoners taken during his wars. These projects not only had the effect of stimulating agricultural production, promoting trade and commerce, and increasing government revenues, they also expanded the numbers of people and the amount of land under the direct control of the monarchy rather than the noble families.

The Sasanian king was also to be revered as the guarantor of law and justice in society. The Sasanians established courts throughout their empire, from the largest cities to the smallest rural districts. They also maintained that, at least in theory, even the humblest subject could appeal directly to the monarch to right a wrong. In practice, the administration of the law was largely in the hands of the Zoroastrian clergy. The law itself was based heavily on the religious principles of Zoroastrianism, royal decrees, and precedents set in earlier cases. A comprehensive manual of the law, known as the "Book of a Thousand Legal Decisions," was compiled during the reign of Khosrow II Parviz. The concern of the Sasanian rulers for their duty of ensuring justice is reflected in many of the legendary stories told about them in later Iranian and Islamic tradition. Among the maxims attributed to Khosrow I Anoushirvan, which later rulers who wanted to emulate him would have done well to keep in mind, were these sayings: "The throne depends on the army, the army on revenue, revenue on agriculture, and agriculture on justice," and "The prosperity of the people is more important than a large army, and royal justice is more beneficial than times of abundance."

As implied throughout the above discussion, religion constituted a prime foundation of royal authority in the Sasanian Empire. The lax and tolerant attitude of the Parthians, which allowed for numerous regional cults and shrines to be maintained by their vassals, was not at all compatible with the kind of centralized state the Sasanians wished to build. Ardashir himself is supposed to have begun the process of destroying the regional religious cults and temples that had appeared under the Parthians and suppressing, by force if necessary, unauthorized religious activity. Shapur's inscription reveals that he was particularly concerned to found sacred fires associated with his dynasty and to provide the sacrifices and priests necessary to support them. The logical culmination of such an attitude would be the establishment of an official state church, and that is essentially what the Sasanians did.

It was not a forgone conclusion, however, that the Sasanians, even though they described themselves as Mazda worshippers, would promote Zoroastrianism as the state religion. At first, they took a definite interest in the teachings of Mani, the founder of Manichaeism. Mani was born in Mesopotamia in 216 and developed his religious teachings as the result of a series of divine revelations he is supposed to have received between 228 and 240, at the very time Ardashir was establishing his rule. As is well known, Mani propagated what was consciously intended to be a universal religion, a highly eclectic system that blended elements of ancient Iranian beliefs, gnosticism, Mithraism, Christianity, and Buddhism. He began preaching in the eastern provinces toward the end of Ardashir's reign, and returned to Mesopotamia when Shapur became king. Shapur honored Mani, gave him a high rank at court, and authorized him to teach his doctrines throughout the empire; Mani accompanied Shapur on some of his campaigns and presented him with the text of one of his scriptures. His faith spread rapidly and had considerable appeal in the eastern provinces and outside the Sasanian Empire. A later king, Bahram I, turned against Mani, ordered his arrest and execution (probably in 274), and persecuted the Manichaeans. This may have been due in part to the fact that Mani was the son of a Parthian nobleman, and his religion became politically suspect because of its strength in the Parthian heartland. More important, the Zoroastrian chief priest, Kartir, had played a critical role in elevating Bahram, rather than one of his brothers, to the throne. Kartir, backed by the Sasanian nobility, exerted tremendous influence over Bahram I and Bahram II and was able to consolidate the position of Zoroastrianism as the state religion.

The establishment of Zoroastrianism had been vigorously pursued by the orthodox priesthood for some time. Probably under Ardashir, they were organized in a hierarchical system headed by a chief priest appointed by the king. The first two of these chief priests were Tansar and Kartir, authors of the texts mentioned earlier. Tansar defended Ardashir's actions on the grounds that he was restoring the true religion and emphasized the harmony of interests between the monarchy and the established church: "Church and state were born from one womb, joined together, and never to be sundered." Kartir recorded how he was made "absolute in authority over the order of priests at court and in every province and place throughout the empire" and boasted that "religious activities were increased, many Vahram fires were founded, and many priests became happy and prosperous." In his words, he had "made the Mazda-worshipping religion and the good priests exalted and honored in the land."[1] He also boasted enthusiastically of the success he attained in the persecution of all rival religions. Manichaeans were hardly the only victims of the Zoroastrian intolerance introduced by Kartir and followed by some of his successors. After Christianity became the official religion of the Byzantine Empire, Iranian Christians, suspect as a political fifth column in Iran, also suffered periodic persecutions. Most Christians in Iran, however, were Nestorians, so this was less of a problem after the Orthodox Church condemned the doctrine as a heresy and persecuted its adherents, some of whom sought refuge in Iran.

One important consequence of the Sasanian religious policy was that the hymns and teachings of Zoroastrianism, which previously existed in oral form, were collected together in official written versions. Several editions of the Avesta were prepared under the auspices of the Sasanian rulers, the last and most authoritative being completed during the reign of Khosrow Anoushirvan. The texts of the Avesta were recorded in a special script to accommodate the ancient Iranian dialect in which they had been composed, but other religious writings, such as the commentary on the Avesta known as the Zand, were set down in the Sasanian vernacular language (Middle Persian or Pahlavi). This was probably a deliberate policy to ensure that the language of the Sasanians would be the standard for the whole empire, and that the Sasanians, rather than previous rulers, would receive credit for fostering religious knowledge. The Sasanian encouragement of literary scholarship also extended to nonreligious learning. Other writings prepared under court and priestly supervision included works on history and the national epic as represented in the *Khwaday-namag* (Book of Rulers) as well as philosophical and scientific texts collected from other areas.

Despite the emphasis on centralized monarchy in Sasanian Iran, aristocratic families continued to be quite powerful. The nobles and the masses of ordinary people were rigidly distinguished from each other. The "Letter of Tansar" praised Ardashir for fixing boundaries between nobles and commoners and forbidding any alliances or marriages between the two groups. The social chasm was reflected in rules pertaining to dress, deportment, gender relations, and property. There was an effort to keep wealth and status concentrated within the great families, and this probably received a religious sanction through the Zoroastrian practice of encouraging next-of-kin marriages (father-daughter, brother-sister). The Sasanian rulers generally sought to co-opt, not destroy, the noble families through the granting of titles and privileges that would attach them to the court and make them dependent on the king of kings. Ardashir, for example, was also said to have defined the various ranks within the aristocracy and their respective privileges. This led to the establishment of a complex, highly structured system of administration for the clergy, military, and bureaucracy headed, respectively, by a chief priest, a commander-in-chief (later four *spahbads* or generals), and a prime minister. Subordinate ranks in each division extended down to the district level. Particularly important posts were often held by members of the royal family itself. The steady increase in the power of the aristocracy, in alliance with the Zoroastrian clergy, would pose special problems for later Sasanian rulers.

CRISIS AND REVIVAL

The reign of Kavad I (488–531) represented a major watershed in Sasanian history. Not only did he have to endure the domination of Hephthalites, who had installed him as king, and defeats at the hands of the Byzantines, he also had to deal with one of the most dramatic socioreligious upheavals in Iranian history. Possibly reviving an older sectarian strain in Zoroastrianism, the priest Mazdak began calling for reforms that would have severely curtailed the privileges of the aristocrats and Zoroastrian clergy. Mazdak's teachings are known only through the reports of his enemies and have undoubtedly been distorted in order to present him in the worst possible light. His basic goal seems to have been to improve the conditions of the rural poor and to protect them from oppression and exploitation by the powerful aristocratic families, which had amassed huge estates and large harems. In Mazdak's view, evil in the world arose from competition for vital resources and their inequitable distribution. He thus taught that land and material goods should be distributed equally; women and children should belong to the whole community. Exactly how Mazdak proposed to do this is unclear, but it most likely involved breaking up estates and distributing land to peasants, giving handouts of food and other goods from the state treasury and temple stores, and liberating women from the harems. Oddly enough, Kavad at first supported Mazdak in his reforms, perhaps in order to break the power of the aristocratic families and win the support of the peasantry for the monarchy.

Naturally, the aristocrats and the orthodox clergy (both Zoroastrian and Christian in this case) were horrified at the appearance of Mazdakism and the social insurrection it had aroused. They determined to resist it with all their resources, and a struggle between Kavad's sons over the succession provided them with an opportunity. The Mazdakites preferred Kavus, who sympathized with them, but Kavad was apparently obliged to name Khosrow, who hated them, as his successor. Either immediately after Kavad's death, or perhaps already acting as if he were king, Khosrow removed any possibility of challenge to his authority by killing all his brothers and their male children except one, who escaped. He then turned with a vengeance on the Mazdakites. Around 528, he summoned Mazdak to the capital, ostensibly to participate in a religious debate, and then seized him and had him tortured to death. This was followed by a bloody purge in which thousands of the Mazdakites were killed.

Since the great social struggle had decimated both the aristocracy and the Mazdakites, Khosrow was in a good position to restore the authority of the monarchy and reorder the empire to his liking. While he was the implacable enemy of Mazdakism, he was willing to address some of the grievances it reflected and certainly did not want to see a complete restoration of aristocratic privilege. The chaotic situation created by the Mazdakite attempts at redistributing wealth was resolved by undertaking a complete land survey and census, with probably a good deal of land being taken over as crown property. The collection of taxes was reformed and regularized. Instead of paying with part of the crop as before, peasants paid a fixed rate in cash. Common people, but not the privileged classes, also paid a poll tax. Khosrow also initiated public works to stimulate agricultural production by repairing canals, building roads, founding villages, and so on. He reformed the administrative structure of the empire, dividing it into four large provinces each under the control of a governor responsible to him. The military was also changed in ways that undercut the power and private armies of the great families. Some soldiers were paid a salary, but Khosrow especially encouraged the use of *dehqans*, soldier-peasants in charge of a village, as the backbone of the army and the main line of defense in frontier areas.

While securing his throne, Khosrow had agreed to an "eternal peace" with the Byzantines, but he was concerned about the apparent revival of Byzantine power under Justinian. Taking advantage of Byzantine preoccupation with the western Mediterranean, Khosrow launched a surprise attack in 540, raided as far as Antioch, and established a naval presence on the Black Sea. The first phase of the war dragged on until 562, when the two parties concluded another peace on more or less equal terms. In alliance with the Turks, whose power had just been established in Central Asia, Khosrow then crushed the Hephthalites and reestablished the Oxus as the border of the empire. He was also able to achieve something of a strategic success against the Byzantines by defeating the Khazars north of the Caucasus and by expelling the Ethiopians from Yemen, transforming southern Arabia into a Persian protectorate. This would have prevented the Byzantines from establishing their own trade links with East Asia either overland to the north or by sea to the south. Fear of being outflanked in this way was probably the reason the Byzantines broke the peace treaty and engaged in a new and inconclusive war against Khosrow during the last years of his reign (572–579).

Because of his accomplishments, Khosrow came to be known by the epithet Anoushirvan ("Of the Immortal Soul"). He and his prime minister, Bozorgmehr, represented the epitome of ideal rulers and wise government. Many maxims and sage proverbs about government and administration were attributed to them. They are perhaps best summarized in the twelve rules of conduct Bozorgmehr gave Anoushirvan and which, according to the later Arab historian Masoudi, Khosrow is supposed to have had inscribed in golden letters: Fear God; be trustworthy and loyal; seek the advice of wise men; honor scholars, the nobles, and the officials; supervise judges and tax collectors strictly; check on the condition of prisoners; assure the safety of roads and markets; punish the guilty according to their crime; provision the army; respect the family; defend the borders; and watch government officials closely to remove the disloyal and incompetent.

Despite Khosrow Anoushirvan's accomplishments, the Sasanian Empire went into rapid decline after his death. One factor was continued discontent among the military nobility, especially in northeastern Iran. This manifested itself in the revolt of Bahram Choubin, a general descended from an old Parthian family, who came very close to overthrowing the Sasanian dynasty. Khosrow II Parviz (591–628) defeated Bahram and retained his throne largely because of assistance from the Byzantine emperor Maurice. When his benefactor Maurice was himself overthrown in a revolt by disgruntled elements of his army in 602, Khosrow Parviz launched another war against the Byzantines. The Persian forces were actually able to take Jerusalem in 614 and Alexandria in 619, and these initial successes apparently caused Khosrow Parviz to think he was destined to rule the world. In actuality, the wars and the extravagant luxury of his court severely overextended his resources. By 627, the Byzantines had reorganized under the emperor Heraclius and were beating back the Sasanians on all fronts. A new revolt, in which some of Khosrow's own sons were involved, then broke out; Khosrow was deposed and murdered. The remaining years of the Sasanian dynasty were marked by internal strife, frequent change of rulers, neglect and disruption of the crucial irrigation systems in Mesopotamia, and serious outbreaks of disease and famine.

FROM THE SASANIANS TO ISLAM

It is a firmly entrenched convention to make the Arab conquest of Iran and establishment of Islam in the 7th century A.D. a great historical watershed and consequently to distinguish sharply between the pre-Islamic and Islamic periods of the country's history. There are many points to commend this view, but it can also be misleading. The last truly imperial dynasty of Iran was overthrown, and Zoroastrianism, the original Iranian state religion, went into a precipitous decline. On the other hand, Arabic did not replace Persian as it did in the case of many other regional languages, and specific elements of Sasanian culture endured, above all in the theory and practice of statecraft. There was certainly nothing new about Iran being enriched by the other cultural traditions of the Near East, and the Arab invasion, not unlike the earlier Greek or Assyrian invasions, served as much as a creative stimulus as a destructive calamity. At the same time, Iran contributed at least as much as it received in the forging of Islamic civilization, and it is reasonable to speak of a distinctly Perso-Islamic culture. The transition from Sasanian to Islamic Iran should thus be seen as one marked by continuity as well as transformation, and the subsequent growth of Islam as a natural development of Iranian history in its regional setting.

Mesopotamia was an area of the utmost importance to the Sasanians. Not only was their capital located there, but it was heavily colonized by Iranians, a center of trade and commerce, the breadbasket of the empire, and the single greatest source of state revenue. Protecting it from Roman and Byzantine attack was essential, but it also had to be guarded against assault from the sedentary and nomadic Arabs living in the area stretching from Hatra to the littoral of the Persian Gulf. The ability of the Arabs, with or without foreign backing, to threaten the Sasanian heartland had been demonstrated as early as 260–263 when Odenathus, the king of Palmyra, harassed the army of Shapur I, which had just defeated the Romans, stripping it of its spoils and even besieging the capital, Ctesiphon. Gulf Arabs also raided Mesopotamia and briefly captured Ctesiphon during the reign of Shapur II. He retaliated with a successful naval expedition against them. To discourage future raids, he had holes bored through the shoulders of the prisoners and tied them together with ropes, thus earning himself among Arabs the name of Dhu'l-Aktaf, "He of the Shoulders." The general policy of later Sasanian rulers was to prevent destructive incursions by Arab nomads by establishing a buffer state on this border ruled by a friendly and loyal Arab dynasty, the Lakhmids, with their capital at Hira. One Lakhmid king, Mondhir III (ca. 505–554), not only protected the flank of the Sasanian Empire by penetrating deep into the Arabian peninsula but carried out successful raids into Byzantine Syria; as the Byzantine historian Procopius put it, he was "discreet, experienced in war, completely loyal to the Persians, energetic, [and] brought the Romans to their knees for fifty years."

Around 580, Noman III became the Lakhmid vassal king. In 602, Khosrow II Parviz deposed Noman, reportedly because of a personal grudge but more likely because Noman had converted to Christianity. The earlier Lakhmid rulers, unlike most of their subjects, had been pagans, and Noman's conversion to Christianity could have been interpreted as carrying a potential risk of a shift in alliance toward the Byzantines. In any case, Hira was thereafter governed by a sheikh from a rival Arab tribe, the Taghleb, under the supervision of a military governor (*marzban*). This led the Bakr b. Wael Arabs to revolt, and they defeated a combined Taghlebid-Sasanian army at Dhu Qar in 611. Although this triumph was celebrated in Arab verse and legend, it was probably little more than a minor skirmish at an insignificant watering hole. Nonetheless, it revealed a definite Sasanian weakness and was a portent of things to come.

In the chaos that followed the failure of the war with the Byzantines, a new element was added to the equation by the appearance of the Prophet Mohammad and the rise of Islam in the Arabian peninsula. Campaigns against renegade Arab tribes that had sought to apostatize from Islam brought Muslim armies under the famous general Khaled b. Walid to the area south of the Sasanian frontier on the lower Euphrates. This was the same region from which the most aggressive clans of the

Bakr b. Wael, the Shayban and the Ejl, had been launching raids into Sasanian territory. It was perhaps inevitable that the two groups should take mutual advantage of Sasanian disarray. Several sources indicate that the chief of the Shayban, Mothanna b. Haretheh, visited Medina, accepted Islam, and made obeisance to the Caliph Abou Bakr in return for recognition of his leadership and the cooperation of Muslim troops in the campaigns—in effect becoming a vassal king on behalf of the caliph.

On orders from Abou Bakr, Khaled joined forces with Mothanna and won a number of skirmishes with the Sasanians, culminating in the fall of Hira in 633. Although these battles sometimes involved Iranian commanders, they were mostly directed against pro-Sasanian Christian Arab tribes and in that sense had something of the character of an Arab civil war as well as a war against the Sasanians. By the spring of 634, when Khaled left to direct Arab operations on the Syrian front, both Muslim and Christian Arabs had more or less united under the command of Mothanna. The Sasanians had also reorganized under a new king, Yazdegerd III, were alert to the problem caused by the Arab raids, and began to counterattack, winning a major victory at the Battle of the Bridge in October 634. After the decisive Muslim victory in Syria at Yarmuk in 636, the second caliph, Omar, was able to transfer forces to the east and resume the offensive against the Sasanians. A pitched battle at Qadesiyya in June 637 ended with the rout of the Sasanian army and the complete collapse of Sasanian defenses in southern Mesopotamia. The capital, which the Arabs called Madaen, was left exposed; it was occupied after a short siege and then looted. Yazdegerd and such Sasanian forces as could escape fled northeast toward the Iranian plateau, hoping to regroup. However, defeats of Sasanian armies at Jaloula, Qasr-e Shirin, and Masabadhan assured Arab control of essentially all of Mesopotamia and most of Khuzistan.

Omar was very reluctant to extend the war to the Iranian plateau and supposedly wished that there could be a "wall of fire" between the Arabs and their Iranian enemies. Apart from any religious motivation it may have had, the war in Mesopotamia had been fought with the objective of dispossessing the Iranian nobility of their property (and perhaps gaining control of the ports involved in maritime trade with India), and Omar wanted time to consolidate and protect what had been gained. His hand was forced, however, by three other factors: His armies were still being harassed by local Sasanian leaders, there was the threat of Yazdegerd counterattacking if he raised a new army on the plateau, and some of Omar's own troops who felt slighted in the distribution of the Mesopotamian spoils were eager to carry out unauthorized raids to acquire more. One band of marauders crossed the Persian Gulf from Bahrain to raid Fars province, but their boats were later destroyed, and they were in danger of being captured. Omar then sent a relief force to rescue them, and it conquered several towns in southern Iran.

Meanwhile, the Iranians had managed to assemble another army at Nehavand, guarding the main pass through the Zagros to central Iran. They were attacked and routed by a large force sent by Omar, probably in the summer of 642. The "Victory of Victories" at Nehavand marked the effective end of organized Iranian resistance. Detachments of Arab forces based in the new camp cities of Kufa and Basra dispersed quickly throughout Azerbaijan, Fars, and Kerman and took possession of the main cities there, usually after signing treaties of capitulation specifying the amount of tribute to be paid. It was not until 650 that their hold on western Iran was consolidated and the subjugation of Sistan and Khorasan began in earnest (accounts of early Arab campaigns in Khorasan are almost certainly exaggerated). The Sasanians were not very popular in eastern Iran, and Yazdegerd failed miserably in rallying the population there. He was murdered by one of his own subjects near Merv in 651. Sistan was conquered after fierce fighting in 652; in Khorasan, many cities and garrisons chose to capitulate in order to minimize the loss of property, to protect the privileges or positions of the local commanders, and to maintain the frontier defenses. By 653, the invading forces had established themselves along the Oxus.

The death of Yazdegerd III marked the end of the Sasanian Empire, but the actual assimilation of its territory under the rule of the caliphs was a much more complicated process than what has been described here. During the initial invasion, many areas were simply bypassed and had to be subdued later; remote areas such as the Elburz principalities and parts of Fars would take much longer to occupy and control. Some local military governors and cities had surrendered and agreed to pay tribute in the expectation that the new rule would be transitory; when this proved not to be the case, they rebelled or attempted to withhold payment of tribute. The number of troops stationed in different places and the effectiveness of the new government varied widely from one locality to another; some provinces were under tight control, others held only tenuously. Internal problems such as the civil war between the followers of the caliph Ali and the Umayyad governor of Syria, Moawiyyeh, enabled some areas to break away and required new campaigns to reestablish caliphal authority over them. In general, it was not until around the year 700 that most of Iran could be said to be under the firm control of the caliphate, and by then the character of the new regime was changing rapidly.

THE RISE OF PERSO-ISLAMIC CIVILIZATION

The armies that destroyed the Sasanian Empire were predominantly Arab in composition, under Arab commanders, directed by Arab caliphs, do not seem to have had religious conversion as a primary motivation, and included Christian as well as Muslim Arabs in their ranks. Nonetheless, it might be more appropriate to describe this process as the "Muslim" rather than the "Arab" conquest of Iran. The conquering forces did include many Iranians; for them, unlike Christian Arabs who could be fit into a tribal structure, Islam was essential as a unifying bond. The process of integrating Iranians into Islam had begun even in the lifetime of the Prophet Mohammad, as is emphasized in later traditions about Salman Pak (Salman Faresi), the semi-legendary first Iranian convert. There were contacts between Mohammad's forces and the Sasanian garrisons that had been established in Bahrain and Yemen; both appear to have either converted to Islam or otherwise collaborated with the Arabs. Several thousand Iranians had joined the Muslim army by 635, and there are reports of how they distinguished themselves at Qadesiyya and shared in the spoils of the battle. Part of Omar's reluctance to extend the conquests may have been that he conceived of Islam as a purely Arab religion and was fearful of the effects even more extensive contacts with Iranians would have in diluting that identity, but this proved impossible to avoid. The pattern of Iranian collaboration with the Arabs in combat and administration, followed by conversion to Islam, was repeated constantly throughout the wars of expansion and the following years. By the time the conquering armies established their new frontier on the Oxus, at least one-fourth of the troops were made up of Iranian auxiliaries and converts.

It is not easy to separate the specific history of Iran from the general history of the caliphate during this period. The most important issue would certainly be the spread of Islam among the general population, the failure of resistance to it, and the emergence of Perso-Islamic culture and principalities. This process played itself out quite differently in northwestern, southern, and eastern Iran. Not enough research has been done to be certain about the details of the experience in all areas, but it does seem clear that events in the province of Khorasan were critical in this regard. The situation there was especially conducive to the blending of Arab and Iranian cultures in an Islamic framework. There had been relatively little fighting to embitter relations between the Arabs and the Iranians, and both people had a mutual interest in defending the frontier against the hostile Turks and Hephthalites of Central Asia. The long distance from the camp cities in Mesopotamia meant that Arab troops had to be garrisoned permanently in Khorasan; this promoted both awareness of Islam among the local population and assimilationist tendencies among the Arab soldiers. The general harmony between the Arab and Iranian elite seems to have produced a particularly effective (and oppressive) system of taxation, which induced many non-Muslims to convert or to flee, as in the well-known case of the Zoroastrians who migrated to India around 720.

Problems connected with both the settlement of the Arab colonists in Khorasan and the spread of Islam among the Iranian population fed into rising discontent with the Umayyad caliphate. As in other places, the idea of removing barriers to conversion and ending various forms of discrimination against non-Arab converts was closely linked to support for a legitimist theory of the caliphate, which emphasized the importance of the ruler's descent from the family of the Prophet Mohammad (an early form of what would eventually become the Shi'ite branch of Islam). All these issues came to a head in a great revolt in Khorasan in 747 directed by a man almost certainly of Iranian descent, Abou Moslem, and which included a broad coalition of Iranians as well as Arab residents of Khorasan in its ranks. Shrewdly exploiting rivalries between other factions, the insurgents defeated the Umayyad governor of Khorasan, pushed Umayyad forces out of Iran, and ultimately destroyed the Umayyad caliphate. After reaching Mesopotamia in 749, the rebel generals proclaimed a descendant of Mohammad's uncle Abbas as caliph.

There continued to be opposition to the new Abbasid caliphate in various parts of Iran, especially after the popular general Abou Moslem was murdered by the second Abbasid caliph, Mansour, in 755. There were revolts by Sonbadh the Magian, perhaps an officer in Abou Moslem's army, at Rayy (756); by Ostadhsis, apparently another renegade former officer, in the area of Herat (767); by Moqanna, the "veiled prophet," in the Zarafshan valley (774–779); by Babak, leader of the Khorramdin sect, in Azerbaijan (817–837); and by Mazyar, a prince of the Karen family, in Tabaristan (839–840). Unlike earlier resistance by local military prefects, which had an essentially secular basis, most of the anti-Abbasid revolts, like the Abbasid revolution itself, are thought to have combined political with religious dissent. The available sources often attempt to depict these revolts as interconnected in an anti-Arab conspiracy intended to destroy Islam and lead to a Zoroastrian restoration; others try to suggest a link between them and later sectarian divisions in Islam. This makes it difficult to assess their nature, which various authorities have interpreted as nationalistic and anti-Arab in character or as the last gasps of organized Zoroastrian resistance to Islam, others as the resurfacing of pre-Islamic Iranian heresies like those of Mani and Mazdak, and still others as simply efforts by Iranian feudal lords to maintain their independence by exploiting religious sentiments. It seems best to view them as a diverse and unrelated series of local rebellions in formerly isolated areas aimed at resisting taxation and stricter control by the centralizing Abbasid government.

Under the Abbasid caliphs, based in Mesopotamia rather than Syria, the influence of Iranians and Iranian culture in the Islamic world rose steadily. This was reflected by their increasing presence in the military, the bureaucracy, and scholarly circles as well as the adaptation of institutions and ideas of Sasanian origin or derived from Sasanian practices to Islamic needs. Not only had the dynasty been founded by men like Abou Moslem, but its intellectual outlook was shaped by those like Ebn al-Moqaffa, who translated Sasanian works of literature and political philosophy into superb Arabic prose, and its affairs were expertly handled by ministers like the Barmakids, descendants of a priestly family from Balkh. (Unfortunately, it cannot be said that the Abbasids repaid such supporters very well: Abou Moslem, Ebn al-Moqaffa, and Jafar Barmaki were all murdered by suspicious caliphs.) The high point in the "Persianization" of the Abbasid caliphate came after the reign of Haroun-al-Rashid (786–803). In 811, a civil war broke out between the caliph Amin and his brother Mamoun. Mamoun's mother was probably Iranian, and he was serving as governor of Khorasan when Amin attempted to replace him. Mamoun was supported by a largely Iranian army that advanced to the Abbasid capital, Baghdad, and installed Mamoun as caliph. He also relied heavily on a minister of Iranian origin, Fazl b. Sahl, and it appeared he was considering moving the capital to Khorasan. The pervasive Iranian influence during this period gave rise to fears among some Arab courtiers that their importance would be eclipsed entirely, but these proved groundless. After Mamoun's death in 833, Turkish slave soldiers began to supplant Iranians as the backbone of Abbasid rule, but by then autonomous Perso-Islamic principalities were beginning to take form in Iran itself.

One of the most capable and aggressive generals in Mamoun's army was Taher Dhu'l-Yaminayn (Taher the Ambidextrous), whose forces were responsible for killing Amin after the fall of Baghdad. Taher came from an Iranian family prominent in Abbasid affairs since the days of the revolution, and Taher himself could be compared to Abou Moslem in his political importance. Unlike Abou Moslem, however, he did not make the mistake of trusting in the gratitude of the caliph for the services he had rendered. Instead of staying too long outside Iran, Taher in 821 requested and received the governorship of Khorasan, which included authority over all provinces east of Iraq. Once there, he is said to have had references to Mamoun dropped from the sermon at Friday prayer services, and he definitely omitted the caliph's name from some of the coins he had minted and commanded his own regional army. Although he died only a year later, his office was inherited by his son and remained in the Tahirid family for some fifty years. The significance of these changes is open to debate. In fundamental ways, a virtually independent Tahirid dynasty had come into being, and the caliphs were either unable or unwilling to contest it. Yet Tahirid authority was still derived from the caliphs, at least in theory, and the Tahirids can hardly be described as enemies of the Abbasids, Islam, or Arabic culture. They might best be understood as the Islamized equivalents of the *marzbans* and great feudal families of earlier eras, nominally subservient to an Abbasid king of kings but largely sovereign within their own realm. In that sense, the pendulum was swinging away from the highly centralized, absolutist, divine-right version of monarchy envisaged by the early Abbasid caliphs—in many respects, from a kind of neo-Sasanian system to a neo-Parthian one.

After the Tahirids, a variety of dynastic principalities began to develop within the Iranian world that were clearly more autonomous both politically and culturally. The most important of these were the Saffarids, the Buyids, and the Samanids. While ethnically and geographically Iranian, all three of these dynasties were completely Islamic in their religious orientation, and there is little doubt that by this time the majority of the Iranian population had converted to one form of Islam or another.

The Saffarid dynasty arose in Sistan, a remote and turbulent province that had always been difficult for the caliphs to govern because of the large number of Kharijites, a militant sectarian group that had turned against other Muslims in the time of Ali, who had taken refuge there. Tahirid efforts to extend their control over the area provoked a reaction that united the Kharijites and indigenous vigilante bands (*ayyars*) under the banner of an adventurer of plebeian social origin, Yaqoub the Coppersmith, and his brothers. Yaqoub drove out the Tahirid governor, consolidated his authority in Sistan, launched raids on neighboring non-Muslim territories, and began to expand into Khorasan, Kerman, Fars, and other provinces. In 873, he overthrew the Tahirids, and it appeared he might even capture Baghdad, but he was repulsed by an Abbasid force in 876. The Saffarids remained a major power until about 911 and a regional one for centuries after that.

The Saffarids are of considerable significance in two respects: They challenged the deferential attitude toward the caliphs that had long prevailed in Iran, and they showed that it was possible to develop a separate, regional, populist cultural identity that could be both Iranian and Islamic. The Saffarids sometimes sent gifts to the Abbasid caliphs, and the caliphs made tactical offers to recognize Saffarid "governorship," but the two obviously detested and distrusted each other. Yaqoub scornfully derided the way the Abbasids had treated their clients, and he did not hesitate to clash with them in pursuit of his own interests. He also mocked the practice of court poets offering him laudatory odes in Arabic, which he admitted he could not understand, and encouraged poets to use the vernacular language.

The Buyid dynasty was likewise founded by a soldier of fortune, Ali b. Bouyeh, and his brothers. They came from another remote and heterodox region, the mountainous area of Gilan known as Daylam. Caliphal authority there was late being established and was always tenuous; just as Kharijites had flocked to Sistan, descendants of Imam Ali and their Shi'ite supporters had often taken refuge in Daylam and shaped the development of Islam there. Several petty dynasties of local rulers came from Daylam, but the Buyids were the most successful by far. Ali b. Bouyeh had hired out his services to a strange generalissimo by the name of Mardawij but later broke with him. Mardawij, who had seized much of western Iran, was descended from the Iranian provincial aristocracy, was a non-Muslim, and had openly vowed to destroy the "empire of the Arabs" and restore Zoroastrianism and the Iranian empire. His grand designs were cut short by his assassination while celebrating a Zoroastrian festival in Isfahan in 935. Ali b. Bouyeh and his brothers then took over most of his territory. Ali sent his brother Ahmad to occupy Khuzistan, and from there Ahmad was able to advance on and enter Baghdad in 945, essentially unopposed. After securing recognition and lofty titles from the caliph Moktafi, the Buyids deposed him and installed Moti, a pitiful Abbasid puppet, in his place. The political history of the Buyid rulers is far too complex to discuss here; suffice it to say that they shared out their empire among the members of the family, generally recognizing one as first among equals, and various Buyids ruled in Mesopotamia and western Iran for more than a century.

Two characteristics of Buyid rule are often cited as being of special importance in terms of anticipating future developments in Iranian history: They were nominally Shi'ites, and they cultivated elements of pre-Islamic Iranian political culture. The Buyids did in fact encourage commemoration of Shi'ite holy days (such as the reported designation of Ali as Mohammad's successor at Ghadir Khomm and the martyrdom of Hosayn during Ashoura), use Shi'ite formulae in the prayer rituals, patronize Shi'ite scholars, claim descent from Sasanid kings, use the title *shahanshah*, wear Sasanian-style crowns, and mint coins bearing Pahlavi inscriptions. Not too much should be made of this, however. Political circumstances compelled the Buyids to maintain the Abbasid caliphate, which they quite possibly saved from destruction by the Fatimid Shi'ites and other enemies. The type of Shi'ism they represented was well within the Islamic mainstream, and they did little if anything to discourage, much less attack, Sunni Islam. The high culture they promoted, as exemplified in the literary works of their most famous minister, Saheb b. Abbad, or their patronage of the anthologist Abu'l-Faraj Esfahani (an Arab of Umayyad ancestry), was almost completely Arabic in composition and orientation. It is even debatable whether the Buyids themselves understood the meaning or implications of the Iranian titles and trappings they used.

The Samanids, who claimed descent from Bahram Choubin, were a family of *dehqans* in eastern Iran, probably originating in the Balkh area. The earliest known ancestor, Saman-khoda, converted to Islam just before the Abbasid revolution. His four grandsons distinguished themselves in support of Mamoun and the Tahirids and were rewarded by being entrusted with strategic territories on the periphery of Khorasan, mostly beyond the Oxus. With the fall of the Tahirids to the Saffarids, the Abbasids in 875 recognized a Samanid, Nasr b. Ahmad, as their legal representative in Transoxiana, followed in 892 by his brother, Esmail. Esmail carried out raids deep into central Asia against the Turkish nomads and won a great victory over them at Talas in 893. The capture of so many Turks was important since it enabled the Samanids to supplement their military forces with Turkish slave troops and to derive considerable revenue from the sale of Turkish slaves to other areas. Esmail also vigorously contested the Saffarids for control of Khorasan, defeating their forces there around 900. The Samanid rulers were widely and justly celebrated for the prosperity of their realm, their effective and judicious administration, and their lavish patronage of all forms of arts and scholarship. As a center of learning and commerce, their capital, Bokhara, was a rival to Baghdad itself.

In many ways, the Samanids were of much more importance than either the Saffarids or the Buyids in the development of Perso-Islamic civilization. Their achievements in this regard are often overlooked on the grounds that they were essentially a Central Asian power that controlled a relatively small part of the Iranian plateau, were Sunni and pro-Abbasid, and presided over a transfer of military power from Iranian *dehqan*s to Turkish slave soldiers. In fact, the Samanids followed quite independent policies (it is very suggestive that they would have chosen to trace their ancestry back to Bahram Choubin, a rebel of Arsacid background, while the Buyids vaunted descent from Bahram Gor, the protégé of a Lakhmid king). Under Nasr II b. Ahmad (913–942), they even considered disavowing their allegiance to the Abbasids in favor of the Fatimids. They later repressed Ismaili Shi'ism in their realm, but tolerated the more moderate Twelver Shi'ism. When they supported Sunnism, they usually did so in its Hanafi form, a school of law founded by a man of Iranian ancestry and one which took a liberal position on issues involving non-Arabs and regional concerns, notably giving great latitude to the use of languages other than Arabic for religious purposes. It was the Samanids, certainly not the Buyids and more than the Saffarids, who revived Persian as a written language (by using Arabic script for a form of Pahlavi) and gave it respectability. In a religious decree authorizing the use of Persian, the Samanid authorities explicitly stated that "here, in this region, the language is Persian, and the kings of this realm are Persian kings." They continued to patronize Arabic scholarship, but they also experimented with the use of Persian for keeping state records, sponsored the translation of important works from Arabic into Persian, promoted a host of famous Persian poets such as Roudaki and Daqiqi, and stimulated interest in the recovery of the Iranian national epic that would find its greatest expression in Ferdowsi's *Shahnameh*. While the Samanids did make increasing use of Turks in their army and at court, they also devised a system for the year-by-year training of their Turkish *gholams* or "pages" to prepare them for military command and administration of a province. This ensured that they were properly acculturated in their new environment, and the successful transmission of the distinctive Samanid Perso-Islamic bureaucratic, literary, and religious values to the Turks meant that these values would be transmitted with them throughout Iran and beyond.

THE TURKO-MONGOL ERA

It was, however, reliance on the Turks, along with financial difficulties and a tendency to overextend themselves, that proved the undoing of the Samanids. Turkish pressure on the Samanids came from two directions, the slave soldiers they had brought into their service and the newly Islamized Turks on their borders. As had happened in the case of the Abbasid caliphs and their slave troops, some of the Samanid Turkish commanders soon began to take personal control of areas to which they were sent. Foremost among these was the general Alptigin, who used his own contingent of slave soldiers to conquer Ghazna, in the eastern part of what is now Afghanistan, around 961. The Turkish garrison at Ghazna, although technically still servants of the Samanids, selected its own commanders and was largely self-governing. Eventually, one of them founded a truly independent dynasty of rulers known as the Ghaznavids (977–1186). The Ghaznavids gained fame for their religious raids (*ghazw*) directed toward the Punjab and Ganges plain, carrying out at least seventeen expeditions into India. Sultan Mahmoud of Ghazna (998–1030) was particularly famous for his wars in India, but he was more interested in filling his treasury than annexing territory. During his raids, many Buddhist and Hindu religious sites were demolished and vast quantities of slaves, jewels, and precious metals carried off as spoils.

Meanwhile, many of the Turkish tribesmen in Inner Asia had become Muslims (usually referred to as Turkomans after their conversion to distinguish them from pagan Turks) and began to found their own states. The first of these was ruled by the Qarakhanid dynasty (992–1211). It was the Qarakhanids who were responsible for destroying the Samanids; they occupied Bokhara in 999 and eliminated the last Samanid pretender in 1005. Although the Qarakhanids were Muslims and regarded themselves as legitimate Islamic rulers, their society and culture remained essentially Turkic and rather isolated from the rest of the Muslim world. The Qarakhanid occupation of Transoxiana marked the beginning of a process that transformed this formerly Iranian cultural zone into a largely Turkish one.

The Seljuks (1038–1194) were the most important of the new Turkish dynasties. Seljuk, the clan chief from whom the dynasty took its name, apparently broke away from the Khazar Turkish confederation and established himself in the area of a market town named Jand, near where the Syr Darya flows into the Aral Sea. Having converted to Islam, Seljuk and the followers he attracted became *ghazis*, or warriors for the faith, fighting against the pagan Turks and offering their assistance as volunteer soldiers at various times to the Samanids, Qarakhanids, and Ghaznavids. At the same time, they cultivated good relations with the populace, and especially the religious leaders, of the cities in the region. As the numbers of their confederation grew, and under pressure from rival groups, the Seljuks sought to move into Khorasan; this eventually brought them into conflict with the Ghaznavids. Under the leadership of two brothers, Chagri and Toghrel, the Seljuks occupied Nishapur and proclaimed an independent sultanate in 1038. They then attacked and destroyed the Ghaznavid army at the Battle of Dandanqan (1040). Chagri took control of the territory in eastern Iran, and Toghrel began to annex new areas to the west. In 1055, Toghrel reached and occupied Baghdad. His successors, Alp Arslan (1063–1072) and Malek Shah (1072–1092), both guided by the exceptionally gifted Persian vizier Nezam-al-Molk (1019–1092), made the Seljuk sultanate the most powerful state in the region, dominating an area from Syria to Central Asia. Alp Arslan won a great victory over the Byzantines at Manzikert in 1071, opening up much of Anatolia to the Turks and to Perso-Islamic civilization.

The Ghaznavids and Seljuks were warriors with little or no experience in administration who had to confront the problem of how to govern the territories they acquired. Not surprisingly, they elected to model their governments after those of the Iranian dynasties they replaced, the Samanids in particular. Of necessity, they relied heavily on the existing Persian bureaucracy for their officials, administrators, and advisors. Under the influence of Iranian statesmen, the greatest of whom was Nezam-al-Molk, they adopted the concepts and values of traditional Iranian theories of kingship and justice, which were outlined in Nezam-al-Molk's famous handbook of administration, the *Siasatnameh*. At the same time, arts, literature, and the sciences all flourished under their patronage. Mahmoud of Ghazna was notoriously determined to project the image of an enlightened ruler, even going so far as to kidnap scholars he could not otherwise persuade to come to his capital. The scientist Biruni, who used knowledge gained during the Ghaznavid operations in India to write a famous book about India and Indian civilization, was perhaps the greatest of the men of learning patronized by the Ghaznavid court. In literature, the Turkish rulers especially encouraged the production of Persian poetry. A galaxy of talented Persian poets thrived during the

Ghaznavid period, including Farroukhi, Manouchehri, and above all Ferdowsi, author of the magnificent epic poem of Iran, the *Shahnameh*. This period also saw the production of what is probably the single greatest example of Persian historiography, Bayhaqi's *History of Masoud*, a beautifully written, detailed, authoritative, and insightful account of the reign of this Ghaznavid sultan (unfortunately, only a small portion of the text has survived). Omar Khayyam, Moezzi, and Anvari are among the best known poets who flourished in Seljuk times.

In their religious policy, the Ghaznavids and Seljuks put their full support behind the revival of Sunni jurisprudence and scholarship, which had been developing in reaction to the rise of Fatimid power and the influence of Ismaili Shi'ite missionaries in Iran. At much the same time that the Fatimids were establishing the Azhar, an official center for training Ismaili authorities in Cairo, a similar institution was appearing in the east, particularly at Nishapur. This was the *madrasa*, a kind of college devoted specifically to the advanced formal study of Sunni law. The Seljuks did not originate this institution, but they did encourage the establishment of *madrasas* throughout their empire. The *madrasas* were supported financially by charitable endowments of real property, known as *waqf*, the revenue from which was used to maintain the buildings, pay teachers, and accommodate the students.

Another important element in the religious trends of this period was the promotion of Sufism. Early Sufism had been a highly personalized and emotional form of Islam that would often manifest itself in ways far removed from the norms of behavior envisaged in the religious law—singing, dancing, or celebration of drunkenness or erotic love as symbols of mystical experience at one extreme, and excessive fasting, devotional exercises, asceticism, and celibacy at the other. By Seljuk times, Sufism was integrated more closely into conventional Sunni Islam, and it was institutionalized. The man most often cited as the architect of the formal reconciliation of Sunnism and Sufism was the Iranian religious scholar and mystic, Abou Hamed Ghazzali (1058–1111). Ghazzali was highly critical of Shi'ism, philosophy, and speculative theology; in the interest of social order, he also argued for acceptance of the authority of the sultanate. Most important, he championed the cause of a liberalized and spiritualized approach to the law which would tolerate many Sufi practices, and of a "sober" Sufism which stayed within the general boundaries of Islamic law. About the same time, Sufism ceased being a highly individualistic activity and took on a collective and institutional form. Students of Sufism attracted to a charismatic Sufi master (the *shaykh* or *pir*) began to group together in an association known as a *tariqa* ("path" or "way"). These orders had their own particular initiation rites, and the members followed the rules of behavior, rituals, and spiritual exercises established by the master. They typically maintained monasteries or hospices in which the followers could reside during spiritual retreats; these would often be built around the tomb of the founder of the order or the tombs of prominent disciples of the order. One such order grew up around the shrine of Jalal-al-Din Roumi (1207–1273) in Konya, where this famous Persian poet and Sufi had moved at the request of a Seljuk prince. Roumi's masterpiece was the *Masnavi*, a long collection of mystical stories in rhyming couplets, which has been called the equivalent of the Koran in Persian. From this point on, classical Persian poetry and Sufism were almost inseparable.

In 1092, the powerful vizier Nezam-al-Molk was murdered, supposedly by one of the Nizari Isma'ili Assassins. Malek Shah died the same year, and the Seljuk Empire began to disintegrate. One reason for this was internal disputes over the succession, which sometimes amounted to virtual civil war. In addition, young Seljuk princes were sent out to act as nominal governors of the provinces. Each was assigned an *atabeg* or guardian chosen from the commanders of the slave soldiers in the Seljuk army. Some of the *atabeg*s in fact took over the provinces for themselves and founded their own petty dynasties. Another element of instability came from a new influx of nomadic Turkomans into Seljuk territory. They were very difficult to control, and wreaked considerable destruction in the countryside. In 1157, they killed Sanjar, the Seljuk sultan, and proceeded to overrun much of the Seljuk Empire.

The eastern areas of the Iranian world were further devastated by the Mongol invasions that began with the campaigns of Genghis Khan in 1219. Although the Mongols were rumored to have been invited to attack by an Abbasid caliph hoping to weaken his rivals, the actual cause for the invasion is generally agreed to have been the murder of emissaries Genghis Khan had sent to the Khwarezmshah, the most important ruler in eastern Iran at the time. The Mongols were not Muslims, had little respect for any sedentary civilization, and were fighting an utterly brutal war of revenge; compared to the incursions of the Turkish nomads, the Mongol invasion was a calamity of the first magnitude. For four years, until 1223, the Mongols wreaked havoc; great cities like Balkh, Merv, and Nishapur were devastated and depopulated, never to recover their previous grandeur. The Mongol onslaught resumed in 1255–1260, as Mongol armies under Genghis Khan's grandson Hulegu swept across

Iran, Iraq, and Syria. Hulegu exterminated the Ismaili Shi'ite enclaves that had been established in Iran and captured and sacked Baghdad in 1258, killing the Abbasid caliph and bringing that most prestigious of Muslim institutions to an effective end. For most of the next 300 years, Iran would be dominated by Mongols and rulers of Mongol descent.

The dynasty established by Hulegu, the Ilkhanate (1256–1353), ruthlessly exploited the sedentary population by extracting as much in taxation as it could and did incalculable damage to the agricultural infrastructure of the country. Its early rulers were also quite hostile to Islam and tried to encourage Buddhism and Nestorian Christianity. Most of their energy was focused on wars with their external enemies, notably the Golden Horde and the Mamluks of Egypt. This began to change under Ghazan Khan (1295–1304), who converted to Islam and, with the assistance of a talented Iranian vizier, Rashid-al-Din, reformed the system of taxation and sought to revive agriculture. Ghazan Khan did not live long enough to make a real difference, and his successors accomplished little. When the last Ilkhan, Abou Said, died in 1335 without an acceptable member of the house of Genghis Khan to succeed him, Iran again broke up into numerous and usually hostile regions under various Mongol officers.

The last of the great Turko-Mongol conquerors was Tamerlane (Timur Lang). Although Turkish speaking, Tamerlane was of Mongol ancestry (and claimed to be related to the house of Chagatay, one of Genghis Khan's sons). Tamerlane combined the fighting spirit of the Mongols with the most militant aspects of the Islamic *ghazi* tradition, and he spent essentially the whole of his adult life (from around 1360 to 1405) engaged in military campaigns that carried him back and forth across much of Asia: establishing his authority in Central Asia (1360–1380); conquering Iran and Mesopotamia (1380–1387); and invading the lands of the Golden Horde (1395), the sultanate of Delhi (1398), the Mamluks (1400), and Ottoman empire (1402). The path of death and destruction he left behind was vast, and it is ultimately very difficult to see what the point of his wars may have been, other than proving his military prowess in as many places as possible. Iran was again united under his rule, but the main effect was to undo the little that had been achieved by the more progressive of the earlier Mongol khans.

It should not be imagined, however, that Iran was a complete desert under Mongol rule; quite to the contrary, certain aspects of Perso-Islamic culture flourished greatly during this period. Even a barbarian like Hulegu had a certain respect (or at least superstitious awe) for some forms of science and learning. Among other things, he patronized the famous

Iranian Shi'ite scholar Naser-al-Din Tousi and provided him with an elaborate observatory near Maragheh in Azerbaijan, where some of the most advanced and sophisticated astronomical work to that time was carried out. The extensive cross-cultural contacts that were made possible by the establishment of the Mongol imperium enriched and broadened geographical and especially historical writing under the Mongols; Ata-Malek Jovayni's *History of the World Conqueror* was an important study of the life of Genghis Khan, and Rashid-al-Din's *Compendium of Histories* was a remarkably well informed and truly universal history of the world. Lyrical and mystical poetry also continued to be in vogue, and two of the very greatest classical Persian poets, Sadi (d. 1292) and Hafez (d. 1390), lived during the Mongol period, albeit in a city, Shiraz, that had escaped the worst of the Mongol catastrophe. Hafez is actually said to have once met the formidable Tamerlane, who wanted to scold him for a verse he had written; undaunted, he held his own in banter with the conqueror. It may also be noted that Mongol patronage made possible the creation of some of the finest illustrated manuscripts and most impressive architectural monuments in Iran.

The assessment of most historians of the Mongol legacy in Iran is not unlike the famous words attributed to a survivor of one of the Mongol assaults: they came, they killed, they burned, they looted, and they left. The devastation and disruption caused by the Mongols in Iran was indeed immense, even allowing for some exaggeration in the historical records, and they eventually disappeared, but not exactly without a trace. Essentially negative, the Mongol impact also opened up creative possibilities. They destroyed the hold of old institutions like the caliphate; they smashed the great urban centers of Perso-Islamic civilization but left bits and pieces of its heritage in the rubble around them; they shifted the cultural balance from eastern to western Iran; they brought new ideas about the nature of the ruling institution and the ruler's prerogatives in making law; they opened the door to religious heterodoxy and innovation; they changed the ethnic mix and demography of the country; and they altered its economy and social life in fundamental ways that increased the importance of tribes and tribal politics. The question was how—and when—these diverse elements could be reassembled into a coherent whole.

NOTE

1. Quoted in Mary Boyce, *Zoroastrians: Their Religious Beliefs and Practices* (London: Routledge and Kegan Paul, 1979), p. 109.

4

Early Modern Iran

Key strands of modern Iranian culture go back to the pre-Islamic, Islamic, and Turko-Mongol periods, but the distinctive features that make it recognizable as a nation-state today really began with the establishment of the Safavid dynasty in the early 16th century. Two factors are of special interest in that regard, the creation of a Shi'ite religious identity and the relations of Iran with neighboring powers and the larger world.

POST-MONGOL IRAN

In the aftermath of the meteoric career of Tamerlane, control of Iranian territory in the 15th century came to be divided between his successors, the Timurid dynasts in the east, and confederations of Turkoman tribes, known as the Black Sheep (Qara Qoyunlu) and the White Sheep (Aq Qoyunlu), in the west. Of these, the Timurids were the most successful in creating a viable and culturally sophisticated state. Rulers of this dynasty continued to carry out military campaigns, as success in warfare was one of the main props of legitimacy for a Turko-Mongol sovereign, but the Timurids were really distinguished as patrons of Islamic scholarship, literature, art, and architecture. Some of them were quite accomplished in these fields themselves, notably the calligrapher-prince

Baysonqor and the astronomer-king Ulugh Beg. A number of the most spectacular and beautiful examples of illustrated Persian manuscripts were produced at the behest of this dynasty. The Timurids chose Herat as their capital and beautified it with many mosques and other monuments; Gowhar Shad, wife of the ruler Shah Rokh, was responsible for endowing the great mosque at Mashhad around the tomb of Imam Reza, which became an important place of pilgrimage for Shi'ite Muslims. The dynasty finally collapsed under the weight of an attack on Herat by Mohammad Shaybani Khan, leader of the Ozbek Turks of Central Asia, in 1507.

Before the Ozbek onslaught, the main threat to the Timurids came from the Black Sheep confederation. The Black Sheep were among the few Turkomans who had sided with the Ottomans against Tamerlane, and they remained rivals of the Timurid house even though Gowhar Shad, wife of Shah Rokh, was the sister of the Black Sheep chief Qara Yousof. After defeating the Mongol Jalayerids in 1410, Qara Yousof was able to take over much of Azerbaijan and western Iran. Shah Rokh recognized one of the later Black Sheep chiefs, Jahan Shah, as governor of Azerbaijan, apparently hoping to co-opt him as a vassal. Jahan Shah, however, rebelled against Timurid authority after Shah Rokh's death, seized new territories as far north as Georgia and south to Kerman, and even briefly occupied the Timurid capital, Herat. He also tried to build up Tabriz as a cultural rival to the great Timurid cities, but it was at best a pale imitation.

The Black Sheep had enemies of their own to the west in the White Sheep confederation, which controlled a large part of eastern Anatolia and northern Mesopotamia. The White Sheep generally acted as allies of the Timurids and maintained a virtual blood feud with the Black Sheep after their amir, Qara Osman, was captured and executed by a Black Sheep ruler in 1435. Their greatest chief was Uzun Hasan, who had far-reaching ambitions to build up an imperial sultanate on a par with that of the Timurids, Ottoman Turks, and Mamluks of Egypt. In 1467, he managed to ambush and kill Jahan Shah, took over most of the former Black Sheep territories, and transferred his capital to Tabriz. Two years later, he similarly defeated and killed the Timurid ruler Abou Said, who had attempted to block the eastward expansion of his principality. In 1472, with the encouragement of Venice, he also challenged the Ottomans but was repulsed. Thereafter, he concentrated on stabilizing his Iranian holdings through reforms aimed at making the transition from a nomadic to a sedentary state, a task continued after his death in 1478 by his sons Khalil and Yaqoub. With the destruction of the Black Sheep, the decline of the Timurids, and the stalemate with the Ottomans, the main threat to the White Sheep principality came from internal power disputes and especially the animosity of Turkoman tribes who resisted the consolidation of state authority and were attracted to a charismatic and militant religious order, that of the Safavids.

THE RISE OF THE SAFAVIDS

The Safavid order had been founded by Sheikh Safi-al-Din (1252–1334), a man of uncertain but probably Kurdish origin, who had become the chief pupil, son-in-law, and eventual successor of a famous Sufi ascetic, Sheikh Zahed Gilani. Safi-al-Din moved the order from Gilan to Ardabil after Sheikh Zahed's death in 1301, perhaps because of competition with Sheikh Zahed's son for control of the movement. Ardabil, a remote but strategic town located about 160 miles east of Tabriz near the Caspian corridor between Transcaucasia and Gilan, had recently been sacked by the Mongols and was a frequent target of raids by Georgian armies. Safi-al-Din and his followers helped organize defenses for the town and supplied such services as providing food and lodging for the poor from the Sufi center (*khanaqah*) they built there. An elaborate shrine grew up around the *khanaqah* and Safi-al-Din's tomb; it served as a place of pilgrimage and headquarters for the order, which continued to be headed by Safi-al-Din's descendants. The activities of the early Safavid spiritual leaders were reportedly viewed with favor by Tamerlane, who provided an endowment for the shrine, allowed the Safavids to collect taxes, and released some prisoners, who became devoted members of the order.

The character of the Safavid order began to change under its fourth leader, Jonayd (1447–1460). Perhaps inspired by the example of the Ottomans, Jonayd militarized the movement and attracted large numbers of disciples, probably from Turkoman tribes, eager to participate as *ghazis* (warriors for the faith) in raids on non-Muslim territories. This invited the suspicion of the Black Sheep ruler Jahan Shah, who forced Jonayd to leave Ardabil. After wandering for some time over Anatolia, Syria, and Mesopotamia, presumably recruiting additional followers, Jonayd was befriended by the White Sheep and Uzun Hasan, whose sister he married. He attempted to return to Ardabil in 1459 but was forced by the still hostile Black Sheep to divert his *ghazi*s to Circassia. To reach that area he had to pass through the territory of a Muslim ruler, the Shirvanshah, who attacked and killed Jonayd in 1460.

Uzun Hasan continued to protect Jonayd's son, Haydar, and allowed him to marry one of his daughters. Haydar invented the distinctive red hat with twelve pleats (in honor of the twelve Shi'ite Imams) that became the distinctive headgear of the Safavids' tribal followers, known thereafter as the *qizilbash* ("red-heads"). The *qizilbash* were fanatically loyal to the Safavid cause and constituted the backbone of their military support. After the crushing of the Black Sheep, however, the White Sheep rulers had little need for Safavid allies, and Uzun Hasan's successors no doubt saw Haydar, with his independent supporters and White Sheep dynastic connections through Uzun Hasan's sister and daughter, as a potential threat. When Haydar attempted to avenge his father's death by attacking the Shirvanshah in 1488, the White Sheep prince, Yaqoub (who was also the Shirvanshah's son-in-law), sent 4,000 troops to help in defeating and killing Haydar. Caught up as pawns in succession struggles among the White Sheep princes, Haydar's three sons were arrested. The oldest was murdered in 1494; the other two boys were spirited off by their devotees to the forests of Gilan, where they remained concealed and under the protection of local Shi'ite notables for several years. For reasons unknown, the second son was passed over as head of the order in favor of his younger brother, Esmail.

Under Esmail, the relationship with his supporters clearly became something more than the usual one between Sufi masters and pupils or a warrior chief and his *ghazi*s. The new propaganda (*dawa*) was a radical form of Shi'ism that emphasized not only that the Safavid house had a special status as descendants of the Prophet Mohammad through the Imam Mousa al-Kazem, but that Esmail was the messianic "Hidden Imam" returning to assert his authority or even that he was an infallible and invincible manifestation of the divine. Numerous sources indicate that his *qizilbash* followers now worshipped him as a godlike being who would protect them in battle, and poems in Turkish attributed to him leave no doubt that this idea was encouraged. Several points should be noted in regard to this astonishing development. Even in an age when Islamic religious concepts were fluid and sectarian divisions not so clearcut as later on, these were extremist (*gholat*) notions well beyond any conventional Sufi or Shi'ite theology. They are not likely to have been initiated by Esmail himself, as he was only five when he was concealed in Gilan and twelve when he emerged in 1499 at the head of a *qizilbash* force. Safavid ideology at that time was likely the product of an elite inner circle of disciples who disseminated the doctrine through a conspiratorial organization. It is less clear whether these ideas were developed specifically to attract *qizilbash* warriors, whose loose adherence to Islam barely disguised a number of their pre-Islamic and generally shamanistic beliefs, or whether the increasing number of *qizilbash* joining the movement to protect their tribal independence inevitably altered its dogmas.

In any case, the new *dawa*, the *qizilbash* troops, and the fortuitous disintegration of the White Sheep confederation as a result of its dynastic disputes added up to a potent formula for change. Some 7,000 hardcore *qizilbash* troops rallied at Erzinjan in 1500 to join Esmail. In short order, they killed the Shirvanshah, exacting revenge for the death of Esmail's father and grandfather; routed the much larger army of Alvand Aq Qoyunlu; and, in 1501, triumphantly entered Tabriz, where Esmail assumed the Persian imperial title of shah. For more than a decade, Esmail did indeed seem invincible in battle. In 1503, he took parts of the central Zagros (around Hamadan) and Fars province. The next year he added the remaining Caspian provinces (Mazandaran and Gorgan) plus central Iran (Yazd). Other areas of western Iran (notably Kurdistan and Khuzistan) recognized Esmail as ruler. Between 1505 and 1508, victories in the Caucasus, eastern Anatolia, and Baghdad gave him control of an empire rivaling that of the White Sheep under Uzun Hasan. It also brought the Safavids to the borders of two dangerous adversaries, the Ottomans to the west and the Ozbeks to the east, both staunch Sunni powers who viewed the Safavid religious propaganda with disdain. In 1510, Esmail attacked the Ozbek forces in a great battle near Merv, during which the Ozbek leader, Mohammad Shaybani Khan, was killed. Esmail had the skull of the defeated khan made into a goblet and sent the straw-stuffed head as a gift to the Ottoman sultan—one of many calculated insults which included ridiculing the Ottomans in poetry, executing prominent Sunnis in the presence of Ottoman emissaries, spreading sedition among Anatolian Turkomans, and meddling in questions of succession to the Ottoman throne.

The Ottoman sultan Bayezid II, who had adopted a conciliatory policy toward the Safavids, was forced to abdicate in 1512 and was replaced by Selim the Grim. Selim immediately suppressed the *qizilbash* in Ottoman territory, killing, jailing, or sending into exile some 40,000 of them. He also blocked trade in silk from Iran (a major source of revenue for the Safavids) and prepared to launch a preemptive attack on Esmail.

Confident the remaining *qizilbash* would join him, Esmail led his forces into Anatolia to confront Selim at Chaldiran in August 1514. The Ottomans were able to neutralize the powerful *qizilbash* cavalry by tying together a barricade of wagons and artillery pieces behind which the crack Janissary troops, armed with muskets, could shelter. In what was essentially a clash between a modern, gunpowder army and a traditional steppe army of nomadic cavalry with a charismatic leader, the *qizilbash* charged fearlessly but could not stand up to the Ottoman firepower. The Safavid forces suffered heavy casualties, especially among the top officer corps; Esmail himself was wounded by gunfire, and his army had to retreat. Selim had hoped to pursue his enemy, but his army balked at facing the fierce Anatolian winter. He returned the next year and briefly occupied Tabriz, deporting some of its artisans, but making no effort to take permanent control of Azerbaijan, probably because of his increasing interest in Syria and Egypt.

The Battle of Chaldiran had many consequences, especially in terms of its impact on Safavid ideology. Later Safavid historians such as Hasan-e Roumlu attempted to minimize the significance of this "slight setback" and its effect on the loyalty and esprit of the *qizilbash*. He hinted, however, at the actual state of affairs when he argued that the defeat was a blessing in disguise since it prevented the exaggerated belief in Esmail's authority among the "unsophisticated *qizilbash*" from causing them to deviate from "the straight path of religious faith" into "serious error." Indeed, the *qizilbash* could hardly have continued to regard Esmail as infallible, and it is a telling fact that over the next ten years, until his death in 1524, Esmail never again dared to take the field with his troops. He lost almost all interest in state affairs and devoted most of his time to drinking. At his death he was succeeded by his ten-year-old son, Tahmasp, who would reign until 1576.

THE MAKING OF SAFAVID IRAN

The defeat at Chaldiran also highlighted and accelerated trends that were defining the character of the Safavid state. Prior to the defeat at Chaldiran, the boundaries of the Safavid possessions were beginning to resemble those of earlier Turko-Mongol states. In its aftermath, eastern Anatolia was permanently lost, and most of the Safavid possessions in Mesopotamia slipped away. The Safavid-Ottoman frontier thus stabilized roughly along the line that marks the current Iranian-Turkish border. In the east, the Ozbeks had regrouped quickly after the death of

Shaybani Khan and defeated a Safavid army in 1512. The Ozbeks and Safavids would continue to struggle with each other for some time, but it was clear that there would be no Safavid presence in Central Asia and that Khorasan would form the easternmost limit of the Safavid state. Turcophone and *qizilbash* elements remained strong in Azerbaijan and government circles, but the Safavid realm had become a largely Persophone one wedged in between the Turkish Ottomans and Ozbeks. The boundaries of the country thus closely resembled those it would continue to have down to the present day, and it is not surprising that writers would then refer to it as "Iran" or that its Persian cultural characteristics would become more important.

Safavid religious policy also set Iran off from its powerful Sunni neighbors; at the same time, it began to shed its extremist *qizilbash* trappings. Immediately after entering Tabriz in 1501, Shah Esmail had announced that the official religion of his kingdom would be Shi'ism—not the *gholat* Shi'ism of the *qizilbash* but a more or less conventional Twelver Shi'ism, to which he had probably been exposed while under the protection of Kar Kia Mirza Ali in Gilan. As indications of this, the names of the Imams were invoked in the Friday sermons and coins were stamped with Shi'ite slogans. This promulgation of Twelver Shi'ism in Iran was undoubtedly the most important and enduring of the Safavid accomplishments, but the problem of how and why it was done needs much additional study before it can be satisfactorily resolved. It is often thought that Iran in 1500 was a predominantly Sunni country and that the transformation to Shi'ism was accomplished by the threat—and at times definitely the application—of force. The change may actually have been not quite so dramatic as this implies. It should be remembered that the real bastions of Sunni Islam in Central Asia were and remained outside the Safavid domain. Heterodoxy had long been common in western Iran, and many Shi'ite communities and principalities are known to have existed there. Moreover, Shi'ism, in the general sense of special affection for the family of the Prophet, had been deeply embedded in popular religion for centuries. There were aspects of Shi'ism, notably its emphasis on legitimacy, that appealed strongly to Iranian sensibilities: The Safavids, for example, skillfully exploited the belief that the Imam Hosayn had married the daughter of the last shah of Iran, and that the later Imams—and the Safavid family—descended from this line. Ultimately, the application of this policy came down not so much to transforming the religious orientation of the Iranian population as to replacing Sunni ulama (religious authorities and jurists) with Shi'ite ones, whom the populace would then follow. To do this, some were co-opted by the offer of material support, while others were imported from other Shi'ite communities (especially Bahrain and the Jabal Amil region of Lebanon); and those who resisted were either executed or, again in the words of Hasan-e Roumlu, compelled "to creep into corners to conceal themselves."

In any case, the benefits to the Safavids of promoting Shi'ism are fairly apparent. The appeal to Twelver Shi'ism broadened the constituency of support for the Safavids; provided the Safavid ruler with an additional element of legitimacy as a descendant of the Imams; diluted the specifically Turkoman-*qizilbash* orientation of the state; created a juridical institution that owed its position, at least initially, to the will of the shah; and gave an ideological basis to the struggle with the Ottomans and Ozbeks. The costs are also clear. First, the injection of the Sunni-Shi'i schism into the wars and political struggles of the time thoroughly embittered relations between the two branches of Islam and led to bloody persecutions on both sides. Second, the Shi'ite ulama soon consolidated an autonomous position and became potentially a threat as well as a prop to Safavid power, a situation remarkably similar to that of the Zoroastrian clergy in Sasanian times. This point is of such importance to all of subsequent Iranian history that it needs some special consideration.

It is a truism that there is no priesthood or church in Islam, but the Shi'ism that developed in Safavid Iran can be said to have acquired the equivalent of both a powerful clerical class and a clerical institution. Many factors contributed to this. The Safavid rulers themselves gave a special recognition and hierarchical organization to the Shi'ite ulama by establishing offices such as that of the *sadr* to oversee religious activities (even though the original purpose was undoubtedly to exercise control over the clerics). Involvement in the administration of charitable endowments (*waqf*), including substantial properties donated by Safavid aristocrats, and the collection of certain religious tithes and fees provided the ulama with a largely independent source of funding. The juridical tasks performed by the ulama required an advanced education and knowledge of Arabic that would of necessity distinguish them from the ordinary Persian- and Turkish-speaking masses. Since the Safavids were suspicious of other Sufi orders, Sufism in Iran provided neither the alternative to Shi'ism nor the focus of popular religion that it did in Sunni states. Great clerical families tended to monopolize religious positions for generations, and their position was further buttressed by marriage and kinship ties among them. Many claimed to be descendants of Imams themselves and thus to have a special status and legitimacy of their own.

Their authority ultimately derived from their knowledge of Shi'ite law, and they had no particular reason to attach special importance to the role of the Safavid shah as either the spiritual guide of a Sufi order or the charismatic leader of the *qizilbash*. Finally, they developed an ideological basis for their authority that owed nothing to the Safavid ruler: In the absence of the "hidden" Twelfth Imam, questions about religious conduct must be decided on a continuing basis by scholars (*mojtaheds*) trained in jurisprudence and juridical methods (*feqh* and *osul-al-feqh*) and sufficiently advanced to exercise independent judgment (*ejtehad*). Ordinary believers were obliged to consult a *mojtahed* and "imitate" his example, a practice known as *taqlid*. This idea did not develop at once, and there was considerable opposition to it within Shi'ism, but once it was established it conferred great influence and authority on the top members of the clerical establishment. *Mojtaheds* typically came to control a patronage system with considerable financial resources and to extend their influence over whole sections of the country through a network of lower-ranking *mollas* or *akhounds*.

ZENITH AND DECLINE OF SAFAVID IRAN

The trend toward greater clerical influence was noticeable as early as the reign of Shah Tahmasp, when there are reports of religious dignitaries who consorted on familiar terms with the shah, who interfered in the running of the government, and whose requests, whether for material benefits or specific actions, were inevitably granted. According to one famous story, the Imam Ali appeared to Tahmasp in a dream in 1532, after which Tahmasp "repented" of drinking wine and his other vices, and he issued a number of puritanical regulations on public conduct. This was almost certainly evidence of the influence the Shi'ite *mojtaheds* were beginning to have on the court and a tacit recognition that the shah was no longer a spiritual guide beyond reproach, but was bound by traditional religious law and convention. (However, it must be admitted that drinking, smoking opium, and debauchery remained favorite pastimes for more than a few of Tahmasp's successors.)

Shah Tahmasp's repentance may also have been part of an effort to distance himself from the *qizilbash* and to secure other sources of support for his rule. For the better part of ten years, the young Tahmasp had been handicapped by overbearing *qizilbash* chiefs acting as his regents as well as by a virtual civil war between various Turkoman tribes. This enabled the Ottomans and Ozbeks to increase the pressure on the Safavid state and chip away more of its territory. Finally, in 1533, Tahmasp managed to execute the most powerful of the remaining *qizilbash* chiefs, Hosayn Khan Shamlu, and began to rule in his own right. Under his leadership, the Safavid army made better use of gunpowder weapons, including muskets and artillery. Tahmasp still could not defeat either the Ottomans or the Ozbeks, but he was able to resist them fairly effectively. In 1548, he moved his capital from Tabriz, which was exposed to Ottoman attacks, to the more secure city of Qazvin. Unable to recover territory that had been lost to the Ottomans, he compensated by expanding into the Caucasus. This proved to be particularly significant, for it gave the Safavids control over a non-Persian and non-Muslim population. Some of them entered the service of the Safavids as vassals, and significant numbers of others were deported to Iran as state slaves on the model of the Ottoman *kapi kullari* (known in the Iranian case as *gholaman*). Just as the Ottomans had augmented the power of the sultan with Christian slaves taken through the *devshirme* system from the Christian population of the Balkans, the Safavid shahs used Georgians, Circassians, and Armenians to create another base of support alongside the *qizilbash*, Persophones, and Shi'ites.

The death of Tahmasp in 1576 was followed by twelve years of chaos, conspiracy, and disintegration. They came to an end with the accession of the greatest of all the Safavid rulers, Shah Abbas (1587–1629). Abbas saw very clearly that the *qizilbash* who had brought the dynasty to power were becoming disloyal and an obstacle to royal authority. He found a number of ways to circumvent them. Some of the troops were still recruited from the Turkomans, but they were chosen for their loyalty to him personally; they became known not by tribal affiliations (like the *qizilbash* Roumlus, Shamlu, Afshars, or Qajars) but as *shahsevans* ("shah-lovers"). Abbas also used the funds accumulated by Tahmasp to reorganize and expand his army, and the availability of state slaves was a major factor in his success. He created a royal bodyguard and cavalry units composed completely of the *gholaman* and armed with muskets. To further offset his dependence on the *qizilbash*, he added Persian musketeers and artillery corps to his standing army. With this new standing army on which he could rely, Abbas was able to centralize the administration of the country and take back control of the tax revenues. He was also able to deal with his foreign problems, beginning with the Ozbeks. In 1598, he defeated the Ozbeks outside Herat and effectively pacified that border. This freed him to confront the Ottomans. In a series of battles between 1603 and 1607, again distinguishing himself by his personal bravery and leadership qualities, Abbas recovered much of the territory that had been lost to the Ottomans. In 1623, he invaded Iraq, recaptured Baghdad, and held it against an Ottoman counterattack. This was naturally of great psychological significance since it restored the Shi'ite shrine cities there to Iranian control.

Abbas also saw the potential advantage of foreign alliances and international trade and took steps that were responsible for opening Iran up to the outside world. He pursued diplomatic relations with the Mughals and European powers in order to put pressure on the Ozbeks and Ottomans. He also began to take an interest in the Persian Gulf as an avenue for trade that would not have to pass through Ottoman or Ozbek territory. Between 1507 and 1515, the Portuguese, trying to consolidate their hegemony in the Indian Ocean, had occupied the island of Hormuz in the straits between the Persian Gulf and the Indian Ocean. Abbas wanted to recover the island, but lacked the naval power to do so. The appearance of the English East India Company and the Dutch East India Company, both of which were competing with the Portuguese and anxious to develop trade with Iran, provided him with an opportunity. In return for trading privileges, the English helped Abbas expel the Portuguese from Hormuz in 1622. Until 1635, the English and Dutch cooperated with each other to defeat the Portuguese, and then began to compete with each other. At any rate, the coming and going of so many European merchants, diplomats, and missionaries, all welcomed and protected by Abbas, gave his Iran a cosmopolitan air.

Shah Tahmasp had succeeded in recapturing the artistic excellence of Timurid Herat by patronizing book production and painting (he was an amateur painter himself). Shah Abbas continued this tradition, but architecture was the crowning cultural glory of his reign. In 1597, he decided to move the capital from Qazvin to Isfahan, an ancient city near the center of the Iranian plateau that had been greatly favored by the Seljuks. Expanding its southern suburbs, Abbas transformed it into one of the most magnificent and beautiful cities in the world. The centerpiece of his well-planned city was an immense meydan, or rectangular park, large enough for polo games, flanked by an arcade of shops. A monumental gateway at the northern end led into the main bazaar, and another at the southern gave access to the Masjed-e Shah (Royal Mosque). The mosque, with its huge dimensions, colorful tiles, imposing dome, and unique plan, is widely regarded as the most impressive in all of Iran. An arcade along the western side of the square flanked Abbas' personal pavilion, the Ali Qapi, which had an open, high-roofed balcony from which the shah could observe the activities in the *meydan*. In the center of the eastern arcade was the shah's private mosque, named for Sheikh Lotf-Allah (a famous preacher and the shah's father-in-law). Abbas also constructed a broad, straight, tree-lined avenue, the Chahar Bagh, to link his gardens and palace to the suburbs beyond the Zayandeh Rud River in the south. These were only the centerpieces of Abbas' creation; Isfahan became virtually a living museum of Safavid culture.

Abbas had accomplished much, but there were flaws in the edifice he had constructed. He enlarged and strengthened his army, but he overtaxed the country to pay for it. He copied some of the institutional practices that had proved useful to the Ottomans, but he also repeated some of their mistakes, such as confining his sons in the harem instead of allowing them to gain experience by governing a province. He also followed the example of several of his predecessors in killing or blinding children he suspected of intriguing against him. The meddling of women, eunuchs, and other palace officials in political affairs continued. He never found any institutional mechanism for maintaining the ruler's authority over the clerical interests. These problems slowly but inexorably weakened the Safavid state. Over the next century, ineffective rulers, demoralization, corruption, political intrigue, a decaying army, loss of territory, the growing independence of the ulama, and religious intolerance began to take their toll.

One of the most dangerous precedents set by Shah Abbas was the conversion of "state lands" (*mamalik*) into "crown lands" (*khasseh*). As a way of centralizing authority and asserting royal control over taxation this was not necessarily a bad policy. However, its effect was to end the system of "fiefs" (*tiyoul*) which had been granted to *qizilbash* leaders in return for administering them and raising the troops to defend them. Under the new system, the shah was more directly responsible for the defense of the provinces. In their zeal for additional revenues, the shahs Safi (1629–1642) and Abbas II (1642–1666) converted practically the whole country to crown lands, thinking they could return strategic provinces to "state land" status in a military emergency. In fact, this policy was a disaster for certain key frontier areas, which were quickly lost to outside powers. It was the great good fortune of the Safavid rulers of this period that they had few foreign adversaries capable of making a concerted attack on Iran, and of those none that deemed it worth the trouble.

This was also the period when the problem of excessive clerical influence became most severe. It is said that Shah Abbas had allowed one *mojtahed* to address him as "founder of a borrowed empire" and as a sign of humility walked on foot in front of another *mojtahed* riding through the main square of Isfahan. He had certainly spent lavishly to refurbish Shi'ite shrines and create charitable endowments, and he made a great show of visiting religious centers like the tomb of Imam Reza, on one occasion traveling the whole way from Isfahan to Mashhad on foot and carrying out such menial tasks as cleaning the mosque and trimming the candles. In the case of Shah Abbas, such actions were probably intended only to cultivate the *mojtahed*s through the use of flattery and financial rewards and to create the impression of piety on his part. Later Safavids, however, were quite clearly subservient to clerical interests. The notoriously timid and superstitious Shah Soltan Hosayn (1694–1722), for example, was thoroughly dominated by the ulama. The great Shi'ite jurist Mohammad Baqer Majlesi (d. 1699) held the top clerical post (then called *mollabashi*) and encouraged the shah to persecute both non-Muslims and Muslims he considered heretical. Ironically, one of the chief targets of this new intolerance was what Majlesi called the "foul and hellish growth" of Sufism, the very form of religion the Safavids had originally championed, and which constituted the bedrock of their movement. Implicit in these developments was the notion that the *mojtahed*s, not the shah, acted as representatives of the Hidden Imam, and that the shah was at best an executive agent on their behalf.

Shah Soltan Hosayn was also astonishingly indifferent to external threats to his kingdom. A new Afghan tribe, the Ghilzai, had appeared on the Safavid eastern border, and the Ghilzai were both aggressive and fanatically Sunni. In 1704, their leader, Mir Vais, had been taken captive after complaining about the notorious behavior of the Safavid governor of Qandahar, and was detained for a while at Isfahan. Shah Soltan Hosayn released him to make the pilgrimage to Mecca; in 1709, having secured a decree from the Sunni religious authorities of Mecca authorizing revolt against the offending governor, Mir Vais returned to Qandahar and expelled the Safavid official. He administered the city himself until his death in 1715. His son Mir Mahmoud attacked and temporarily occupied the province of Kerman in 1719. In 1721, he launched another invasion of Iran. After repelling the Safavid army that attempted to block him, Mir Mahmoud besieged Isfahan for six months in 1722, reducing the population to starvation and forcing Shah Soltan Hosayn to abdicate. Although puppet Safavid shahs were maintained in various parts of Persia until 1773, the Ghilzai invasion had effectively ended Safavid rule.

THE POST-SAFAVID INTERREGNUM

The Afghan hold on Iran was very tenuous, and it was not long before power began to shift back to the *qizilbash* tribes. A number of the Qajar and Afshar tribesmen had been relocated to defend the borders of Khorasan and Gorgan, and these (along with some Kurdish tribes in the same area) rallied to the support of the Safavid pretender in northern Iran, Tahmasp II. In 1727, as the country was in the process of being further dismembered by the Ottomans and Russians, Tahmasp designated Nader Khan Afshar as his military commander. Nader Khan, an ambitious man of undistinguished background, proved to be one of the most remarkable generals since Tamerlane, whom he clearly admired and sought to emulate. He routed the Ghilzai army in Khorasan in 1729, defeated the Ottoman forces in western Iran in 1730, and recovered Herat from the Abdali Afghans in 1732. Meanwhile, Tahmasp had attempted to lead another attack on the Ottomans, which was repulsed, and had been obliged to sign unfavorable treaties with both the Ottomans and the Russians. Nader Khan persuaded the *qizilbash* leaders to depose Tahmasp and had himself recognized as regent for Tahmasp's son, Abbas III. Nader then defeated the Ottomans in another series of battles between 1733 and 1735. Since the Russians were primarily interested in preventing the Ottomans from acquiring former Safavid territories near their border, they gradually withdrew their forces, and in 1735 signed the Treaty of Ganjeh, establishing boundaries and arranging a defensive alliance with Nader.

Early in 1736, Nader Khan called for an assembly of notables, held near his hunting encampment on the Moghan Plain. In what was obviously a prearranged plan, Nader Khan announced that he would retire to Khorasan, having defeated Iran's enemies, and that the assembly could elect a new Safavid ruler. Instead, the assembly insisted that Nader Khan become shah (not surprisingly, since one of the best-known proponents of continuing the Safavid dynasty had been strangled to death in full view of the assembly). Nader accepted, but on condition that Shi'ism be abandoned as the official religion. Shi'ism could still be practiced, but in the form of what Nader called the "Jafari Faith," that is, stripped of practices offensive to Sunnis, such as cursing the first three caliphs, and reduced to being simply a school of law comparable to the four Sunni *madhhabs*. The rationale for this abrupt change in religious policy has occasioned much speculation, but the intent was probably to disperse still further the religious prestige accorded the Safavid house.

It was also clearly a prerequisite for Nader's larger plans, most immediately a peace settlement with the Ottoman Empire. An Ottoman ambassador attended the assembly, and the terms of a treaty were drafted and approved there. It included provisions defining the status of the Jafari Faith, allowing Iranian Muslims to participate in the pilgrimage rituals on the same basis as other Muslims, authorizing an exchange of ambassadors, and otherwise normalizing relations. With all issues settled, Nader was crowned shah on 8 March 1736.

Having secured peace on his western borders, Nader Shah turned his attention to the east. After a long siege, he captured Qandahar in 1738. From there he advanced toward India via Kabul and Peshawar, captured Lahore, defeated a large Mughal army at Karnal, and entered Delhi in March 1739. After arranging for his son to marry a Mughal princess, extracting a huge amount of cash and treasure (most famously the Koh-e Noor diamond and the Peacock Throne), and arranging the cession of all lands west of the Indus to Iran, Nader left the Mughal emperor as ruler and returned to Herat. He next attacked the Ozbeks, defeating them and establishing the Oxus as the northeastern boundary of his kingdom, with Mashhad as its capital. Southern Iran also attracted Nader's attention, as he attempted to build up a fleet in the Persian Gulf and planned an invasion of Oman.

After 1741, however, Nader's problems began to mount and his behavior became increasingly harsh and erratic. His brother had been killed fighting in the Caucasus, and Nader's efforts to avenge his death aroused Russian suspicions of his intentions. He was ultimately obliged to withdraw, which encouraged the outbreak of revolts in several Iranian provinces. In 1743, the Ottomans rejected the provisions of the proposed treaty that would have recognized the Jafari Faith, and war resumed on the western front. Nader Shah called another religious assembly at Najaf to reconfirm the renunciation of Safavid Shi'ism, but this had no discernable effect on either the Ottomans or the Iranian populace. Hostilities continued until 1746, when provisions about the Jafari Faith were dropped and a treaty otherwise similar to the one drafted ten years earlier was signed.

Nader's achievements, although quite impressive, proved very ephemeral. Although he defended the borders of his empire with great vigor, he acted in the Turko-Mongol tradition and seems to have had no sense of a separate Iranian identity. By concentrating so much on military adventures, Nader Shah had failed to create any durable administrative and bureaucratic apparatus for his empire. Not even the spoils of India were sufficient to finance his ambitious enterprises, and he was compelled to renounce a remission of taxes he had promised and to impose heavy new taxes on the Iranian population. He alienated many of his original followers by incorporating Afghan and Ozbek auxiliaries into his army and granting them special favors. To make matters worse, there had been an attempt to assassinate Nader in 1741. His son, Reza-qoli, was implicated and was blinded as punishment. There were also frequent efforts to bring about a Safavid restoration and many revolts, sometimes led by men Nader had once trusted. Nader consequently reacted very harshly to any perceived challenge, so much so that it was rumored he had gone insane. In June 1747, a group of his officers, fearing that he was about to have them killed, murdered Nader Shah while he was sleeping in his tent.

Nader's nephew, who was probably involved in the murder plot, was enthroned as Adel Shah and authorized the execution of all of Nader's surviving sons. However, Nader Shah's army and empire were already falling apart, and none of the subsequent Afsharid rulers (1747–1796) are of any real significance for Iranian history.

5

From the Zand to the Qajars

In the confused situation after the murder of Nader Shah, two main tribal groups, the Zand and the Qajars, struggled for supremacy in Iran, with the Qajars ultimately prevailing. During this period the task of rebuilding a political and cultural identity for Iran was begun, and the country entered the first phase of its encounter with European imperialism and the impact of Western culture, decisive factors in Iran's subsequent development.

THE ZAND HEGEMONY

The Zand were of obscure but Iranian origin and had nomadized in the central Zagros. They had assisted Nader Shah in his wars with the Ottomans, but most were relocated to Khorasan after 1732. Under the leadership of their chief, Karim Beg (later Karim Khan), they defected from the Afsharid army after the accession of Adel Shah and returned to their tribal homeland. There, the Zand initially cooperated with another returning tribe, the Bakhtiaris, in establishing a hegemony over western Iran and installing a young Safavid boy as Shah Esmail III at Isfahan in 1751. Karim Khan then broke with the Bakhtiari chief, Ali

Mardan, defeated him in a battle, and became the *vakil* or regent for the putative shah.

The Qajars were one of the *qizilbash* tribes that had risen to prominence under the Safavids. They had come to be divided into two main branches and several clans, which at this period were concentrated in the area of Gorgan. Their alliance with Nader Khan in support of Tahmasp II was an uneasy one, since some of the Qajar tribal chiefs had ambitions of their own. Mohammad-Hosayn Khan, head of the Develu clan, apparently intrigued with Nader's son Reza-qoli; he was responsible for encouraging Reza-qoli to execute Tahmasp and his sons (carrying out the grisly deed himself) and was one of the chief conspirators behind Nader's assassination. Mohammad-Hasan Khan, head of the rival Qoyunlu clan, broke with Nader and Mohammad-Hosayn Khan and, with the support of various Turkoman tribes, engaged in a virtual blood feud with both. He revolted after Nader's murder and managed to take control of much of northern Iran. After 1752, the Zand and the Qajars fought with each other, struggled to suppress challenges from within their respective areas, and attempted to annex other provinces to their domains. The details of the conflict are too complicated to survey here; suffice it to say that by 1763, the Zand had prevailed and controlled all of Iran save Khorasan, which they were more than willing to leave in the hands of the Afsharids.

The triumphant Karim Khan made Shiraz his capital and ruled from there until his death in 1779. Karim Khan was particularly concerned to enhance security in the Persian Gulf and promote commercial contacts there with the maritime powers. In 1763, he granted the British East India Company the right to establish a base at Bushire, the port of Shiraz. His desire to capitalize on the European trade with India by diverting it to Iranian ports was a major factor in his decision to go to war with the Ottomans and attack Basra in 1775. In other respects, Karim Khan's policies seemed to be a conscious repudiation of all those associated with the time of Nader Shah. He never took a title such as shah and continued to act as a *vakil*, but now as *vakil-al-raaya*, regent "for the people" rather than on behalf of a Safavid prince. He supported Shi'ite religious practices. He kept taxation modest and fairly implemented. He rarely resorted to cruel or excessive punishments. He rebuilt and beautified Shiraz in much the same way Shah Abbas had developed Isfahan.

Karim Khan has earned an enviable reputation among both Iranian writers and modern historians as one of the most well-liked and benign sovereigns the country has ever had. At first glance, that perception may be difficult to understand, since so much of his life was still spent in fighting for territory, suppressing rebellions, and engaging in an assortment of personal vices, all rather like the activities of his less highly regarded peers. As later events proved, esteem for Karim Khan was hardly reflected in any reservoir of loyalty among the populace to the Zand dynasty. In all probability, the memory of the modest comforts of Karim Khan's Iran as an idyllic respite from the country's usual troubles was magnified by the calamitous nature of the events that preceded his reign and those that followed his death. At least in the popular imagination, Karim Khan came to represent a tradition of the ruler as magnanimous and paternalistic, common among Iranian tribes at least since the days of Cyrus, while most of his near contemporaries were associated with the typical Turko-Mongol model of avaricious and violent rulers ruthlessly exploiting a subject population.

THE QAJAR DYNASTY

Karim Khan Zand had held various Qajar notables hostage at Shiraz as insurance against sedition on the part of their respective clans. Among them was Aqa Mohammad Khan, son of the Qoyunlu chief, Mohammad-Hasan Khan, mentioned above. As a young boy, he had been captured by his father's nemesis, Adel Shah, and was castrated before being released (hence his title *aqa*, "chief eunuch"). Karim Khan is said to have treated Aqa Mohammad with the utmost respect and frequently consulted with him on political matters. Aqa Mohammad was allowed to go out hunting for recreation, and he used this as an opportunity to escape back to his tribal lands once he learned that Karim Khan was dead.

While Zand princes struggled over the succession to Karim Khan, Aqa Mohammad proved himself a master of tribal politics. He gradually consolidated his position as leader of his clan in Mazandaran, applied a judicious mix of force and conciliation to unify the two branches of the Qajar tribe, and acquired plunder and prestige by carrying out successful raids on areas south of the Elburz and into Gilan, which attracted support from still other tribal groups. In 1784, he fended off a Zand attempt to seize Mazandaran and went on to capture Isfahan from them. He occupied Tehran in 1786 and made it into a base for extending Qajar control over northern Iran.

Lotf-Ali Khan Zand made an attempt to recover Isfahan in 1791 but was undone by treachery in his own ranks; not only repulsed from Isfahan, he was denied entry back into Shiraz and had to flee to Kerman, where he made a last stand against the Qajars. Aqa Mohammad Khan besieged the city, which fell in October 1794, but Lotf-Ali Khan managed to escape south to Bam. Aqa Mohammad Khan was so enraged at Lotf-Ali's escape and the assistance the people of Kerman had provided him that he reportedly had the eyes of most of the city's male inhabitants gouged out and handed over the women and children to his troops as slaves. After Lotf-Ali Khan was betrayed and captured, Aqa Mohammad ordered the decapitation of 900 prisoners, whose skulls were used to build a pyramid commemorating the event; Lotf-Ali Khan himself was abused, blinded, and sent to Tehran to be executed. These, unfortunately, were only among the first of the atrocities to be attributed to Aqa Mohammad.

In 1795, Aqa Mohammad demanded that King Erekle II (Heraclius) of Georgia, a former vassal of Nader Shah, likewise recognize his suzerainty. When Erekle declined, putting his faith in an alliance with Russia, Aqa Mohammad invaded the country, defeated the Georgian forces, and sacked Tbilisi. After this victory, Aqa Mohammad formally assumed the title of shah in 1796. He then set out for Khorasan, where he deposed Nader Shah's grandson, Shahrokh. The latter died after being horribly tortured to force him to reveal where the crown jewels he was known to possess were hidden. Catherine the Great had retaliated for the devastation of Georgia by sending a Russian force to take Derbent, but her successor, Tsar Paul I, had them recalled. Aqa Mohammad Shah took advantage of this by launching a second invasion of the Caucasus. During that campaign, on 16 June 1797, he was disturbed by a quarrel between two servants, whom he ordered to be executed. As it was Friday, a Muslim holy day, he was persuaded to postpone the execution until a more propitious time and left the servants to go about their duties. When he fell asleep, they and a third collaborator stabbed him to death. Since this bizarre episode took place during a war against non-Muslims, the cruel and vindictive, but undeniably efficient and effective, monarch thus earned the epithet of the "Martyred Shah."

At least when it came to matters of state, Aqa Mohammad left little to chance. Well aware of the problems caused by succession disputes (a major factor in the decline of both the Afsharids and the Zand), he had already designated his nephew, Fath-Ali Khan (then known as Baba Khan), as his heir and made elaborate arrangements to ensure his accession. After learning of Aqa Mohammad Shah's murder, Fath-Ali traveled from Shiraz, where he was serving as governor of southern Iran, to Tehran in July 1797 and was subsequently crowned on 19 March 1798. The next year, he confirmed his son Abbas Mirza[1] as crown prince and assigned him to govern Azerbaijan, a critical province since it was threatened by both the Ottomans and the Russians. Abbas was not the oldest son, and perhaps not the most capable, but his mother was the daughter of the chief of the Develu Qajars, so he was the choice best suited for maintaining the unity of the Qajar tribe.

Although Aqa Mohammad Shah's precautions had secured the throne for Fath-Ali, the latter still had to face several challenges to retain it. Aqa Mohammad's brother, Ali-qoli Khan, contested the succession but had little support and was blinded after he refused to pay obeisance to Fath-Ali Shah. Zand, Safavid, and Afsharid pretenders to the throne were easily defeated. A more serious threat came from a Kurdish chief, Sadeq Khan Shaqaqi, whose actions at the time of Aqa Mohammad Shah's murder had been suspicious to say the least. He had made off with the crown jewels and raised a large army to try to capture Tehran. Fath-Ali's forces decisively defeated him in August 1798. Fath-Ali's own brother, Hosayn-qoli Khan, persistently demanded a share of the government; he was finally put to death in 1803.

The event that signaled most clearly Fath-Ali's hold on the throne and his determination to act in an independent, even arbitrary, fashion was the overthrow of the powerful prime minister, Ebrahim Kalantar Shirazi. Ebrahim Kalantar had been the mayor of Shiraz under Karim Khan but turned against Lotf-Ali Khan and collaborated with the Qajars. Aqa Mohammad Shah had made him prime minister, and Ebrahim Kalantar provided significant assistance in binding southern Iran to the Qajar north, organizing the Qajar administration, holding the army together after Aqa Mohammad's murder, and ensuring the accession of Fath-Ali Shah. Using trumped-up charges of conspiracy, Fath-Ali dismissed Ebrahim Kalantar as prime minister in April 1801 and had him arrested, mutilated, and eventually executed, along with most of his family. There may well have been reasons of state for removing Ebrahim Kalantar from office, but this was poor reward for the many services he had rendered to the Qajars.

Fath-Ali Shah was generally milder in his policies than Aqa Mohammad Shah, although the execution of Ebrahim Kalantar by literally boiling the unfortunate minister in oil showed that he could be just as brutal in his treatment of those he disfavored. He left much of the business of governing the provinces to Abbas Mirza and his other sons, and rivalries among them greatly affected the course of events during his reign. As noted by several European visitors, Fath-Ali Shah reveled in playing the role of Iranian monarch to the hilt; he delighted in holding resplendent court ceremonies, patronizing the arts (especially those that depicted him in paintings and monumental carvings like those of his imperial predecessors), cultivating religious scholars, and maintaining a truly huge harem—in some ways, he was almost a caricature of the most extreme Orientalist fantasies about opulent Eastern potentates. The reality was that he was presiding over a battered Iran whose financial, military, and strategic importance was fast diminishing and over a court that the British emissary Sir John Malcolm described as "weak, proud and deluded." The disparity would be painfully apparent by the end of his reign.

IRAN AND THE EUROPEAN POWERS

Foreign affairs dominated the remaining period of Fath-Ali's tenure as shah (1797–1834). In 1799, the last king of Georgia had gone beyond merely seeking a defensive alliance with Russia and actually turned over his kingdom to become a Russian protectorate, and Russian troops occupied Tbilisi. This coincided with a renewed expansionist and anti-Islamic sentiment at the Russian court under Tsar Alexander I. In 1802, Prince Tsitsianov, himself of Georgian origin, launched an aggressive campaign in the Caucasus. His capture of Ganjeh was a serious blow to Qajar prestige and a potential threat to Gilan and Azerbaijan. When Tsitsianov moved on Erivan, a gateway to Azerbaijan, in 1804, Fath-Ali Shah sent Abbas Mirza to oppose him, thus beginning the First Russo-Persian War (1804–1813).

The conflict with Russia, as well as the sense of legitimacy and importance derived from contacts with foreign ambassadors, made Fath-Ali Shah receptive to the approaches of other European powers, and Iran was rapidly caught up in the diplomatic maneuverings of the Napoleonic era. The British East India Company sent John Malcolm to Tehran in 1800 to secure, mostly through lavish gifts and promises of future subsidies, an agreement aimed at excluding French influence and obtaining Iranian cooperation against a perceived mutual enemy, Zaman Shah Dorrani, the amir of Afghanistan. Fath-Ali Shah was later chagrined to find that the British were unwilling to extend the treaty to include assistance against the Russians, with whom they were then allied against France. Napoleon took advantage of this to conclude the Treaty of Finkenstein in May 1807, in which France and Iran agreed to an alliance against Russia and Britain. The diplomatic contacts were accompanied by the dispatch of a French military mission under Claude-Mathieu de Gardane to assist the Iranians in their struggle with Russia. Barely two months later, however, Napoleon made peace with Russia at Tilsit, and French influence in Iran began to collapse. The British Foreign Office took control of Iranian affairs from the East India Company and sent a full ambassador, Sir Harford Jones, to undermine the French in Tehran. Jones offered the Qajars a subsidy and military assistance against Russia, which was confirmed by a formal treaty in 1809. British military advisors arrived and some efforts were made to strengthen the Iranian army, but they made little progress before Britain and Russia became allies again in 1812. Despite the presence of some British officers, the Iranian forces encamped at Aslanduz were surprised by a Russian attack on 31 October 1812 and badly beaten. The best the British could do under the circumstances was to help mediate the Treaty of Golestan in 1813, an agreement that was nonetheless quite disadvantageous to Iran, as it confirmed the loss of most of the former provinces in the Caucasus and prohibited an Iranian naval presence on the Caspian Sea. It also involved Russia in Iranian internal affairs by pledging Russian support to guarantee the accession of the crown prince to the throne. Meanwhile, a new British ambassador, Sir Gore Ouseley, negotiated the Definitive Treaty of 1814 to replace the 1809 treaty. Among other things, it pledged that Britain would provide troops or a subsidy if Iran were attacked by a European power; and stipulated that Iran would not permit enemies of Britain to cross its territory en route to India and would assist Britain if Afghans attacked India (but Britain would be neutral in a conflict between Iran and the Afghans). In addition, only British officers (or those from countries friendly to Britain) would be used to train Iranian troops.

By 1826, disputes over the ambiguous delineation of territory in the Treaty of Golestan had increased tension between Iran and Russia. The large numbers of Muslims fleeing to Iran to escape Russian rule further inflamed public opinion in Iran, and religious leaders began to call for a holy war in the Caucasus. Abbas Mirza, never feeling quite secure in his designation as crown prince and wanting to distinguish himself in competition with his brothers (some of whom had led successful skirmishes in Khorasan and against the Ottomans), joined the war party. He launched an attack on Russian positions in July 1826. After some initial successes, mostly due to the incompetence of the Russian commander as well as to Abbas Mirza's success in modernizing his army, the war turned against the Iranians, and the Russians advanced as far as Tabriz. This was largely because Fath-Ali Shah had declined to supply either men or funds for the effort, insisting that Abbas Mirza rely on his own resources as governor of Azerbaijan. Britain also refused to provide assistance under the terms of the Definitive Treaty of 1814 since it maintained that Iran was the aggressor in the war. In February 1828, Abbas Mirza was obliged to accept the humiliating Treaty of Turkmanchai. Iran not only lost the disputed territories in the Caucasus, it had to grant economic concessions and privileges of extraterritoriality for Russian subjects and property in Iran and pay the enormous sum of 20 million roubles in war reparations. The hardest task Abbas Mirza may ever have had to perform was informing his notoriously parsimonious father of the latter provision.

The provisions of the Treaty of Turkmanchai were put to a severe test as a result of the actions of the first Russian minister to Iran after the war, A. S. Griboedov. Griboedov was contemptuous of "Asiatics" and expressed his domineering attitude in various ways, including pressuring Iran to join Russia in fighting the Ottomans. Public sentiments were already disturbed by the reverses of the war and the sight of drunken Cossack guards in the streets of Tehran. Griboedov's efforts to arrange repatriation of former Christian inhabitants of the Caucasus, without much regard to whether they had become Muslims or to their position in Iranian society, led to trouble. For reasons that are not entirely clear, one of the shah's own eunuchs and two Armenian women from the harem of a former prime minister known for his anti-Russian sentiments were held at the Russian legation. No doubt encouraged by the minister, who had been forced to turn the women over to Griboedov, an influential *mojtahed* in Tehran whipped up the fury of a mob by demanding that the women be rescued and that the eunuch, if he had renounced Islam, be executed as an apostate. On 11 February 1829, the Tehran bazaar closed in protest, and a mob broke into the Russian legation and killed the entire staff save one. Engaged as it was in war with the Ottoman Empire, the Russian government decided not to retaliate. The tsar accepted the apologies of the shah, and the incident blew over. Nonetheless, it was important as an early indicator of the passions that could be aroused by a foreign presence in Iran, particularly when it involved a clash with religious sensibilities and cultural values.

After 1831, Abbas Mirza redeemed a reputation tarnished by his defeats in the Caucasus by successfully putting down revolts in central Iran and winning a number of victories over enemies in Khorasan. He was apparently planning, with full Russian support, to compensate for the territorial losses in the northwest by taking Herat and restoring the Iranian border in the east to the status it had enjoyed under the Safavids. However, he died in the midst of these activities, on 25 October 1833; his father, Fath-Ali Shah, died almost exactly a year later, on 24 October 1834. The unexpected loss of crown prince and king so close together left the question of succession in doubt, but both the Russians and the British joined in supporting Abbas Mirza's son, Mohammad Mirza. Indeed, a British officer, Henry Lindsay Bethune, commanded the forces that installed Mohammad Shah in Tehran and defeated his uncle Hasan-Ali Mirza Farmanfarma, the governor of Fars.

Alarmed by the rise of Russian influence in Iran and the implications for India of a Russian-supported Iranian advance to Herat even as the Russians themselves were showing signs of moving into Transcaspia, the British sought to curry favor with the new shah, supplying money and a military mission to assist him. Neither had much effect; as prince, Mohammad Mirza had made a vow to return to Afghanistan, and as shah he intended to fulfill it. In 1836, he led an Iranian army to Khorasan and began campaigns to subdue the Turkoman tribes in the area. This was followed in 1837 by an advance to Herat and a siege of the city. Without much regard to the terms of the Definitive Treaty, a British officer, Eldred Pottinger, helped organize the defense of Herat. After another British emissary, John McNeill, failed to persuade the shah to give up the siege (he was encouraged to persist by a Russian envoy), Britain occupied Kharg Island in the Persian Gulf and threatened to go to war unless the shah ended the siege and gave up the Afghan territories he had acquired. Faced with rising costs and the failure of another effort to capture the city, Mohammad Shah finally relented and abandoned the siege in 1838. It was not until 1842 that the outstanding issues of the war were resolved and Britain removed its forces from Kharg.

After the Herat fiasco, Mohammad Shah had little interest in further adventures and tended to be dominated by his controversial prime minister, Hajji Mirza Aqasi. In 1840, he was faced with the revolt of Aqa Khan Mahallati, the leader of the Ismaili Shi'ites, whom Fath-Ali Shah had made governor of Kerman. Aqa Khan was forced to flee to India in 1842, where he was given protection by the British. His brother failed in an attempt two years later to establish himself in the province of Baluchistan. Another war with the Ottomans almost broke out in 1842 as a result of border clashes and an Ottoman crackdown on Iranian Shi'ites in Karbala, but was averted by the intervention of the Russians and the British. To avoid further disputes, a border commission was convened in 1843 and drafted the Treaty of Erzurum, signed in 1847, which defined

the basic outline of Iran's western border (although the details were quib-
bled over for the rest of the century and into the next). Mohammad Shah
died in 1848 and was succeeded without challenge by his son Naser-al-
Din.

RELIGIOUS ISSUES IN QAJAR IRAN

In terms of internal affairs, religious developments in early Qajar Iran
were of great importance. First of all, the advent of the Qajars coincided
with the definitive triumph in Iran of what is known as the Osuli school
of Shi'ism over its rival, the Akhbari school. Akhbari Shi'ism had revived
in Safavid Iran during the early 17th century, to some extent as a focus
of opposition to the increasing power of the *mojtaheds*. Following the
teachings of Molla Mohammad-Amin Astarabadi (d. 1624), the Akhbaris
held that the traditional reports (*akhbar*) about the Imams constituted the
fundamental and self-sufficient source of guidance for the Shi'ite community during the occultation of the Twelfth Imam. Since these were
necessarily complete and had already been collected and codified by
earlier Shi'ite scholars, and they were to be understood and interpreted
literally, there was need for neither Sunni legal methods like consensus
and analogy nor for the practice of *ejtehad* on which the authority of the
mojtaheds rested. The Osulis maintained that religious regulations needed
rational proofs and constant reinterpretation, which could only be supplied by trained scholars capable of using *ejtehad*. This justified both the
division of the Shi'ite community between those who gave guidance (the
mojtaheds) and those who were obliged to seek and follow it (the *moqal-
leds*) and the institution of a clerical hierarchy. During the 18th century,
the Akhbari school was dominant, but it came under concentrated attack
from the great Osuli *mojtahed* Mohammad-Baqer Behbahani (d. ca. 1792),
who successfully resisted all challenges to the authority of the *mojtaheds*.

Not even the strongest of the Safavid rulers, with the advantage of
considerable religious charisma in their own right, had been able to ignore the prestige and influence of the *mojtaheds*. The Qajars owed their
rule solely to force of arms and, although apparently marked by a genuine sense of piety, lacked even a modicum of religious legitimacy; they
had little choice but to attempt to justify themselves as defenders of
Shi'ism and lavish attention on religious projects such as building
mosques and providing charitable endowments. From the beginning,
they prudently chose to display the greatest deference to the wishes and
interests of the religious leaders. Behbahani's son, Mohammad-Ali, for

example, was extremely wealthy, had his own entourage of armed followers to enforce his judgments, and carried out a virtual war against Sufi religious rivals. Aqa Mohammad Shah, who hoped to send him into exile, was unable to force him out of his stronghold at a religious shrine in Tehran, and Fath-Ali Shah treated him as an honored advisor. Not even the seemingly miraculous ability of an Akhbari, Mirza Mohammad, to produce, as promised, the head of the Russian commander in the Caucasus sufficed to break the hold of the Osulis on the early Qajar court. There were, of course, occasional challenges from rival religious figures, notably Sufis, and when absolutely necessary the rulers would break with the religious establishment. Beyond that, the ability of the *mojtahed*s to shape government policy or, alternatively, to arouse public opinion would be amply demonstrated in coming events.

There was, however, one extremely significant challenge to the religious status quo in Qajar Iran. In the spring of 1843, as the result of a series of religious visions, a certain Sayyed Mirza Ali-Mohammad Shirazi proclaimed himself to be the *bab* or gateway to the hidden Twelfth Imam as well as his representative. He gathered around him eighteen disciples, who set out in July 1844 to disseminate the ideas and writings of the Bab throughout the Shi'ite world.

A highly esoteric, messianic, and millenarian faith, Babism drew most directly on the ideas of Sheikhism, a variety of Shi'ism derived from the teachings of Sheikh Ahmad Ahsai (1753–1826). Ahsai had claimed that true religious knowledge (such as his own) came directly from Mohammad and the Imams through dreams; he emphasized a theosophical and allegorical approach to religious thought and placed intuition and mystical insight above formal learning. He and his followers insisted in particular on the role of the "Perfect Shi'ite," who served as an infallible religious guide in each generation. Mirza Ali-Mohammad had been associated with the Sheikhi faction led by Kazem Rashti; after the latter's death a number of his followers attached themselves to him as the Bab.

Whereas earlier Sheikhism had sought to exist within the bounds of Twelver Shi'ism, the Babis began to propound more extreme doctrines reminiscent of militant heterodox movements in early Islamic Iran. In one phase, they suggested that the Bab was preparing the way for the return of the Hidden Imam and the final war against unbelief; in another, that he was initiating an entirely new cycle of religious understanding, with a revelation that would supercede the Koran and traditional Islam. There was a strong anticlerical element in Babi teachings as well as an interest in radical social change and reforms. This was dramatically il-

lustrated in the behavior of one of the Bab's most devoted and controversial followers, Qorrat-al-Ayn, a remarkable woman who dared to
appear unveiled and give public religious instruction. She reportedly
claimed to be an incarnation of Mohammad's daughter Fatema, celebrated the birth of the Bab as a religious holiday, and declared existing
Islamic laws to be abrogated.

The Babis sought zealously to win over powerful government figures
to their cause. At the same time, they seemed to be willing to resort to
assassinations and armed rebellion if necessary. As disturbances
throughout the country mounted, the Bab was summoned in July 1848
to Tabriz to explain his teachings before Naser-al-Din Mirza and a council of religious dignitaries. What happened at this interrogation is disputed, but it seems that Mirza Ali-Mohammad claimed that he was
himself the Hidden Imam, in which case the political authority of Naser-
al-Din and the religious authority of the scholars would both have been
invalidated. This assertion was rejected after the council ascertained to
its satisfaction that his knowledge of Arabic and various religious dogmas was deficient. He was then beaten and sent back to detention at
Chehriq fortress. The subsequent outbreak of Babi rebellions in several
areas of Iran persuaded Naser-al-Din, now the shah, and his minister,
Mirza Taqi Khan Amir Kabir, to order the execution of the Bab. He was
brought before a firing squad at the citadel of Tabriz; the first volley
merely severed the rope holding him, and the Bab almost escaped in the
cloud of smoke. He was eventually discovered and put again before the
firing squad, which then performed its duty flawlessly. Over the next
two years, primarily after a failed attempt on the life of the shah in 1852,
as many as 3,000 Babis were put to death.

The execution of the Bab and the ruthless suppression of his followers
naturally led to a reworking of the movement's ideas, theology, and
goals and eventually its split into the Azali and Bahai sects. As these
flourished mostly in exile or among non-Iranians, the subsequent history
of Babism-Bahaism is largely outside the scope of this book. The forces
of dissent and reform which the Babi movement represented remained
potent, however, and assumed other forms that were of consequence in
Iran. Azali Babism, some of whose leaders used the Shi'ite practice of
dissimulation (*taqiyya*) to conceal their affiliation and penetrate clerical
and government circles, was especially important in this regard. Azalis
in Iran and abroad continued to be actively opposed to Qajar rule and
are thought to have made important contributions to the development
of modern Iranian nationalism and constitutionalism. Bahais, however,

were regarded by the Shi'ite establishment as apostates, technically subject to the death penalty, and they have frequently been targets of clerical fury.

REFORM AND REACTION

Prior to the accession of Naser-al-Din Shah, there had been only the barest of efforts in Iran at reform of government and society, whether of a modernizing or Westernizing nature. Apart from the reorganization of the army under Abbas Mirza with the assistance of European advisors, the major achievement in this regard was the dispatch of groups of students to study in Europe: two to London with Sir Harford Jones in 1811, a group of five to England in 1815, and another group of five to Paris in 1845. Although few in number and specialized mostly in narrow technological studies, these students were of some importance in spreading awareness in Iran of the material achievements and intellectual foundations of European civilization. For example, one of the best known was Mirza Mohammad-Saleh, who received a general education at Oxford. After returning to Iran, he established a printing press, issued the country's first newspaper, published a number of books describing the history and governmental institutions of Great Britain as well as his experiences there, and served as a teacher for the sons of other notables.

Despite this somewhat unpromising background, a veritable floodgate of reform was opened after 1848. The new shah, Naser-al-Din, was only sixteen and highly reliant on Mirza Taqi Khan, the official who had been assigned as his tutor and who had worked tirelessly to bring Naser-al-Din to Tehran to be crowned after the death of Mohammad Shah. Naser-al-Din Shah appointed Mirza Taqi Khan as his prime minister; instead of using the usual title, he was called Atabak (regent), Amir Nezam, or, as he is best known, Amir Kabir. Mirza Taqi Khan Amir Kabir was a man of humble origin (his father had been a cook) who had risen steadily through the ranks of government service on the basis of his obvious talents and accomplishments rather than just personal connections. Two experiences had served to set him apart from the routine courtiers and to prepare him to be a visionary reformer. He had been a member of the delegation sent to St. Petersburg to apologize to the tsar for the murder of Griboedov, and this gave him the opportunity to familiarize himself with Russian methods of government and administration, schools, factories, businesses, and cultural life. He had also served with distinction on the commission that drafted the Treaty of Erzurum, which put him in a position to acquaint himself with the program of wide-ranging legal and administrative reforms in the Ottoman Empire known as the Tanzimat (Regulations).

After becoming prime minister, Amir Kabir had to deal with a number of distracting problems: the revolt of a Qajar prince, Hasan Khan Salar, and some Turkoman tribes in Khorasan; the Babi insurrection; and Russian protests over a Turkoman pirate attack on their naval base at Ashurada in the Caspian. Nonetheless, he was able to initiate a program of reforms aimed at strengthening Iranian government and society that was astonishing both in its scope and its conscious avoidance of creating dependencies on Russia or Great Britain for its implementation. Amir Kabir had been responsible for the financial and logistical operations of the army in Azerbaijan and was well aware of the country's military needs. He sought to modernize the training of the tribal contingents of the army and to expand the recruitment base by instituting a kind of conscription system for rural areas and creating non-Muslim military units. He tried to make sure soldiers were paid what they were due rather than having salaries siphoned off by the officers, and he prohibited the practice of forcing civilians to provide supplies for the army. To alleviate Iran's reliance on Britain and Russia for military needs, he sought to develop Iran's own munitions industry and to bring in advisors from other countries such as Austria and Italy. To address the problem of government finances, Amir Kabir attacked such time-honored but essentially corrupt practices as the sale of offices and the exchange of "gifts" (i.e., bribes) for official services. He also sought to regularize the system of taxation and the customs regime; salaries of bureaucrats were reduced; extravagant pensions were eliminated. He greatly increased government intervention in economic life to stimulate agricultural and commercial activity: cash crops such as cotton and sugarcane were introduced; numerous factories were established; artisans were encouraged to learn new manufacturing techniques; urban renewal projects in the capital and major cities were begun. He began publication of an official gazette that was used to circulate news about government regulations, to inform readers about political and scientific developments in the world, and to cultivate a new style of Persian prose free of the absurdly complex rhetoric and bombast that had once been favored.

Potentially the most revolutionary of Amir Kabir's innovations were in education and law, both of which encroached on the traditional domain of the Shi'ite clergy in Iran. He brought religious courts under closer scrutiny and control by government authorities, punished corrupt religious judges, and tried to limit the practice that allowed criminals to avoid arrest by taking sanctuary (*bast*) at a religious shrine. His single greatest accomplishment was undoubtedly the establishment of the Dar-al-Fonoun, a government-sponsored military and technical college in Tehran which opened in December 1851. It would use foreign instructors, again chosen from countries without strategic interests in Iran, and offer classes, mostly in French, on topics such as medicine, pharmacy, military tactics, engineering, and mineralogy as well as basic instruction in European and Middle Eastern languages, history, mathematics, and so on. The school was a training ground for an entire generation of the Iranian elite and the model for the other advanced educational institutions that would follow.

Tragically, Amir Kabir was no longer prime minister when the Dar-al-Fonoun held its opening ceremony. As in so many other cases, not only in Iran, the values of honesty, efficiency, integrity, and genius were not appreciated by those who most conspicuously lacked them. Amir Kabir's efforts to weed out corruption, restrain fiscal abuse, and overturn traditional interests inevitably made him a host of enemies. A faction centered around his chief bureaucratic rival, Aqa Khan Nouri Etemad-al-Dowleh, and the shah's mother, Mahd-e Olya, intrigued against Amir Kabir from the day he was appointed prime minister. They reportedly convinced the young and naïve shah that Amir Kabir was building up the army as the prelude to a coup. On 16 November 1851, Naser-al-Din Shah abruptly dismissed Amir Kabir from office. Although Amir Kabir had followed a distinctly independent course in foreign policy, both the Russians and the British were disturbed by his fall. They appreciated his stabilizing influence on Iran since their primary objective was to avoid any disorder there that might draw them into conflict and upset the equilibrium of power in Europe. The Russians had the added worry that Amir Kabir's replacement, Aqa Khan Nouri, had once received British protection and might favor Britain over Russia. The Russian ambassador made the mistake of declaring that Amir Kabir was under his protection and sending armed guards to his house. This flagrant breach of Iranian sovereignty only aggravated the shah's suspicions and sealed Amir Kabir's fate, from which not even his marriage to the shah's sister could save him. He was packed off to a kind of house arrest at the Qajar provincial palace of Bagh-e Fin near Kashan. On 10 January 1852, an executioner sent from Tehran had Amir Kabir dragged into the bathhouse, where the arteries in his arms and legs were severed, and he was left to bleed to death.

The new prime minister, Aqa Khan Nouri, not only turned back the clock on most of Amir Kabir's reforms and cultivated the vices Amir Kabir had tried so hard to repress, he promptly involved Iran in an international crisis. Tensions with Britain rose during the Crimean War since Nouri seemed to be allying himself with the Russians against the Ottomans and the British. In 1855, Nouri got into an ugly row with the British ambassador, Charles Murray, over the employment at the British legation in Shiraz of one of Nouri's rivals, Hashem Khan. After Nouri encouraged rumors of an affair between Murray and Hashem's wife, who was also the shah's sister-in-law, Murray broke off diplomatic relations and withdrew the British mission. Nouri then decided to endorse the shah's wish to try once more to recover Herat for Iran in violation of a treaty Britain had secured in 1853. This time, the Iranian campaign was successful, and Herat was captured in October 1856. The British immediately declared war on Iran, which they pursued from the Persian Gulf rather than risking an attack on Herat. They occupied Kharg Island in December and landed forces at Bushire in January 1857. Mohammereh was bombarded and occupied in March, by which time the Iranians had already agreed to the Treaty of Paris mediated by Napoleon III. Britain's problem throughout the war had been that it wanted to remove Herat from Iranian control, but without inflicting a defeat severe enough to produce chaos in Iran or drive the country entirely to the Russians. The terms agreed to at Paris were therefore remarkably generous; Iran had to give up claims to Herat and all other Afghan territory and Murray was returned as minister, but there were no reparations imposed and Nouri was allowed to retain his office.

In 1858, Naser-al-Din dismissed Nouri for matters unrelated to the Anglo-Persian War. He declined to name another prime minister and began to supervise more government affairs himself. It must be said, however, that he accomplished little beyond the construction of the country's first telegraph lines, linking Tehran with Kermanshah and Bushire. Moreover, a combination of drought, a horrible famine, failure of the silk crop, and a general decline in trade severely depressed the country's economy. Anxiety in the country was further increased by the rapid advances the Russians were making in Central Asia, with the capture of Tashkent (1865), Khoqand (1866), and Bokhara and Samarqand (1866–1868).

Meanwhile a new circle of reformers was beginning to form around a dynamic and talented member of the Iranian diplomatic service, Mirza Hosayn Khan Moshir-al-Dowleh. He had served in the two places that traditionally exerted the most powerful influence on Iranian reformists, the Caucasus (as a consul in Tbilisi from 1852 to 1858) and the Ottoman Empire (as minister in Istanbul after 1858). The fact that he was in the Ottoman Empire during the height of the Tanzimat, a period when Britain was the chief defender of the integrity of the Ottoman Empire against Russian encroachments as well as the leading proponent of liberal reforms of Ottoman legal, administrative, and financial institutions as a remedy for the empire's problems, was clearly of great importance in shaping his views of Iran's needs. He also developed friendships with intellectuals such as Fath-Ali Akhoundzadeh, a controversial advocate of Iranian nationalism and secularism, and Mirza Malkom Khan, an early proponent of consultative institutions of government and development of the country's economic infrastructure. Moshir-al-Dowleh kept up a steady stream of memoranda and letters to Naser-al-Din Shah informing him of the changes taking place in the Ottoman Empire and the desirability of reform in Iran. In 1870, Naser-al-Din Shah, who was given to frequent and ostentatious displays of piety, decided to make a visit to the Shi'ite shrines in Ottoman Iraq in the company of Moshir-al-Dowleh. This was a fortuitous development for the reformers, as Baghdad was then governed by one of the most talented of the Ottoman Tanzimat statesmen, Midhat Pasha, and the visit served to introduce the shah to the modernizing and Westernizing changes taking place there. Shortly after returning to Iran, Naser-al-Din recalled Moshir-al-Dowleh and made him minister of justice, commander of the army, and eventually prime minister.

The appointment of Moshir-al-Dowleh touched off another wave of reform in Iran, but it soon became apparent that it was of an altogether different character from what had taken place under Amir Kabir. While making many needed legal, administrative, and military changes, Moshir-al-Dowleh concentrated on the economic development of the country. Instead of doing so in a way that emphasized self-reliance, he and his supporters deliberately encouraged the involvement of foreign powers, especially Great Britain. The rationale for this, grounded in his observations of the Ottoman experience and probably sincere if in retrospect misguided, was that the recent Russian advances into Central Asia constituted a potential threat to Iran, and the British needed to be given inducements to offset it; moreover, Russia could be expected to oppose the kind of reforms Moshir-al-Dowleh wanted to make, while Britain should support them since a stronger Iran as a buffer state was in its interest. The prime example of the agenda Moshir-al-Dowleh had in mind was the Reuter Concession of 1872. This proposed to give the entrepreneur Baron Julius de Reuter, a naturalized British subject, the exclusive right for seventy years to develop almost all of Iran's mines and other natural resources; to construct dams, roads, railways, bridges, and other public works; and to set up a national bank. To persuade Naser-al-Din of the benefits of such projects, he encouraged the shah to make the first of his expensive and ultimately counterproductive visits to Europe in 1873.

Popular disapproval, fierce Russian opposition, and lukewarm British support resulted in the cancellation of the Reuter Concession and precipitated the fall of Moshir-al-Dowleh. Unfortunately, a veritable Pandora's box had been opened. More and more Iranian officials began to lobby for the granting of one concession or another to Europeans, and in most cases the line between a patriotic desire to build up the country and an interest in personal profit was blurred. Competition for such awards exacerbated the already endemic factionalism and grudges within the Iranian bureaucracy. Economic rivalries complicated the play of Russian and British interests in Iran, which had previously been based on essentially strategic concerns. Unnecessary projects were started because the grant of a concession to a national of one country had to be matched by a comparable grant to a national of the other; useful projects had to be abandoned if the objections of one of the powers could not be overcome. Revenues from such schemes did the country little good as they mostly disappeared into the expenses of the court, financing for the shah's trips to Europe, and other trivialities. Desire for cash among government officials led to rapacious tax collection and increased corrupt practices such as the sale of offices and pensions. Vital aspects of national life passed into foreign hands: the military (with the establishment of the Russian officered Cossack Brigade in 1879); transportation (steamer services on the Karun River by the Lynch Brothers in 1888); banking (allowing Reuter to open the Imperial Bank of Persia in 1889). Even the borders of the country—with Russia, Afghanistan, and British India—were being determined by outside powers, with Iran being reduced to little more than a spectator. In little more than a decade, Iran had begun a precipitous slide toward weakness, bankruptcy, and dependency.

NOTE

1. It may be noted that the term *Mirza* after a personal name means "prince"; when it prefaces a name, it is simply an honorific.

6

The Forging of the Nation-State

During the last decade of the 19th century and the first decade of the 20th century, the forces in Iran opposed to foreign domination, arbitrary rule, and corruption in public life took the first bold steps toward national revival only to see them ruthlessly reversed by further humiliations. World War I was a particularly bleak period in the history of modern Iran, but it was followed by a vigorous assertion of Iranian sovereignty and state building under the new Pahlavi dynasty.

THE TOBACCO REBELLION

If any one event can be said to mark the beginning of Iran's history as a modern nation-state, it is probably the so-called Tobacco Rebellion of 1891–1892. Naser-al-Din Shah's incessant need for money, especially after his expensive third trip to Europe in 1889, had led the minister Ali-Asghar Khan Amin-al-Soltan to negotiate a concession with Major Gerald Talbot, a British subject, which would enable the latter to form the Imperial Tobacco Corporation. In exchange for an outright payment to the shah plus a yearly rent and 25 percent of the profits, the company would obtain exclusive rights for fifty years to the production, sale, and export of all tobacco in Iran. Since tobacco was so widely used in Iran, this would inevitably affect virtually all classes in all parts of the country. Articles critical of the concession began appearing in the reformist newspaper *Akhtar*, published in Istanbul, in late 1890, as did a highly inflammatory leaflet, apparently authored by Jamal-al-Din Afghani (Asadabadi), the famous ideologue of pan-Islamism and critic of British colonialism, who had recently returned to Iran from Russia in January 1891.

After the arrival of company agents that spring, disturbances broke out in Shiraz, the center of the tobacco trade, with merchants closing down the bazaar in protest and a fiery cleric, Ali-Akbar Falasiri, stirring up a riot and calling for a holy war against the tobacco company. Similar incidents then took place in a number of other cities. Both Afghani and Falasiri were expelled from Iran and wound up in Iraq, where they issued appeals to the foremost Shi'ite jurist of the time, Mirza Hasan Shirazi (Falasiri's father-in-law), to take action against the shah and the concession. Shirazi wrote a letter to Naser-al-Din Shah complaining about the concession and the mistreatment of Falasiri, but neither it nor subsequent correspondence with Qajar officials had any discernable effect. Late in 1891, Shirazi asked a prominent cleric in Tehran, Mirza Hasan Ashtiani, to act on his behalf in the matter. Shortly thereafter, in December 1891, a *fatva* said to have been written by Shirazi and prohibiting the use of tobacco was circulated in Tehran (it is now generally thought to have been forged, but Shirazi never disavowed it). As a juridical ruling by a supreme Shi'ite authority, it could hardly be ignored, and touched off a widespread, almost universal, boycott of tobacco. In January 1892, under pressure from the boycott and increasingly violent demonstrations, the shah agreed to cancel the concession, and Shirazi sent a telegram ending the boycott. As compensation for the company's losses, Iran had to pay some £500,000, which drove the country further into debt and ultimately required it to take out loans from British and Russian banks.

The successful resistance to the tobacco concession figures prominently in what can be called the modern nationalist mythology of Iran, especially in terms of the role of the clergy. In that view, the Tobacco Rebellion represented the emergence of a coalition of reformist intellectuals and merchants led by an outraged clergy in an urgent effort to mobilize the masses against corrupt government and foreign domination, a statement of national indignation at the selling of the country to the interests of imperialism, and a heroic prelude to the later Constitutional Revolution and other national struggles. Some of these sentiments, still rather undefined, were present in the Tobacco Rebellion, and it certainly prefigured many later movements in terms of its composition, organization, tactics, and methods. Nonetheless, there are many problems with such an interpretation. The clergy did not act as a monolithic group, and several prominent religious figures did not support the boycott; those involved were not so much leaders as agents and activists for other interests. Their attack was really focused more on the concession itself than on the larger issues, and most were anxious to resolve the matter when demonstrations threatened to get out of hand. The masses were aroused more by exploitation of simple xenophobia than by incipient nationalism. The cancellation of the concession may have helped some merchants, but it also entailed financial losses for tobacco growers and drove the country to take out a foreign loan to pay the compensation to the company. Opposition to the concession also came from within the government, as some officials, probably out to embarrass Amin-al-Soltan, worked against it. It has even been suggested that Naser-al-Din himself did not favor the concession or was frightened by popular opposition to it, so that the protest was orchestrated to provide him with cover for cancelling it without angering the British.

The most immediate significance of the rebellion was that it demonstrated the extent to which British and Russian competition for influence in Iran was being waged through proxies in the arena of trade and commerce. The fact that it was this particular concession, and not the grant of concessions in general, that inspired the rebellion strongly suggests Russian involvement in instigating or directing it. The Russians were alarmed by the scope of the concession as evidence of rising British influence; their ambassador condemned it in September 1890; and they encouraged resistance to it, as evidenced through their contacts with both Afghani and Mirza Hasan Shirazi as well as their actions in Tehran and Tabriz. Without doubt, the rebellion had the effect of diminishing British and increasing Russian influence in Iran, and Amin-al-Soltan adjusted his policies accordingly. It also demonstrated the ability of the clergy to shape public opinion; the British took due note of this and increased efforts to offset the pro-Russian clerics by co-opting sympathetic members of the clergy to work on their behalf.

THE REIGN OF MOZAFFAR-AL-DIN SHAH

The failure of the tobacco concession and the rise of Russian influence weakened the position of reformers and modernists at the Qajar court.

Naser-al-Din Shah took less and less interest in government affairs and left them in the hands of Amin-al-Soltan. The years after 1892 were thus marked primarily by political plots and intrigues, increasing debt and economic hardship, and a breakdown of law and order in the provinces. On 1 May 1896, Naser-al-Din was shot to death as he was arriving at the shrine of Shah Abd-al-Azim outside Tehran to celebrate the beginning of the fiftieth year of his reign. The assassin was Mirza Reza Kermani, a former Azali Babi and an associate of Afghani (who probably instigated the murder as revenge for his expulsion from Iran).

Naser-al-Din was succeeded by Mozaffar-al-Din, who, as crown prince, had long served as governor of Azerbaijan. Mozaffar-al-Din brought with him an entourage of officials he had come to rely on during his tenure in that province and who are thus usually referred to as the Turk or Tabrizi faction. With the collaboration of another powerful member of the Qajar family, Abd-al-Hosayn Mirza Farmanfarma (related by marriage to Mozaffar-al-Din as both son-in-law and brother-in-law), they were able to engineer the fall of Amin-al-Soltan in November 1896. Mozaffar-al-Din, however, was almost exclusively interested in replenishing the empty treasury he had inherited from Naser-al-Din, and his new minister, the reform-minded Amin-al-Dowleh, was unable to float the necessary loans in Britain. As a result, he was dismissed and Amin-al-Soltan was recalled to office in 1898.

Amin-al-Soltan turned to Russia for financial assistance and in January 1900 negotiated a large loan. Part of the proceeds was to be used to pay off existing foreign loans, and further borrowing from other countries was prohibited for ten years, thus ensuring Iran's complete indebtedness to Russia. The loan would be repaid with proceeds from the new customs administration Amin-al-Dowleh had set up under Belgian supervision. The grateful shah rewarded Amin-al-Soltan with the new title Atabak-e Azam (he is now generally known simply as Atabak). Negotiations for a second loan began in 1901 and were concluded in 1902. It was made contingent on revision of the customs regime. The new tariff system, drawn up by Joseph Naus, the Belgian customs director who acted in effect as the minister of finance, drastically lowered duties on goods imported from Russia and raised those on British products (notably tea).

The British objected strenuously to these developments, but other entanglements prevented them from doing much about them. British investors were also wary of Iran in the wake of the tobacco fiasco. To reassure them and to avoid a total Russian monopoly, Atabak did cooperate with the new British envoy, Arthur Hardinge, in setting up what was to become without question the most fateful of all the economic concessions granted by the Qajars to foreign nationals. On 28 May 1901, Mozaffar-al-Din Shah signed an agreement giving William Knox D'Arcy, an Australian mining millionaire, exclusive rights for sixty years to the exploitation of the gas and petroleum resources of the entire country except for the five northern provinces. In return, D'Arcy provided £40,000 in cash and stocks plus 16 percent of future profits. At the time, this was actually a rather speculative gamble, and by 1905 D'Arcy was nearly bankrupt. The British navy, however, was considering switching from coal to oil for fuel and helped arrange for the Burmah Oil Company to back D'Arcy. Finally, after almost giving up, the new company struck oil on 26 May 1908. This led to the formation of the Anglo-Persian Oil Company in 1909, with the British government taking a controlling interest in 1914 to secure its wartime needs. The profound importance of this development naturally led to a complete reassessment of Britain's interests in Iran.

The various loans, concessions, and financial reforms did little to ease the economic crisis in Iran. Mozaffar-al-Din squandered much of the proceeds on expensive trips to Europe. The efforts of Naus to impose the new tariffs and cut back on government expenditures antagonized both Iranian merchants and the affected government officials. Babi disturbances, religious agitation, bread riots, political intrigue, and the loss of both British and Russian confidence led to destabilization and the downfall of Atabak in 1903, followed by the appointment of his enemy, the harsh and authoritarian Ayn-al-Dowleh, as minister. The defeat of Russia by Japan in 1904 and the subsequent Russian Revolution of 1905, however, introduced an entirely new element into Iranian political thinking and, by removing the threat of Russian intervention, emboldened the various opponents of government policies to form a more diverse coalition with a more radical agenda than any seen thus far.

CONSTITUTIONAL REVOLUTION

In the late 19th and early 20th centuries, constitutional government came to be viewed by many as a panacea for a country's political troubles. The spectacular Japanese defeat of Russia, coming soon after the promulgation of a constitution in Japan, seemed to be a vindication of this theory and contributed to the outbreak of constitutional revolutions in Russia (1905) and Iran (1906), among other places, as well as the restoration of the Ottoman constitution (1908). All of these revolutions were aimed at curtailing the arbitrary exercise of power; none of them sought to abolish the existing monarchies. In Iran, however, there were some substantial and instructive differences between its constitutional revolution and that of its Ottoman neighbor.

In the case of the Ottoman Empire, a long history of reformism preceded the revolution of 1908. Ottoman intellectuals lived in a cosmopolitan environment and had direct contact with the European sources of constitutional thought. In keeping with the tradition of Ottoman reformism, the constitution was imposed mostly from the top down rather than by popular demand, with the military playing a key role. The revolution had a strong secular impulse because it was aimed at both the despotic Sultan Abd-al-Hamid and the Islamist ideology he had used to justify his autocracy. The adoption of a constitution was also intended to help solve the problem of ethnic and religious minorities in an imperial system. In Iran, the intellectual foundations for constitutionalism were much shallower and formed largely through the intermediary influence of activists in Istanbul, Tbilisi, and Baku. Reform-minded officials in Iran had enjoyed only very limited success over the past century, and there was no effective military force to back demands for change. Support for the revolution came from a very eclectic mix of government officials, journalists, intellectuals, religious dissidents, clerics, merchants, and tradesmen. They had varying motives, ranging from genuine patriotism to pure self-interest, and frequently shifted positions as a matter of political tactics. Constitutional ideology and principles did not so much precede the revolution as develop out of it. From the start, the revolution had a religious dimension, and over time this tended to create problems with minority groups rather than solve them.

In its first phase, the revolution was primarily a protest movement against the policies of Ayn-al-Dowleh and Naus and reflected economic issues. Throughout 1904 and 1905, a number of secret or semi-secret political societies (*anjomans*) were organized and began issuing propaganda and making plans for instituting in Iran the kind of constitutional regime that seemed to have produced such a miraculous transformation of Japan. With the lessons of the Tobacco Rebellion in mind, members of some of the *anjomans*, although they included non-Muslims, Azali Babis, Bahais, and secularists, concluded that it was essential to have support from the Muslim clerics for their movement. They were quite successful at attracting support among the young religious students (*tollab*) and enjoyed the sympathies of two high-ranking clerics, Mohammad Tabatabai and Abdallah Behbahani, who agreed in November 1905 to coordinate their activities. What they needed was some cause to rally public opinion, and this was provided by an incident the following month. On 12 December, the governor of Tehran, Ala-al-Dowleh, ordered two prominent merchants to be bastinadoed for not complying with a government order to lower the price of sugar. After protesters were attacked and labeled Babis, Tabatabai and Behbahani led a group of about 2,000 people to take *bast* (an Iranian custom of granting sanctuary and protection against arrest to anyone taking refuge in a religious building) at the shrine of Shah Abd-al-Azim. At first they demanded only the dismissal of Ala-al-Dowleh, but this soon escalated, under the prodding of the *anjoman* activists and even some court factions, to the removal of Ayn-al-Dowleh and Naus and the establishment of a "house of justice" (*adalat-khaneh*). The shah refused to move against his ministers but agreed on 10 January 1906 to the creation of the *adalat-khaneh*, which he understood to mean an agency "to carry out the religious law (*sharia*) and ensure the security of the subjects." In July, the police attempted to arrest some of the more vocal critics of the government, including the popular preacher Jamal-al-Din Vaez Esfahani, and a religious student was killed during the ensuing protests. Rather than risk an outright confrontation, Tabatabai and Behbahani organized a new *bast* by clerics and religious students in Qom.

On 23 July 1906 a group of merchants, in solidarity with the clerics and probably at the instigation of Behbahani (who had long been viewed as pro-British and was on good terms with the British *chargé d'affaires*, Evelyn Grant Duff), asked to take *bast* on the grounds of the British Legation in Tehran. Over the next week, they were joined by virtually the entire bazaar community—merchants, artisans, small tradesmen—of Tehran, anywhere from 13,000 to 20,000 people. This marked an important new phase in the revolution. The merchants were now solidly committed to the cause of reform, and members of the *anjomans* openly addressed the crowds at the Legation and sought to educate them in political issues. Under their guidance, the movement took on a distinctly national dimension and formulated as a main demand the election of a representative assembly (*majles*). On 29 July, Ayn-al-Dowleh resigned, and the request for a national consultative Majles was granted a few days later, on 10 August. This brought to an end the *bast* of the religious leaders in Qom as well as that at the British Legation.

After some opposition from the court, an electoral law was signed in September. It granted suffrage to all male Iranian citizens over the age of thirty who owned property, irrespective of their religion (thus including many non-Muslim merchants and tradesmen but generally excluding peasants and the poor). A disproportionate number of seats in the Majles were allotted to Tehran in order to expedite the proceedings. The Majles held its first meeting on 7 October and drafted a basic constitution, the Fundamental Laws, by the end of the year. It authorized the creation of a Senate, with still unspecified duties and half of whose sixty members would be appointed by the shah. Basic power, however, was vested in the Majles, elected every two years as the representative of all the people, with authority over legislative, financial, and diplomatic matters. The Fundamental Laws were signed by Mozaffar-al-Din Shah, literally on his deathbed, on 30 December 1906. Iran had thus made surprisingly rapid progress toward the construction of a democratic and pluralistic society, but three major obstacles to further progress appeared in 1907.

First of all, Mozaffar-al-Din died on 6 January 1907. His successor, Mohammad-Ali Shah, had interceded during the early phase of the rev-olution on behalf of the protesters, but mostly because he wanted to see the fall of Ayn-al-Dowleh, whom he suspected of intriguing to block his accession to the throne. Beyond that, he was adamantly opposed to rad-ical reform, the Majles, and constitutionalism. Once Mohammad-Ali Shah was crowned and felt secure on the throne, he began to work against all of them.

Second, members of the British legation, if not the British government, had been openly sympathetic to the constitutionalists, so much so that some observers came to regard the movement as British-controlled. Grant Duff had not only allowed the *bast* on the legation grounds, he had provided advice to the leaders of the movement and interceded on their behalf with the shah. Whatever illusions the constitutionalists might have thus acquired about British support, however, were rudely shat-tered on 31 August 1907 with the conclusion of the infamous Anglo-Russian Agreement. Great Britain and Russia were seeking to ally against the rising power of Germany and as part of their rapprochement needed to defuse potential areas of conflict between them. Insofar as this affected Iran, the agreement pledged "to respect the integrity and independence of Persia" but proceeded to carve the country up into exclusive Russian and British spheres of influence. Russia was free to conclude any political or economic arrangements, without British competition or interference, in the area north of a line from Qasr-e Shirin to Yazd to the intersection of the Russian, Afghan, and Iranian border. Britain had a similar zone south of a line from the Afghan border to Bandar Abbas. The two parties could apportion government revenues from the Iranian customs, its post and telegraph service, and its fisheries to make sure existing loans from the Russian and British banks were paid off. Since Britain already dominated the Persian Gulf area (and was probably plotting for a puppet regime in southwest Iran), this effectively left the constitutional government in control of little more than the central desert basin. Engaged in the struggle for the constitution, the Majles was unable to respond in any meaningful way to this travesty.

Finally, divisions began to appear among the constitutionalists themselves, primarily in the form of a split between secular nationalists and conservative Islamists. There had been an effort by some leaders to conceal or paper over these differences by taking a gradualist approach and using nebulous terminology like *adalat-khaneh* or *majles* or *mashroutiyyat*, based on Arabic and vaguely Islamic-sounding words rather than borrowing terminology from European languages. As a result, the movement attracted supporters like Behbahani and Tabatabai and even came to include their conservative clerical rival, Fadl-Allah Nouri. In the First Majles, however, a numerically small but well-organized and determined faction of progressives, reflecting the thinking of the truly radical *anjomans* in Tabriz, pushed an agenda based on ideas of popular sovereignty, secularism, and nationalism. Under the leadership of Hasan Taqizadeh, they dominated the Majles, and their ideas were effectively disseminated among the masses by popular orators such as Malek-al-Motakallemin and by writers like Ali-Akbar Dehkhoda in the famous newspaper *Sour-e Esrafil*. Their influence was clearly reflected in the Supplemental Laws which were drawn up to complete the constitution. They included articles affirming popular sovereignty, an independent judiciary, the equality of all citizens without regard to religious identity, mandatory education under state control, and freedom of the press.

Alarmed by the secularist drift of the parliamentary discussions, the leader of the religious conservatives, Nouri, drafted an article requiring laws passed by the Majles to be approved by a committee of clerics. When this was modified to give the Majles control over appointments to the committee, Nouri broke his alliance with the constitutionalists, organized a *bast* of his own at Shah Abd-al-Azim in June 1907, and, with the encouragement of the court, stepped up propaganda about the un-Islamic nature of the constitutionalists' proposals. Nouri argued that only Shi'ite Muslims should be allowed in the Majles; that all legislation should be in conformity with existing religious law; and, stung by criticism of the clerics in the press, that freedom of expression should be limited. In tandem with Nouri, the shah resisted signing the Supplemental Laws.

This produced a furious response from Taqizadeh and other radicals, as well as sizable counter-demonstrations and efforts to raise militias to enforce the wishes of the Majles. Then, on 31 August, the prime minister, Amin-al-Soltan Atabak, was assassinated. The assassin immediately committed suicide, and his motivation remains a mystery. He was from Tabriz and apparently had ties with a radical *anjoman* there. However, Atabak had been moving closer to the position of the Majles, so some have alleged that the shah may have orchestrated the murder in hopes of discrediting the radicals. If so, the plot backfired; huge crowds celebrated the death of a tyrant and so intimidated the shah and Nouri that the Supplemental Laws were approved on 7 October 1907. Their secular and liberal provisions were preserved largely intact, although as a gesture of accommodation with Nouri they did affirm Twelver Shi'ism as the official religion and included a provision for review of legislation by religious scholars.

For a while it appeared that the shah and the Majles might be able to develop a working relationship, but tensions rose again as specific measures were undertaken to implement the constitution. The Majles asserted control over the finances of the court and entertained a proposal to create a national army that would be independent of the shah. Mohammad-Ali Shah also became convinced that members of the Majles were conspiring to depose him in favor of another member of the Qajar family, probably his uncle Zell-al-Soltan, the longtime governor of Isfahan. When the Majles demanded that the anti-constitutionalist courtiers Sad-al-Dowleh and Amir Bahador be sent into exile, the shah struck back in what appeared to be an attempt at a coup d'etat. On 15 December, the prime minister, Naser-al-Molk, was arrested and a gang of rowdies from poor areas of Tehran were employed to attack the Majles building. Nouri and his followers rushed to their support, and they took over the nearby Toupkhaneh Square. However, members of the *anjomans* acquired weapons and successfully defended the Majles. Under pressure from the British and Russians (who did not want any one side to vanquish the other), and urged to compromise by moderate officials, the shah hesitated to press further, and the coup, if that is what it was intended to be, failed.

The collapse of the royalists during the Toupkhaneh incident encouraged the radicals to press their advantage. In so doing, they alienated the moderate cleric Behbahani with their ideas about judicial reform.

Their increasing hostility toward Mohammad-Ali Shah also alarmed the British and Russians, as did their diplomatic flirtation with Germany. Economic hardships were also beginning to erode popular support. Meanwhile, the shah was busy building up his own military force and was soon in a much stronger position. He arrested several Qajar aristocrats believed to be sympathetic to the Majles and issued an ultimatum that some of the most vocal radicals be sent into exile. The Majles rejected the ultimatum, and members of the *anjomans* again mobilized to protect it. On 23 June 1908, a detachment of the Cossack Brigade cleared the defenders out of the adjacent Sepahsalar mosque, invested the Majles building, and shelled it. Several prominent constitutionalists, including the orator Malek-al-Motakallemin and the editor of *Sour-e Esrafil*, Jahangir Khan, were rounded up and executed; numerous others, notably Behbahani and Tabatabai, were arrested; still others either took *bast* at the British Legation or fled into exile.

The June coup began the period of the revolution known as the "lesser despotism." The bombed-out Majles symbolized the collapse of the constitutional movement in Tehran, where Nouri now praised the monarchy and argued that constitutions were contrary to Islam. The victory of the reactionaries, however, was hardly complete. From the safety of the shrine cities in Iraq, high-ranking members of the Shi'ite clergy criticized the shah for his action. Constitutionalists in exile worked to swing public opinion in Europe, especially Great Britain, in favor of their cause. Opposition to the royalists was very strong in provinces like Gilan, Khorasan, and, above all, Azerbaijan. In the south, leaders of the powerful Bakhtiari tribe declared support for the Majles and took control of Isfahan. Not surprisingly, the center of the resistance was in Tabriz. Members of the *anjomans*, volunteers from the Caucasus, Armenians, tradesmen, religious students, and peasants and tribesmen from the surrounding countryside banded together to oppose the hated Ayn-al-Dowleh and the reactionary cleric Mirza Hasan. The heroic but unlikely leader of the resistance in Tabriz was a former rogue (*louti*) and liveryman named Sattar Khan. The royalists occupied part of the city, but Sattar Khan and the opposition fighters barricaded themselves in other neighborhoods and withstood a ten-month siege. By February 1909, the royalists had surrounded Tabriz and the population was facing starvation. Relief then came from an unexpected source. The constitutionalists had long feared that the Russians would intervene in support of Mohammad-Ali Shah; instead, the Russians demanded that the shah accept a cease-fire and restore the constitution. On 29 April, with the encouragement and approval of Great Britain, Russian troops entered Tabriz, breaking the siege and allowing the supply of food. The Russian motivation is not entirely clear, but was probably aimed at maintaining the entente with Britain and out of concern over the effects the fall of the city would have on opinion in Transcaucasia and elsewhere.

Meanwhile, there had been a coup in Rasht, where a revolutionary government was set up under Eprem Khan, the leader of the Armenian Dashnak Party, and Mohammad-Vali Khan Sepahdar, a former Qajar commander who had defected to the constitutionalists at Tabriz. On 5 May, they sent an armed force to Qazvin, which was joined there by resistance fighters fleeing Tabriz after the Russian occupation, and the combined constitutionalist forces then prepared to move on Tehran. At the same time, a Bakhtiari force under the tribal leader Samsam-al-Saltaneh was moving toward Tehran from the south. After attempts at reaching a compromise settlement failed, the two armies entered the capital on 13 July. Three days later, a special assembly (*majles-e ali*) deposed Mohammad-Ali Shah, who went into exile in Russia.

With the approval of the Russians and British, Mohammad-Ali's young son Ahmad was made shah, with the respected head of the Qajar tribe, Azod-al-Molk, acting as regent. A "Temporary Directorate" was constituted to manage affairs until a new Majles could be elected. A special tribunal was also convened to prosecute prominent anti-constitutionalists. Among those convicted and executed was the conservative clerical leader, Fazl-Allah Nouri.

The Second Majles, which convened on 15 December, was quite different in composition from the First Majles, as the electoral law had been changed to expand the franchise and increase the representation of the provinces. This actually had the effect of diminishing the influence of the radicals, who had difficulty competing with landlords, tribal lords, and the wealthy in mobilizing voters to support candidates of their choice. By 1910, the divisions between the moderates and radicals (now the Democrat Party) had become very embittered, and the animosity was reflected in the assassination of Behbahani on 15 July, almost certainly at the instigation of Taqizadeh, and the subsequent expulsion of Taqizadeh from the Majles and his exile to Istanbul.

The major problems faced by the Second Majles were the need to restore order and to deal with financial problems. Despite the polarization of its politics, it managed to deal with both in a positive manner but at the cost of antagonizing the Russians and British. In each case, it turned to other countries: As a police force, it created a Gendarmerie with Swedish officers, and to solve the financial crisis it employed an American,

Morgan Shuster, as its economic advisor. The Shuster appointment proved especially contentious. The Russians had become increasingly hostile, refusing to withdraw their troops from Qazvin, demanding the continuation of the Cossack Brigade, and insisting on the dismissal of governors they disliked in Azerbaijan and Khorasan. Shuster, working closely with the Democrats, proved to be far too effective and intrusive into areas the Russians regarded as their own (and, to his surprise and dismay, he was not very popular with the British either). When the former shah tried to return to Iran from Russia in July 1911, Shuster offered a bounty for his capture and helped finance the army that eventually defeated him. In October, in accordance with instructions from the Majles, he attempted to confiscate the residence of Shoa-al-Saltana, brother of the former shah and a Russian protégé, in the face of stiff Russian opposition. He appointed officials in the area of Iran assigned to Russia and whom the Russians found objectionable, notably a British subject well known for his vehemently anti-Russian sentiments. He further embarrassed Russia and the British government by publishing a letter critical of both in the London *Times*.

At British suggestion, and after the U.S. ambassador in Russia had disavowed any interest in the matter, the Russians broke off diplomatic relations, sent troops to Rasht, and issued an ultimatum for Shuster's dismissal and reimbursement of its costs for invading Iran! The insulting demands were rejected by the Majles on 1 December. The Russians brutally suppressed resistance in Rasht and Tabriz, and their forces then began advancing on Tehran, with Britain building up its forces in the south. Faced with the grim prospect of the occupation of the capital, the government ministers, backed by the police force under Eprem Khan, demanded that the Majles accept a revised ultimatum. When it did not, they declared the Majles dissolved, even though there was no constitutional basis for this action, and locked the doors to the building. The Second Majles and the Constitutional Revolution thus came to an end on 24 December 1911. Sporadic resistance to foreign occupation continued in the provinces for a few months, but petered out after the Russians retaliated by shelling one of the holiest sites in Iran, the shrine of Imam Reza in Mashhad, in March 1912.

IRAN AND WORLD WAR I

The regency that had been established upon the deposition of Mohammad-Ali Shah came to a formal end with the coronation of Ahmad Shah in July 1914. Any hopes that the young king might restore the tarnished prestige of the Qajar monarchy were quickly dashed. Since 1909, Ahmad had been subject to pressure from the constitutionalists on one side and reactionaries like his grandfather Kamran Mirza on the other. This left him largely without genuine political convictions; he was always much more interested in finding excuses to travel abroad, to build up his personal fortune (often through corrupt means), and to avoid all tedious responsibilities. Even if he had been gifted with a stronger personality, he would have had great difficulty in coping with the hardships imposed on Iran by the outbreak of World War I only a few weeks after his coronation.

Technically, Iran was a neutral and nonbelligerent country during the Great War. However, the entry of the Ottoman Empire on the side of the Central Powers, coupled with the extensive involvement of its Russian and British enemies in Iranian affairs, made it inevitable that Iran would be caught up in the conflict. First of all, Iran's northwest province, Azerbaijan, became a battleground between Russian and Ottoman forces. By 1915, Russian troops had been stationed in Qazvin and were in position to occupy Tehran. Second, Britain was determined to protect the vitally important operations of the Anglo-Persian Oil Company in Khuzistan and initiated an invasion of Ottoman Iraq, using Iranian territory around Ahvaz as a base of operations, in order to shield the pipelines and other installations from Ottoman attack. Third, German agents in Iran were active in support of their Ottoman allies and creating problems for the British and Russians there. The most famous of the German operatives was Wilhelm Wassmuss, who was able to threaten the British consulate and communications station at Bushire and stir up anti-British tribal revolts in Fars province. To bolster its control of the area, Britain organized a subservient local militia, the South Persia Rifles, in 1916 and extended its own ties with sympathetic tribes, mainly the Bakhtiaris in Fars and the Arabs under Sheikh Khazal in Khuzistan. Finally, there was considerable sympathy for Germany among Iranians, and a group of politicians attempted to persuade Ahmad Shah to follow the Ottoman example and enter the war on the side of Germany. This failed, partly because of the presence of Russian troops and partly because of the influence of pro-British politicians on the shah. For a while, a "Committee for National Defense" in Qom and Kermanshah cooperated with Germany against the Russians and British but eventually collapsed.

The war thus turned out to be a disaster for Iran. It revealed the glaring and humiliating inability of the puny military forces at the disposal of the Iranian government, limited to the Cossack Brigade (about 8,000 men) and the Gendarmerie (about 7,000), to do anything to protect the country's national sovereignty. It highlighted the vacillation, corruption, and self-interest of much of the ruling elite. It imposed great economic difficulties, exacerbated by food shortages and famine, especially in the areas of northwestern Iran where Russian and Ottoman troops had been engaged. In many ways, the country was actually disintegrating. In addition to the presence of foreign troops operating on its soil and the promotion of tribal unrest, the already tenuous control of the central government over the provinces was slipping away. The most important case was in Gilan, where a local leader named Kouchek Khan, head of the Islamic Union (Ettehad-e Eslam) guerilla movement (also called Jangalis or "Foresters"), had seized control of the region in 1917. Despite the hardships that the country had endured, Britain managed to prevent Iran from presenting its case at the Paris Peace Conference.

As a result of the Russian Revolution in 1917, and in accordance with the Treaty of Brest-Litovsk (March 1918), Russian troops were to be withdrawn from Iran, but Turkish forces were still active in Azerbaijan and the Caucasus. To fill the void left by the departing Russians, the British decided to send a small contingent of troops under Major General L. C. Dunsterville into northern Iran (humorously known as the "Dunsterforce" and later Norperforce). Dunsterville was able to repulse Kouchek Khan and take the Caspian port of Enzeli, from where he attempted, unsuccessfully, to help the anti-Bolshevik and anti-Ottoman forces in Baku. In June 1919, the Bolsheviks terminated the special privileges and concessions the tsarist government had extracted from Iran. What these events seemed to signify was the total collapse of Russian influence in Iran, leaving Britain as the sole foreign power to dominate Iran in both the north and the south.

THE ANGLO-PERSIAN AGREEMENT OF 1919

The British foreign secretary, Nathaniel Curzon, and his minister in Iran, Percy Cox, sought to translate this perception into a reality through the Anglo-Persian Agreement of 1919. Curzon was the author of a celebrated book, *Persia and the Persian Question*, which combined a vast mine of information about Iran with a rather shallow and demeaning view of Iranians. He was a leading member of the school of thought that viewed Russia as an expansionist power and held that British India consequently needed to be defended by a shield of British-dominated border states. In that scheme Iran was doubly important because of British interests in the Persian Gulf and Iranian oil. These concerns were reflected in the agreement, negotiated with three ministers well known for their Anglophile sentiments, Prime Minister Vosouq-al-Dowleh, Foreign Minister Firouz Mirza Nosrat-al-Dowleh, and Minister of Finance Sarem-al-Dowleh. It pledged that Britain would "respect absolutely the independence and integrity of Persia" yet stipulated that Britain, with Iran footing the bill, would supply "whatever expert advisers" were needed for the administration of the country, provide the officers and supplies necessary to create a credible Iranian army, assist in improving trade and communications through the construction of railroads and other projects, and set up a joint committee to revise the tariff system. To help finance these arrangements, Britain offered a loan of £2 million, payable over twenty years at 7 percent interest. The rationale for the agreement was that a greatly weakened Iran was going through a period of duress from internal and external challenges and needed the protection of a foreign power while it reorganized, with Britain being the power best suited for this purpose. Most Iranians, as well as other countries such as France and the United States, saw the agreement as a transparent effort to turn Iran into exactly the kind of protectorate, awash with imperious bureaucrats and opportunists on the payroll of the host country, that Britain had created in Egypt under Lord Cromer.

Whatever the merits of the agreement, its fate was sealed by the obtuse methods employed to secure it. Its terms were shrouded in secrecy, the Majles was never convened to approve it as required by the constitution, and it was never submitted to the scrutiny of the League of Nations. It was also known that the British had been paying a monthly stipend to Ahmad Shah largely so that he would keep Vosouq-al-Dowleh in office, and rumors circulated that bribes had been paid to the Iranian negotiators to facilitate the agreement (an allegation that has since been proven to be true). News of the agreement fanned the flames of the separatist movements in Azerbaijan and Gilan, aroused the indignation of the nationalists, and was denounced by other governments. It also alarmed the new Soviet regime and confirmed its fears that Britain would use its hegemony in Iran to assist White Russian forces and anti-Bolsheviks in the Cossack Brigade. In 1920, troops from the Red Army, in pursuit of White Russian refugees and ships, occupied Enzeli and began collaborating with Kouchek Khan, forcing the small British force there to withdraw to Qazvin. The Soviets let it be known they would not remove their forces as long as British troops were in Iran.

This made it very clear, even to Iranians who might otherwise have been sympathetic to the agreement, just how little "security" the British could really offer Iran against a determined adversary. At the very moment British authority in Iran seemed to reign supreme, the country was wracked by tribal and provincial unrest, the government lacked all credibility, and the deployment of British forces had provoked, not prevented, the intrusion of another foreign power. In Britain itself, not everyone agreed with Curzon on the importance of making deeper commitments in Iran. The political climate after the war required that Britain limit its military and economic involvement abroad. It was facing difficulties in Egypt, Palestine, and Iraq, and the India Office preferred to concentrate resources on the defense of India's own borders rather than diverting them to buffer states. The British government was thus obliged to undertake an evacuation of its forces from Iran by April 1921. It dispatched General Edmund Ironside with the mission of removing Norperforce and transferring its military duties to the Cossack Brigade after removal of its remaining Russian officers. In the face of mounting opposition to the agreement, Vosouq-al-Dowleh resigned in July 1920. His successor, Moshir-al-Dowleh, scrupulously avoided putting any part of the agreement into practice and insisted on adherence to the constitutional requirement that the Majles approve it, which effectively delayed its implementation.

THE COUP OF 21 FEBRUARY 1921

Although Curzon remained committed to the agreement, other British officials realized that it was dead and came around to the idea that British interests in the Persian Gulf and India could be better protected by a stable if independent Iran rather than through a de facto protectorate. British policy aimed at a graceful withdrawal of its forces from Iran while leaving behind a government capable of preventing either domestic chaos or drawing in the Bolsheviks. The question was how such a government could be formed and who should lead it. That problem was abruptly solved on 21 February 1921 when a contingent of the Cossack Brigade from Qazvin under the command of Colonel Reza Khan marched into Tehran, took control of government offices, declared martial law, and ousted the ineffectual cabinet, then under Fath-Allah Akbar Sepahdar. As a result of this coup, Sepahdar was replaced as prime minister by Sayyed Zia-al-Din Tabatabai, with Reza Khan as commander of the army and later minister of war.

The events that led to the coup of 21 February have been studied extensively by historians, but the circumstances of many critical events are still unclear, and there are widely varying interpretations of them. At present, the preponderance of the evidence indicates that the coup took place without the knowledge or complicity of the Foreign Ministry in London but with the active involvement of British officials on the scene, notably General Ironside and the British minister, Herbert Norman, acting largely on their own initiative. Ironside had been searching for a capable Iranian officer to lead the Cossack Brigade, the only significant military force in Iran, and thought there was no one better suited for the job than Reza Khan, whom he had urged Ahmad Shah to appoint as commander. Ironside was summoned to a meeting in Cairo and left Iran shortly before the coup, probably having assured Reza Khan that the British would not oppose him should he wish to take action. Norman had also been attempting to find a suitable replacement for the compliant Vosouq-al-Dowleh and, after several less than successful efforts, had apparently taken notice of Sayyed Zia, a journalist for a paper regarded as the virtual mouthpiece of the British Legation in Iran. It is not certain how much collaboration there was between Ironside and Norman nor exactly how Reza Khan and Sayyed Zia, both of whom were of obscure background and not members of the political elite of the time, managed to forge an alliance and coordinate the coup. In the view of many Iranians, everything must have been orchestrated by the British, but as it turned out these developments hardly worked to Britain's advantage.

Sayyed Zia was apparently under the impression that the coup had been staged for his benefit (he declined to use the title prime minister and preferred to think of himself as "dictator" in the Roman sense of the word) and proceeded to announce an ambitious program of reforms while carrying out actions that thoroughly discredited him. Although he moved to annul the Anglo-Persian Agreement, he could not shake the common perception that he was a British puppet. Curzon had hoped to bring someone like Firouz Mirza Nosrat-al-Dowleh to power and, despite the urgings of Norman, had little interest in supporting an upstart like Sayyed Zia, especially after his hopes for the agreement were dashed. Sayyed Zia also made the mistake of arresting many members of the old political elite, including both supporters and opponents of the agreement, primarily in order to extort money from them. When they were released from jail, they issued public denunciations of Sayyed Zia and intrigued against him relentlessly. Sayyed Zia also quarreled with Reza Khan over the employment of British officers. Reza Khan, who would tolerate no interference by civilian politicians in military affairs, forced Sayyed Zia to resign on 23 May. The latter immediately left Iran, no doubt in fear that the many enemies he had made were out to kill him. Qavam-al-Saltaneh then became prime minister, and a new Majles convened in June 1921, the first to be seated since 1915.

REZA KHAN AND THE FALL OF THE QAJARS

In contrast to the empty promises of Sayyed Zia, Reza Khan took concrete actions that showed he was capable of restoring order and national integrity. Five days after the coup (26 February 1921), the Soviet-Iranian Friendship Treaty was signed. In addition to securing peaceful relations and the removal of Soviet forces, this was useful to Reza Khan in another respect: It pulled the rug out from under the separatist movements the Bolsheviks had been supporting in Gilan and Mazandaran. This facilitated Reza Khan's assertion of government control over those areas; his troops defeated the Jangalis, and the unfortunate Kouchek Khan, attempting to flee, froze to death in the remote Elburz Mountains in November 1921.

Reza Khan also pursued a policy of consolidating all military forces under his command and with Iranian officers. He dismissed the Swedish officers of the Gendarmerie, replacing them with Iranians, and incorporated the Gendarmerie itself into the army. Despite British efforts at obstruction, he was also able to absorb the remnants of the South Persia Rifles into the army. He was careful to ensure that his troops received adequate pay; to that end, he had the Ministry of War take over some tax collecting functions and, in 1922, agreed to bring in an American financial advisor, Arthur C. Millspaugh, to keep the financial house in order. Between 1921 and 1923, Reza Khan used this new, reorganized, and enlarged army with great effect in putting down challenges to the authority of the central government.

Reza Khan's military successes enhanced his prestige and standing in the eyes of the public and with many of the political factions in Iran. On 28 October 1923, Ahmad Shah named him as the new prime minister and promptly left Iran to return to Europe, where he had spent much of his time since 1919. Reza Khan also retained his post as minister of war and continued his efforts to suppress the tribes and rebellious elements in Kurdistan, Azerbaijan, Fars, Mazandaran, Luristan, Gorgan, Khorasan, and Baluchistan. None of these campaigns was easy, but the riskiest move by far was the decision in 1924 to attack Sheikh Khazal of Mohammareh in Khuzistan (then called Arabistan). It was rumored that Ahmad

Shah was inciting Sheikh Khazal in order to make trouble for Reza Khan, and the British certainly regarded him as a key protégé in the web of petty emirates they had created around their interests in the Persian Gulf. Khazal had refused to pay taxes, written the Majles to complain that Reza Khan was a menace to the shah, and plotted to have Khuzistan incorporated as part of the British mandate in Iraq; Britain warned Reza Khan against intervening and sent gunships to the area. Unintimidated, Reza Khan called the bluff and marched on Mohammareh in person. In the end, the British were more concerned about damage to their oil installations than Sheikh Khazal's autonomy and did nothing to defend him. He quickly surrendered and was later arrested and sent into a comfortable exile in Tehran. Probably no other event so enhanced Reza Khan's reputation as his willingness to confront the British lion in one of its chief lairs.

These events took place against the background of a growing debate over the future of the Qajar monarchy. The Fifth Majles, which convened in 1923, was dominated by politicians sympathetic to Reza Khan, notably those of the liberal, reformist, nationalist, and secularist Revival Party (Hezb-e Tajaddod). They quickly approved a bill mandating compulsory military service, which Reza Khan had wanted but could not get through the conservative Fourth Majles. They passed a number of other measures that clearly had Reza Khan's approval, including the abolition of titles of nobility used by the Qajars and the adoption of European-style family names (as Reza Khan now became Reza Pahlavi). In 1924, obviously inspired by the example of Mustafa Kemal (Ataturk)'s abolition of the sultanate in Turkey, some of the more radical reformists floated the idea of abolishing the Qajar monarchy in favor of a republic. There was considerable opposition to this idea, especially among the religious leaders, who then held that a republican form of government was inimical to Islam. Having secured the reformist legislation he wanted from the Revival Party, Reza Khan began to shift toward the conservative parties, meeting with religious dignitaries in Qom and dramatically threatening to withdraw from public life if controversy over republicanism did not cease.

The matter then proceeded to the obvious and logical compromise: abolish the Qajar dynasty but not the monarchy and make Reza Khan the shah. On 14 February 1925, the Majles conferred the title of commander-in-chief, normally reserved for the king, on Reza Khan. On 31 October, after Ahmad Shah had indicated an interest in returning to Iran, the Majles voted to depose him and make Reza Khan head of state while a Constituent Assembly drew up arrangements for a new regime. On 12 December 1925 the Constituent Assembly amended the constitution to confer the monarchy on Reza Khan and his descendants. The new Reza Shah Pahlavi crowned himself in an impressive ceremony at Golestan Palace in Tehran on 25 April 1926.

THE REIGN OF REZA SHAH

Reza Shah Pahlavi has to be placed among the most remarkable figures in Iranian history, not necessarily for his accomplishments but for his sheer strength of will and force of personality. He was born on 16 March 1878 in Elasht, a small, obscure village in the Elburz Mountains. His father died shortly after he was born, and his mother then decided to move the family to her former home in Tehran. His uncle was a member of the Cossack Brigade and helped arrange for the young Reza (somewhere between the age of twelve and fifteen) to join that force. At a time when literacy was relatively rare, he managed to teach himself to read and write. His military abilities were also exceptional, and he moved steadily through the ranks to become commander of the Hamadan detachment by the time he was forty. It was then that he was noticed by Ironside and recommended as the best man to be in charge of the Cossack Brigade. After the coup, he showed that he could hold his own against the wiliest politicians of the day and literally made himself shah.

Reza Shah's goal as ruler can be summed up in one phrase: to complete the job of making Iran into a modern nation-state. Because of his military background, he had an intuitive understanding of the basic requirements for this, especially the need to build up a professional army and to crush any sign of tribal resistance or provincial separatism. Even before becoming shah, he had managed to consolidate the existing military forces, to secure adequate funding, to begin sending cadets abroad for advanced military training, and to introduce a system of conscription. By the 1930s, he had built up an army of over 100,000 men equipped with mechanized transport and aircraft. He also improved communications and logistical support. Iranians had long hoped to build a national system of railroads but had been frustrated by foreign interference and the immense difficulties of construction in such a mountainous country. Reza Shah started the Trans-Iranian Railroad in 1927, and it was completed in 1938. He also allocated considerable funding for highways, and by 1940 over 15,000 miles of roads had been built.

The ultimate purpose of Reza Shah's overriding interest in the military was certainly not to undertake foreign adventures or even to protect the country against invasion. It was intended to maintain domestic security and, above all, to break the power of the tribes. This typically involved disarmament, arrest or execution of the tribal chiefs, integration into the bureaucratic and administrative system, imposition of taxes, and forced settlement. Thus the Bakhtiari tribe, which had played such an important role in the Constitutional Revolution, was prevented from dealing directly with the British or Anglo-Persian Oil Company, had its leadership decimated, and had the territory in which it nomadized split between the governors of Isfahan and Khuzistan. In the great tribal rebellion of 1929 in Fars, the Qashqai, Boir Ahmadi, and Mamasani tribes were all defeated. Many critics have lamented the undeniable hardship all this inflicted on the tribal peoples, once proud and free, with their unique culture and handicrafts, but now constrained to live in inadequate villages and take up unfamiliar occupations. This view, however, has more than a small element of the romantic myth of the noble savage in it; it is unlikely that many peasants or other sedentary people regretted the end of tribal depredations. Certainly, a government with its own army no longer needed to rely on the goodwill of tribes to govern or to allow them to become pawns of foreign powers.

In terms of his social and economic policies, Reza Shah was heavily influenced by the ideas of his sometime political allies in the Revival Party and by the contemporary example set by Mustafa Kemal Ataturk in Turkey. Both essentially advocated an extremely nationalistic state that was both unified and modernized.

National unity not only involved a strong military and central government, it also required the obliteration of competing ethnic, regional, and religious identities. Thus, there was a pronounced effort to build up a pervasive sense of Iranian nationality by glorifying the pre-Islamic periods of Iranian history and holding up Persian language and culture as normative. Archaeological work was encouraged, a special cultural institute attempted to purge Persian of its borrowings from Arabic grammar and vocabulary, classical authors like Ferdowsi who were regarded as Iranian nationalists in spirit were singled out for special celebration, and the use of minority languages like Kurdish and Turkish was discouraged in numerous ways.

Modernization involved the creation of a bureaucratic state apparatus, an educational system, economic development, and social reforms. It thus led to the establishment of new government ministries, restructuring of the administrative system from the central government to the provinces and down to the district and local level, with a corresponding increase in the size of the bureaucracy, as well as the founding of schools and universities and investment in transportation, factories, and other elements of the infrastructure. Reza Shah's approach to economics was strongly etatist, as was Ataturk's, and encouraged the formation of state monopolies and public sector industries rather than private investment and entrepreneurship. Critics have argued that the state investments were also made with an eye to inflating national pride rather than meeting genuine economic needs.

In terms of social change, Reza Shah's greatest achievement, apart from settling the tribes, was his move toward the emancipation of women. In general, Reza Shah believed that women should be educated, should have access to the workplace, and should have the same basic rights as men. It was at his specific insistence that female as well as male students were admitted to the University of Tehran when it opened in 1936. His involvement of the state in women's issues intensified after his visit to Turkey in 1934. This was undoubtedly encouraged by his discussions with Ataturk, who had begun an all-out attack on the custom of women having to wear veils in public, a small but highly symbolic indicator of their social status. Reza Shah had long attempted to set an example by having his own wife and daughters appear unveiled and in mixed company. In 1934, a law was passed that actually prohibited female students and teachers from wearing the *chador*, a traditional full-length covering used by women when they went out in public. In 1936, the law was extended to apply to women in many other public facilities, but the use of the *chador* was never completely outlawed, as was the veil in Turkey, and it remained in common use despite the efforts to discourage it. In this respect, as in other cases, Reza Shah's reforms did not go nearly as far as did Ataturk's. The liberation of women was strongly opposed by the Shi'ite clergy, and most male politicians, including the reformists, had little interest in this issue. If anything, arguments over the *chador* diverted attention from more important questions like the right of women to vote. Whereas Turkey was among the first countries in the world to give women the franchise, they never obtained that right in Reza Shah's Iran. Furthermore, Reza Shah was no more tolerant of criticism and political opposition from women than from men and actively suppressed women's organizations that displeased him.

The development of a genuine sense of common national identity was the most elusive of Reza Shah's objectives. It not only required denial of the actual ethnic diversity of the Iranian population but also, like the liberation of women, inevitably raised the problem of religion in the Pahlavi state. This was particularly true because the most obvious bond among the vast majority of the population was the Islamic and more specifically Shi'ite religion. Yet to many of the intellectuals favored by Reza Shah, Islam was foreign (Arab) in origin, anti-nationalist in outlook, and responsible for the material backwardness of the country. They were well aware of the difficulties religion had caused during the Constitutional Revolution and tended to be very anticlerical and secularist in their views.

In many accounts, Reza Shah is also depicted as determined to break the hold of Islam and the clerical class on Iranian society, but this is a bit of an exaggeration. His attitude toward religion was quite mild as compared to that of a fervent secularist like Ataturk (or Iranian intellectuals like Ahmad Kasravi and Ali-Akbar Dehkhoda). Indeed, in many ways he reflected the traditional view of religion and state as bonded together. In his addresses upon being named shah and at his coronation, he pledged to uphold Twelver Shi'ism and explicitly stated that he saw religion as "one of the most effective means of ensuring national unity" among Iranians. However, he did not care for ignorant clerics or hidebound visions of religion; unlike some of his religious critics, he saw religion as the servant of the state, rather than the state as the servant of religion. Thus he encouraged the development of Qom under the Ayatollah Abd-al-Karim Haeri as a center of religious studies, the licensing and certification of religious scholars, and the formalization of the hierarchical ranking system among the clerics. On the other hand, his educational reforms and the introduction of a civil judicial system (even though it incorporated many principles derived from traditional religious law) intruded greatly into areas that had previously been controlled by clerics. Above all, Reza Shah certainly did not countenance opposition or criticism from the clerics. There are many anecdotes about his brutal treatment of those he regarded as troublemakers. The most famous is undoubtedly the story that he stormed into the great mosque in Qom in 1928, muddy boots and all, to horsewhip a cleric who had complained about the queen visiting the shrine without wearing a veil. This, however, was really provoked by an individual instance of lèse-majesté and was hardly an assault on the clerical institution. The fundamental ambivalence of relations between state and religion under Reza Shah is indicated by a detail often omitted in the story: Haeri intervened to make sure there were no demonstrations or public speeches against Reza Shah for his violation of the shrine.

Mohammad-Ali Foroughi, a leader of the Revival Party and Reza Shah's first prime minister, once remarked that it was impossible to understand or judge Reza Shah without having lived through the events that produced him. The subordination to foreign interests, poverty, insecurity, factionalism, and disorder rampant in Iran during the late Qajar period profoundly shaped his view of the world. This should be kept in mind when considering two of the least appealing aspects of his reign. First of all, he was undeniably acquisitive when it came to material goods. He was notorious for using both fair means and foul to acquire land and made himself the greatest landlord in the country, eventually owning some 3 million acres in the Caspian provinces. He also built up an immense personal fortune and is said to have stashed away as much as £30 million in British banks (at a time when the country's entire revenue from oil royalties was £1 million or less). Second, he was severely repressive of any threat to his authority, real or imagined. This applied not only to genuine enemies but to anyone who might be a potential competitor. The list of victims was very long. He particularly disliked socialists and communists; they were repressed in 1927 and their activities outlawed in 1931. In 1937, fifty-three organizers of a new communist party were arrested. Politicians who had crossed Reza Shah at some point wound up in exile, jail, or worse. Mohammad Mosaddeq, one of four Majles delegates who spoke against Reza becoming shah, was imprisoned and then completely excluded from public life. Hasan Modarres, a moderate cleric who had opposed the bills authorizing conscription and abolishing the Qajar monarchy, was forced into exile and, by most accounts, murdered. Even politicians who supported Reza Shah but for one reason or another fell into disfavor could suffer the same fate: Sardar Asad, the Bakhtiari defender of the constitution and Reza Shah's minister of war, was jailed and murdered in 1929; Firouz Farmanfarma (Nosrat-al-Dowleh), minister of finance, was accused of misusing state funds in 1930, placed under house arrest, and strangled to death in 1938; Abd-al-Hosayn Timourtash, a key ally in the Revival Party and a former confidant, was charged with embezzlement and bribery in 1933 and died under suspicious circumstances; Ali-Akbar Davar, the brilliant architect of the new judicial system and a pillar of support for many of Reza Shah's policies, felt he had fallen into disfavor with the shah and committed suicide in 1937.

In terms of foreign policy, Reza Shah was determined to maintain Iran's independence and to restore its sense of national pride by elevating its stature in the world and insisting it be treated with respect. This was the motivation behind any number of his actions, from insisting on the use of the name Iran instead of Persia to banning photographs of things that were picturesque but might give an impression of backwardness (camels, for example) to breaking off diplomatic relations with countries if its newspapers published unflattering articles about him or his country. Iran maintained good relations with most countries, and it was particularly successful at increasing its influence with Turkey, Egypt, and other countries in the region. The greatest accomplishment in this regard was the conclusion of the Sadabad Pact in 1937, by which Iran, Iraq, Afghanistan, and Turkey recognized their mutual borders and agreed to cooperate in the event any of them were attacked by outside powers.

The notion that Reza Shah had been put in power by the British and was actually their creature rather than an independent nationalist is so embedded in recent Iranian political mythology that it might as well be true, but it really does not fit the facts. As noted above, the British, and only some of their officials on the scene in Iran at that, had at most a minor role in the coup and none at all in making him shah. He did not hesitate to confront the British over their intrigues with Sheikh Khazal, or to stop their dealings with the Bakhtiaris, and his reign marked a definite diminution of British influence in Iran. On 26 November 1932 he also defied the British by cancelling the concession for the Anglo-Iranian (formerly Persian) Oil Company. This was a very bold move for the time, and it was brought about by his anger over the less than forthright accounting practices of the company, which had resulted in Iran being paid about twice what it had received in 1917 even though production had increased almost tenfold. This was a quarrel with the British government as well as the company, and Iran successfully defended its action at the World Court. Negotiations for a settlement began under the auspices of the League of Nations, with Hasan Taqizadeh representing Iran. A new concession was signed on 29 April 1933. Despite harping by later critics that Reza Shah had "backed down" or that it was a bad agreement, the deal was probably about as good as Iran could have expected to receive. In exchange for agreeing to extend the concession for sixty years, Iran got stricter accounting procedures, linked royalties to production, received a guarantee of a minimum payment of almost £1 million (calculated in gold to guard against currency fluctuations), and reduced the amount of territory covered by the concession.

REZA SHAH AND WORLD WAR II

No matter how strongly Reza Shah wanted to preserve Iran's independence, there was little chance he could actually resist a determined effort by major powers like Britain or the Soviet Union to violate it. In that sense, his fate was sealed the day Germany invaded Russia. In the years before the war, Reza Shah had been attempting to interest other countries in Iran, especially with a view to finding an alternative to Britain (or Russia) for the exploitation of oil resources. He had first turned to the United States, but the American financial advisor to Iran, Arthur Millspaugh, had proved a disappointment and was dismissed in 1927. Subsequent efforts to obtain American loans and oil investments had produced no results, largely due to British efforts to block them and to Soviet objections. In the 1930s, Reza Shah turned to Germany and quickly developed extensive political and economic ties.

As long as the Ribbentrop-Molotov non-aggression pact of 1939 between Germany and the Soviet Union was in effect, British policy was basically to do its best to curry favor with Reza Shah in order to limit both German and Soviet influence in Iran; this included both a large loan and increased payments for oil. Hitler's attack on the Soviet Union, however, meant that Britain and the Soviet Union needed once more to become allies, and the goodwill of the Iranians was less important than protection of the oil fields and use of Iran as a transportation corridor. The Allies thus issued ultimatums for the expulsion of German nationals from Iran and use of the Trans-Iranian Railroad; after Reza Shah refused, they invaded the country on 25 August 1941, once more setting up a Russian zone in the north and a British zone in the south.

The BBC immediately began broadcasting vicious propaganda aimed at embarrassing and discrediting Reza Shah. Yielding to the inevitable, he abdicated on 16 September. The British and Russians toyed with the idea of restoring the Qajar monarchy, but unable to agree on a candidate or to find one who would accept under such disgraceful conditions, they finally consented to continue the dynasty by transferring the crown to Reza Shah's son Mohammad-Reza Pahlavi. Reza Shah himself was sent into exile, going finally to South Africa, where he died in 1944.

7

Mohammad-Reza Shah

The long reign of Mohammad-Reza Shah (1941–1979) was marked by frequent reversals of fortune for the ruler and tremendous changes for Iran. In its later years, Iranians tended to take the wealth and prestige the country had attained under his rule for granted, largely forgetting the centuries of misery, neglect, and isolation that had preceded it and concentrating instead on the manifest shortcomings of his increasingly autocratic style of government and the lack of opportunities for political participation. The strange mix in late Pahlavi Iran of hubris and megalomania with repression and social tension culminated in one of the most dramatic revolutions of the 20th century.

THE WAR YEARS

Although the British and Russians had opted not to restore the Qajar monarchy after their invasion of Iran, they had effectively turned back the clock to the late Qajar era. In many ways, it was as if Reza Shah had accomplished nothing. Foreign troops were again on Iranian soil, the country was divided into British and Soviet zones, foreign ambassadors dictated essential policies, the tribes brought out weapons they had hidden away and reasserted their autonomy, demands for ethnic and provincial separatism were revived, the economy was in shambles, and factionalism was rampant. Imprisoned communists were released and, with Soviet support, founded the influential Tudeh Party. A host of politicians from the pre–Reza Shah period resurfaced, many of them bent on revenge for twenty years of intimidation or exclusion from public life. Even the failed Sayyed Zia-al-Din Tabatabai made his way back to Iran, hoping his pro-British credentials would secure him office.

These developments might have suggested that the young Mohammad-Reza Shah Pahlavi was fated to go the way of an Ahmad Shah soon enough. There was indeed little he could do but bide his time; nonetheless, several factors made his position stronger than it might appear. First of all, the continuation of the Pahlavi dynasty received something of an official stamp of approval from Britain and the Soviet Union with the signing of the Tripartite Treaty in January 1942. Second, the shah was able to retain control over what was left of Reza Shah's army (almost half the personnel had deserted after the Allied invasion, but it was still a potent force in terms of domestic control). Third, the many civilian politicians arrayed against him were unable to unite, either to drive a wedge between the shah and the army or to forge a stable political coalition as a credible alternative to him. Finally, the entry of the United States into the war and its consequent involvement in Iran as part of the effort to resupply the Soviet Union introduced a new variable into the political equation. Some Iranian politicians actively encouraged American interest in the country by bringing back Millspaugh as a financial advisor and by putting another American, H. Norman Schwarzkopf, in charge of the Gendarmerie. For their part, American policy makers were beginning to realize that the United States would become an importer of oil after the war and thus took a greater interest in the Persian Gulf region. As time went on, they tended to see the shah and the military, rather than the constantly feuding politicians, as the best guarantee of security in the country, and Mohammad-Reza Shah did his best to encourage that impression. He would have a splendid opportunity to do so shortly after the end of the war.

IRAN AND THE COLD WAR

The 1942 Tripartite Treaty, like the 1907 Anglo-Russian Agreement, had the Soviet Union and Britain make rather empty promises "to respect the territorial integrity, sovereignty, and political independence of Iran," to "defend" it against aggression (even as they occupied its territory), and to "safeguard" its economy (which was being wrecked by the war). However, it also included the specific stipulation that British and Soviet forces would leave Iranian territory within six months of the end of the war. That pledge was confirmed at the 1943 Tehran Conference as part of a joint Anglo-American-Soviet statement which offered economic assistance as a reward for Iranian contributions to the war effort. As the end of the war approached, however, it seemed that the Soviets and, to some extent, the British were actually in no hurry to leave. Instead, they seemed to be reverting to the traditional pattern of dominating their zones of influence in the country through their own troops and political proxies. Both were also interested in limiting the American presence as much as possible in order not to jeopardize their own interests, but the Soviets were particularly concerned that an Anglo-American condominium in Iran not serve to exclude them.

In 1944, when Prime Minister Mohammad Saed seemed receptive to negotiations with American oil companies for a concession in Iran, the Soviets immediately demanded an oil concession in all the northern Iranian provinces their troops then occupied. Saed declined and suggested that consideration of any concessions be deferred until after the war. The real issue, of course, was not oil (there was none in that area) but geopolitics. After the Soviets pointedly suggested that "a more trustworthy" person head the Iranian government, Tudeh demonstrators demanded Saed's removal from office. Although a majority of the Majles was opposed to the idea of a Soviet oil concession, a majority could also not resist the opportunity to make political capital out of the crisis and. brought down Saed's government. On 2 December 1944, the Majles mooted the concession issue by prohibiting cabinet members from discussing the grant of any concession while foreign troops were in Iran. Credit for this measure is often given to the hero of the nationalists who introduced the bill, Mohammad Mosaddeq, but the idea had already been suggested two months earlier by the Saed cabinet and was fully supported by his replacement as prime minister, Morteza Bayat.

Whether in response to the frustrated oil negotiations, fear of a hostile Anglo-American alliance that would exclude the Soviets from Iran, or ambition to bring part or all of Iran into an orbit of "friendly" countries around itself, the Soviet Union began to buttress its position in Iran much more aggressively. One method was to build up the Tudeh Party as an instrument of communist influence throughout the whole of the country, concentrating on class issues to build up a political constituency, and use it to reflect pro-Soviet positions in the Majles. Because the Majles was divided into several factions that depended on shifting coalitions to form a government, the political clout of the Tudeh delegates was magnified considerably. A closely related but ultimately different method was to encourage separatist movements among the non-Persian ethnic groups in areas under Soviet control, the most important being the Democratic Party of Azerbaijan (DPA) led by Jafar Pishevari (a communist who had lived for a while in the Soviet Union) and the Democratic Party of Kurdistan. Armed by the Soviets, the DPA took over Tabriz on 10 December 1945 and declared the foundation of an "Autonomous Government of Azerbaijan" under Pishevari; a similar "Mahabad Republic" was declared in Kurdistan a few days later. Finally, the Soviets attempted to stall on the withdrawal of their troops from Iran, avoiding discussion of the issue at both the Yalta and Potsdam conferences. It was finally agreed that the troops would be withdrawn by 2 March 1946, but right up to that date the Soviets actually continued to increase the number of their troops in Azerbaijan. This produced what has come to be regarded as the first crisis of the Cold War.

In January 1946, Iran went before the United Nations to charge the Soviet Union with interference in its internal affairs and to demand that it honor the commitment to withdraw its troops from Iran. Britain and the United States strongly backed the Iranian position; they had already withdrawn their troops and insisted the Soviets do the same. When they did not, Britain responded by cultivating tribal and other elements that could be used to protect its interests in southwestern Iran; the United States began to move military forces into position to deal with the crisis. Either a war in Iran between the former allies or another partitioning of the country seemed possible, but in May the Soviets suddenly agreed to withdraw their forces.

President Harry Truman's firmness on the issue of Soviet withdrawal from Iran probably helped persuade Stalin to reverse course, but the politics of the Iranian prime minister, Ahmad Qavam, also played a critical role. Qavam, the former Qavam-al-Saltaneh and brother of Vosouq-al-Dowleh, was one of those veteran politicians of the late Qajar era with an amazing reedlike ability to bend with whatever current was strongest while staying on good terms with rival powers. He had at times been perceived as pro-British and pro-American but was well liked by the Soviets, who made no secret of the fact that they wanted him to be prime minister and would deal only with him on the withdrawal question. He had spent the period from his designation as prime minister in January

1946 to the formation of his cabinet in March involved in discussions with the Soviets based on what looked very much like a policy of appeasement. On 5 April, the parties agreed that the Soviets would withdraw in exchange for Iran dropping its complaint at the United Nations, solving the provincial separatist problem in a "peaceful" way, and bringing before the Majles a proposal for a Soviet oil concession in the northern provinces. The fact that the Majles was bound not to consider concessions while foreign troops were present was a powerful inducement for the Soviets to remove their forces so that the vote on the concession could take place. After the troops were withdrawn, and thus could not be returned without provoking a major international crisis, Qavam delayed bringing up the matter of the concession in the Majles, pointing to the need to hold new elections as an excuse. Finally, on 22 October 1947, the new Majles voted overwhelmingly to reject the concession (102–2) and, with much less enthusiasm, excused Qavam for his technical violation of the 1944 law prohibiting such discussions.

Qavam's linking of the concession with the withdrawal of Soviet forces has been interpreted after the fact as an extremely clever ploy that resulted in the removal of the forces at no cost to Iran. However, his simultaneous handling of the related problem of the Soviet proxies in Iran raises the possibility that he had miscalculated the actual degree of Soviet influence in Iran and had genuinely set out to ingratiate himself with the Soviet Union. Qavam made numerous concessions to the Azerbaijanis, actively collaborated with the Tudeh during the elections, arrested pro-British politicians, and brought many pro-Soviets and communists into his government. The British were convinced that Qavam had, in the words of an embassy dispatch, "definitely sold his country to the Russians" and began to encourage tribal rebellions and demands for autonomy in Fars and Khuzistan to offset the pro-Soviet governments in Azerbaijan and Kurdistan. It was only when faced with rising political criticism, British hostility, American skepticism, and the prospect of further national disintegration that Qavam abruptly reversed course in October and turned against his Tudeh allies. In December 1946, he agreed to military action to destroy the separatist governments. The Soviets, with an eye on the elections and the concession, did not intervene, and the Azerbaijan and Mahabad governments collapsed in a matter of days. It was not Qavam, however, who received the glory for this; it was Mohammad-Reza Shah, who had refused to sign the agreement Qavam wanted to make with Pishevari and who now led the army into Tabriz to crush the opponents of the central government. Like his father, he was able to use his control of the military and defense of national integrity to bolster his image as a leader.

THE MOSADDEQ ERA

Qavam was forced out of office shortly after the vote on the Soviet oil concession. This gave Mohammad-Reza Shah an opportunity to assert his political authority more boldly. The shah also gained a great deal of public sympathy when he was shot and wounded during a failed effort to assassinate him while he was visiting the University of Tehran in February 1949. He was then able to declare martial law and crack down on religious militants, communists, and other opponents. In March he convened a supportive Constituent Assembly which proposed to change the constitution by creating a Senate, with half the members appointed by the shah, and by giving the shah the right to dissolve Parliament. Other indications of the rise in the shah's prestige included the passage of laws restricting criticism of the royal family in the press and returning crown lands to the monarch.

Opposition to Mohammad-Reza Shah and the royalists developed around three main groups. On the left, the Tudeh Party was rising rapidly in popularity, especially among university students and workers. Although outlawed after the attempt on the shah's life, it still had considerable political clout, which it would soon manifest through strikes and street demonstrations. On the right were religious factions that objected to secular developments and foreign influence in society. The most important of these was the Fedaiyan-e Eslam, which had been formed in 1945 and gained notoriety by assassinating one of Iran's most outspoken secularists, the historian Ahmad Kasravi, on 11 March 1946. The organization was greatly strengthened in the late 1940s by a tactical alliance with the conservative religious leader Ayatollah Abu'l-Qasem Kashani. In between these extremes were a number of liberal, anti-royalist, and nationalist factions which banded together in 1949 under the guidance of Mohammad Mosaddeq to form the National Front (Jabheh-ye Melli). Mosaddeq, who had built up quite a reputation for his personal integrity, acid wit, and brilliant oratory, was famous for his opposition to all foreign economic concessions as well as his demands for honest government and the subordination of the shah to the constitution. In 1949, he led a protest against efforts by court officials to rig the elections for the Sixteenth Majles. He had also managed to bring Kashani into the

National Front, and the election of Mosaddeq and other National Front candidates was helped, albeit inadvertently, by the Fedaiyan. The latter had assassinated Abu'l-Hosayn Hazhir, the minister of court in charge of the voting, and in the subsequent Tehran special election they guarded the ballot boxes against tampering.

Despite the efforts of the opposition, the new Majles was dominated by a clear royalist majority. Nonetheless, Mosaddeq and the small but vocal minority of National Front members soon found an explosive political issue that put the shah on the defensive. They denounced a proposed revision of the 1933 agreement with the Anglo-Iranian Oil Company (AIOC) and began to demand the termination of the concession and nationalization of the company. This idea had almost universal appeal in Iran, including the approval of the religious groups and the Tudeh, which enabled the National Front members to use popular pressure in the streets to compensate for their numerical weakness in the Majles.

The shah's response was to name Ali Razmara, a general with a reputation for toughness, as prime minister. While seeking to push the oil proposal through the Majles, Razmara also tried to court the leftists and intimidate the bourgeois elements in the National Front and Majles by improving relations with the Soviet Union, introducing a bill to distribute land to peasants, and proposing to implement provisions for provincial assemblies. The more he moved in this direction, the more the National Front and its supporters pushed the oil negotiations as the most pressing issue facing the nation. Razmara's insistence on a more realistic solution to the oil question cast him, despite his other policies, in the role of a puppet for the shah and the British. On 19 February 1951, a special committee in the Majles, chaired by Mosaddeq, recommended full nationalization of the AIOC. Razmara rejected this proposal. Shortly thereafter, on 7 March, a member of the Fedaiyan assassinated Razmara at a mosque in Tehran.

The chaotic atmosphere created by the murder of Razmara, coupled with the reappearance of Tudeh demonstrators in major cities throughout Iran, made it impossible to resist the call for taking over the AIOC. The nationalization bill was passed in the Majles on 15 March and in the Senate a few days later. Unable to control the Majles, Razmara's succesor as prime minister, Hosayn Ala, resigned. It was rumored that the shah and the British were planning to bring back Sayyed Zia for the post, but this was preempted in an unusual way: One of the exasperated conservative members of the Majles, Jamal Emami, suggested half-facetiously that since Mosaddeq was responsible for pushing the legislation, he should also be the man to implement it as prime minister. Emami apparently thought that Mosaddeq was a chronic obstructionist who liked to criticize but would never take responsibility for anything and would fail if he did. To his surprise, Mosaddeq accepted the offer and the Majles quickly requested that the shah appoint him, thus making it difficult for the shah to follow the normal procedure of offering a nomination himself. Yielding to the inevitable, but never forgetting or forgiving the slight, the shah accepted Mosaddeq as prime minister on 29 April and signed the nationalization bill on 2 May. Mosaddeq then secured legislation to dismantle the AIOC and replace it with the National Iranian Oil Company (NIOC). In June, he sent the army to take over the company's facilities in Khuzistan.

Britain reacted furiously to Mosaddeq's triumph, despite his pledge to compensate the company for its losses. British interest in Iranian oil was not only strategic and a matter of imperial pride; the substantial revenues it derived from taxes on the company and its share of the dividends were quite important to the depressed postwar British economy. Nationalization of domestic companies (as the Labour government in Britain had itself been doing) was one thing, the British argued, but the nationalization of the AIOC was a violation of agreements between nations, which entitled the British government to be a party to the dispute. The British consequently lodged a complaint with the International Court of Justice, but the court ruled (July 1952) that it lacked jurisdiction and urged the parties to negotiate a settlement. Similarly, Britain asked for the United Nations Security Council to intervene, but Mosaddeq went to New York in September 1951 and argued persuasively before a sympathetic Security Council that the matter was a private controversy and not a threat to peace requiring UN action. Britain had also increased its military forces in the Persian Gulf, but using them against Iran was not really an option since it would be almost certain to face American criticism and Soviet opposition. The muddled handling of the crisis contributed to the defeat of the Labour government and the return of Winston Churchill and the Conservatives to power in Britain; they would pursue a tougher but more subtle anti-Mosaddeq policy.

The most intense pressure Britain could put on Iran was economic, not military, and this was applied quite successfully. When the Iranians took over the company, none of the British employees accepted an offer to work for the NIOC; they were withdrawn under armed British escort, which effectively shut down much of the company's operations. Britain also organized a boycott and blockade so that there were virtually no takers for what oil Iran was still able to produce, thus putting tremendous economic strain on a country so heavily dependent on oil revenues. Iranian reserves in British banks were frozen, and Britain used its diplomatic influence to persuade the Truman administration in the United States not to provide emergency aid or loans to Iran. When Mosaddeq visited Washington after his presentation at the United Nations, he was informed that no loan could be made until the dispute was settled. As the economic situation in Iran worsened and no resolution of the crisis was in sight, its domestic politics became much more volatile and tensions between various factions mounted.

By 1952, it was apparent that Mosaddeq was both unwilling and unable to reach a settlement on the nationalization issue: unable, out of fear that he would be excoriated for any compromise just as all his predecessors in oil negotiations had been (and quite possibly killed); unwilling, because the popularity he derived from the oil controversy was a vehicle for his larger agenda of hobbling, if not ousting, the shah. In an effort to expand the debate and gain maneuvering room, and under the influence of his chief political deputy and eventual foreign minister, the radical journalist Hosayn Fatemi, Mosaddeq adopted an increasingly authoritarian and decidedly left-of-center political approach. He manipulated the elections for the Seventeenth Majles by giving more weight to the votes of the educated elite and increasing representation for urban areas like Tehran where the National Front was strongest. When it became clear that the vote was still not going the way he wanted, he suspended the election as soon as a quorum of delegates had been chosen and before opposition returns from the provinces could come in. Even then, the National Front only controlled about thirty out of seventy-nine seats. In another dramatic gesture to drum up popular support and detach the military from the shah, Mosaddeq attempted in July 1952 to name his own minister of war (technically his prerogative but a matter that had been traditionally left to the shah as commander-in-chief). The shah rejected the nominee, and Mosaddeq resigned. The National Front, backed by the Tudeh, then organized violent street demonstrations that compelled the shah to bring Mosaddeq back to office on 21 July (Siyom-e Tir according to the Iranian calendar).

After the victory of Siyom-e Tir and the positive decision of the International Court of Justice the next day, Mosaddeq was at the peak of his power and acted like it. He turned down another proposed settlement for the oil crisis that had been endorsed by both Churchill and Truman and included as a sweetener the offer of an immediate loan from the United States. In October, he broke diplomatic relations with Britain on the grounds that it was interfering in Iran's internal affairs (the Rashidian brothers, reputed pro-British agents, and General Fazl-Allah Zahedi had recently been arrested for plotting a coup). He took over the Ministry of War himself and pushed through a number of measures intended to humiliate the shah, even forcing the shah's twin sister, the politically active Princess Ashraf, into exile. He reduced the budget for the palace and the military, and encouraged the press to depict the court as corrupt and treasonous. He obtained a decree from the Majles giving him "emergency powers" that made him, for all practical purposes, a dictator, first for six months and then for another year. He used this to implement a number of populist measures such as land reform and taxing the wealthy. When members of the Majles finally balked in July 1953, and their refusal to attend sessions resulted in the lack of a quorum, Mosaddeq called for the extra-constitutional step of dissolving it and holding a national referendum to give him a vote of confidence. The balloting for the referendum was not secret as there were separate boxes for voting for or against the proposal. Not surprisingly, Mosaddeq won almost unanimously. There was talk that another referendum would be held to abolish the monarchy and declare a republic in its place.

In fact, support for Mosaddeq was rapidly evaporating. The secularist and populist measures he had begun to implement, as well as the mounting economic difficulties, had alienated conservatives, bazaar merchants, and the religious leaders with whom they were aligned. Kashani objected to the extension of Mosaddeq's emergency powers as well as the influence of radicals like Fatemi; he left the National Front, soon to be followed by other groups. Virtually the entire religious establishment—Kashani, the pro-royalist Ayatollah Behbahani, and the normally apolitical Ayatollah Boroujerdi—came to be arrayed against Mosaddeq. Mosaddeq was thus increasingly dependent on the support of the Tudeh to back his policies through street demonstrations. They did so only for tactical reasons, not out of any fondness for Mosaddeq, and their presence further alarmed conservatives. Mosaddeq's reduction of the military budget, purge of the officer corps, and other efforts to weaken the army also caused the military to side with the shah. Royalist officers began meeting to plot how to undermine Mosaddeq and encourage further fracturing of the National Front. They would receive some significant assistance in this regard from the United States.

In his handling of the nationalization crisis, Mosaddeq had banked heavily on two premises that both proved to be false—that he would be able to sell Iranian oil despite British opposition and that he would receive support from the United States. On the nationalization itself, the United States was not unsympathetic to Mosaddeq and hoped to find a reasonable settlement without antagonizing its British ally. In the context of the Cold War, however, Washington's paramount concerns were that order be maintained in Iran, the Tudeh kept out of power, and the Soviet Union given no pretext for intervention. Mosaddeq's apparent intransigence, coupled with the leftist shift in his policies and the increasingly visible role of the Tudeh, shattered any faith that Mosaddeq could serve these interests. Mosaddeq himself only confirmed that impression when he tried to use the threat of a communist takeover to justify a request for American aid in May 1953.

In fact, under the new Eisenhower administration, the United States had already decided to align itself decisively with Britain and the shah against Mosaddeq. In February 1953, American and British officials had agreed on a covert operation, code-named AJAX, to overthrow him. It had been conceived by the British MI-6 in collaboration with General Zahedi and other sympathetic Iranians and would be implemented by the U.S. Central Intelligence Agency (CIA), which sent an agent, Kermit Roosevelt, to Iran. The basic strategy was to create an atmosphere conducive to a coup by spreading propaganda about Mosaddeq, stirring up more public disorder and tribal unrest, and using fear of the Tudeh to induce Kashani and others to turn completely against Mosaddeq. One of the most effective tactics was reportedly hiring thugs to pose as Tudeh demonstrators and act in an incendiary manner to frighten the noncommunist public.

After Mosaddeq's referendum, the shah rather reluctantly gave his approval for the covert operation. He withdrew to a resort on the Caspian and, on 16 August, signed decrees dismissing Mosaddeq as prime minister, which he had a constitutional right to do, and appointing Zahedi in his place. Mosaddeq received advance intelligence of this and had the army officer delivering the dismissal document arrested. He tried to suppress news of the dismissal decree and used radio broadcasts to depict the incident as an abortive coup (his opponents, however, managed to circulate copies of the decrees in Tehran to show that Mosaddeq was exercising power illegally). Either to dramatize the situation or for fear the plot had failed, the shah immediately left the country. The National Front began an obvious move to abolish the monarchy; Fatemi even called for the "traitor" shah to be hanged. On 17 and 18 August, crowds of Tudeh demonstrators tore down statues of Reza Shah and demanded the creation of a republic. It is alleged that the mobs were augmented by provocateurs sent by the conspirators, but their numbers were certainly small compared to the number of genuine communists involved. Fearful that a Tudeh revolution was in the making, Mosaddeq ordered the police and army to clear the streets, thus removing from the scene the group most likely to have shielded him from what was coming next. On 19 August, a large and rowdy crowd shouting pro-shah slogans marched on the Tehran bazaar, attacking pro-Mosaddeq institutions such as the offices of the national radio along the way. They were led by professional roughnecks from the poorer districts of Tehran (including a particularly colorful character known as Jafar the Brainless), who had been recruited by Kashani and the royalists and financed at least in part by funds from the CIA. Simultaneously, units of the army led by Zahedi surrounded Mosaddeq's residence and, after a fierce battle, forced him to surrender. This paved the way for the shah's return to Iran on 22 August. Zahedi became prime minister, holding the office until 1955. Mosaddeq was convicted of treason, imprisoned, and then placed under house arrest until his death in 1967; Fatemi was captured, despite Tudeh efforts to protect him, tried, and executed.

The importance of the events of 1953 in shaping Iranian perceptions of the Pahlavi regime and of American involvement in Iranian affairs can hardly be exaggerated. For a segment of the Iranian population, the revered Dr. Mosaddeq was a true patriot and a political martyr, and the collapse of the National Front nothing less than a political catastrophe for the country. American involvement in the coup is invariably cited as a prime example of its harmful meddling, either through malevolence or stupidity, in the affairs of other countries. These ideas have been so deeply embedded in the Iranian psyche that it is probably useless to try to point out their many defects or the harsher realities they serve to conceal, but some effort should be made to put them in a broader historical context. In most respects, Mosaddeq's adventure was flawed from the beginning and probably doomed to failure under any conceivable circumstances; there are certainly many reasons to doubt it would have led to the utopia his enthusiasts have envisaged.

No one would deny that the AIOC had exploited Iran mercilessly or that Mosaddeq enjoyed the broadest possible support in confronting the company: It did not allow Iranians or independent agents to check the books; it calculated Iran's share of the profits according to a disadvantageous formula (after paying taxes to Britain and making investments in operations outside Iran); it treated its Iranian employees shabbily; it reportedly made more in profits the last year of its operation than it had paid Iran since the beginning of the concession. American officials thought that the concession was an abomination and that the British were blockheads for not making better offers to head off a crisis. However, nationalization was not necessarily the best solution to this problem. Mosaddeq had a poor grasp of economic realities; he vastly overestimated the importance of Iranian oil production to the world at a time when the market was actually glutted. As a result, he did not realize how easily Britain could block its sale and other countries make up the deficit in production. He also did not take into account that nationalization would deprive Iran of its legitimate claim to investments made by the AIOC in other countries with profits derived from its Iranian operations. From a strictly financial point of view, some of the deals he turned down would have been more profitable than what could be arranged under full nationalization.

Mosaddeq's politics were sometimes as misguided and self-defeating as his economics. He prided himself on being a democrat and a constitutionalist, but he did not hesitate to violate these principles when it suited his purpose. He contributed as much as anyone to the notion that Iranian political disputes are best settled through demonstrations in the streets rather than through haggling with a recalcitrant parliament. Although he toyed with populism, he was basically an elitist who wanted to restrict the franchise and keep public affairs in the hands of a privileged oligarchy. A scion of the old aristocracy, he was motivated as much, if not more, by dislike of the Pahlavi upstarts as by anger at foreign influence. His high-handed methods alienated the religious and military groups he desperately needed to stabilize his government. Even though as a nationalist he worked zealously to remove British influence from Iran, he nonetheless sought to involve the United States in Iran on his behalf; and it often seems his followers' grudge is not aimed at the principle of American interventionism but at the fact that the United States, following its own assessment of its interests at the time, intervened in support of the shah rather than Mosaddeq.

Most important, it was ultimately Iranians who brought Mosaddeq down, not a few American secret agents with a suitcase of cash. There is abundant evidence that in 1953 many Iranians, probably a large majority, were sympathetic to the shah or relieved, either because of the financial crisis or the continuing public disorder, to see Mosaddeq overthrown. Although Mosaddeq claimed to represent the "nation" and the "people," the National Front had less than 10 percent of the seats in the Sixteenth Majles and could not even command a clear majority in the blatantly manipulated Seventeenth Majles. The ease of the coup should have made it obvious just how small and culturally isolated the liberal, secular, and intellectual nationalist elite around Mosaddeq really was, and how exaggerated its belief in its social influence had become (and would continue to be). In many countries around the world, such elites have managed to make their peace with modernizing military autocracies and gradually become part of the governing establishment. In Iran, the relationship between the two was and remained adversarial and full of distrust, to the detriment of both.

With the advantage of hindsight, the most important lesson of 1953 was the key importance of religious groups and the traditional classes in Iran's political struggles. One of the conspirators against Mosaddeq had noted that for every thousand supporters Mosaddeq could rally, someone like Kashani could muster ten thousand. That was why detaching Kashani from Mosaddeq's coalition was so vital to the success of the coup. It was Kashani and the religious groups who had helped put Mosaddeq in power in the first place, and they were essential to bringing him down. Ultimately, this lesson seems to have been lost on both the shah and most of Mosaddeq's devotees, who would have to learn it again the hard way in 1979.

THE NEW AUTOCRACY

The rest of the 1950s were relatively uneventful for Iran. The Zahedi administration moved quickly to put an end to the oil crisis. The 1954 agreement—negotiated, ironically enough, by Ali Amini, the same minister of finance who had served Mosaddeq—recognized Iranian ownership of the petroleum but made contractual arrangements with foreign companies for its production and marketing. It also determined the compensation to be paid to the AIOC and determined the allocation of production among members of an international consortium (40 percent to AIOC, 40 percent to American companies, and the rest to European companies). American aid to Iran increased substantially after the agreement, and Iran followed an unambiguously pro-Western and anti-communist policy, participating in both the Baghdad Pact and its successor, the Central Treaty Organization (CENTO). In 1957, a domestic security apparatus, SAVAK, was formed to keep the Tudeh and other opposition groups under control.

By 1960, the shah's control over Iranian political life was substantially complete, but his dependence on American financial aid and support influenced many of his decisions. He sensed that the newly elected Kennedy administration favored "progressive" leaders in developing nations and thus began to promote a degree of liberalization in Iran. The elections for the Twentieth Majles were comparatively fair and returned some delegates from outside the two "official" parties created by the shah, but it remained a conservative institution. Two reformists clearly favored by the United States came to office in 1961, Ali Amini as prime minister and Hasan Arsanjani as minister of agriculture. Amini dissolved the new Majles, brought a variety of politicians into his cabinet, forced the head of SAVAK into exile, and loudly condemned corruption in the economy and government. Arsanjani was the architect of the 1962 Land Reform Act, which required certain large landholdings to be sold to the state and redistributed to the former tenants, potentially the most important example of social engineering ever undertaken in Pahlavi Iran. Unfortunately, Amini was undercut by the National Front's rather short-sighted and ill-considered but persistent criticism of him over the question of dissolving the Majles and holding new elections and by the shah's concern that he was becoming too popular; he was forced to resign in July 1962.

After Amini's fall, Mohammad-Reza Shah attempted to co-opt the drive for social change through his own "Revolution of the Shah and the People," better known as the White Revolution. This was based on six reform measures submitted to a referendum in January 1963. They included a watered-down version of land reform, nationalization of forests, privatization of state industries, a profit-sharing plan for workers, creation of a "literacy corps" to combat rural illiteracy, and the extension of the franchise to women. Despite the seemingly benign nature of these proposals—and the almost unanimous vote of approval they received in the referendum—there was significant opposition to them. Some of it represented little more than political opportunism, such as the National Front's boycott of the referendum and criticism that the measures should come from the Majles. The rest was based on the self-interest of those adversely affected, most notably the religious establishment, which had reasons to object to both land reform and the right of women to vote.

These concerns were at the heart of an outburst of three days of rioting, involving several segments of society but largely inspired by religious leaders, in a number of Iranian cities in June 1963. The ease with which the security forces suppressed the disturbances, coupled with the reactionary nature of the motivation behind them, resulted in many observers dismissing them as an unimportant distraction. This also intimidated much of the opposition and increased the government's tendency to rely on authoritarian measures to deal with dissent. A year later, when a controversy erupted over proposals to acquire American military equipment and give diplomatic immunity to American military personnel in Iran, there was little public disorder. Only one major religious leader, Rouhollah Khomeini, made a serious effort to arouse indignation over them; many people may have agreed with him, but few were willing to take the protest to the streets. Khomeini was promptly arrested and then sent into exile.

From the mid-1960s on, politics in Iran revolved completely around the will of the shah. The Majles continued to function, but it was little more than a symbolic legislature dominated by the two government-sponsored parties and rubber-stamping whatever the shah wanted. From 1965 to 1977, there was only one prime minister, the rather bland but utterly loyal Amir Abbas Hoveida. In 1975, even the pretence of a two-party system was abandoned, as the shah decided Iran would become a monolithic, one-party state under the banner of the Revival (Rastakhiz) Party. Membership in the party became virtually a requirement for any position of importance in the Pahlavi administration or the public sector of the economy. The idea was that the party would rally mass support for the Pahlavi regime, eliminate or absorb other political groups, and allow the new technocratic, bureaucratic state to penetrate every corner of society. Instead, this authoritarian intrusion created tremendous resentment among many classes of the population.

The legislation, material development, and social projects of this period are certainly not without interest and importance, especially in terms of their contribution to increased rights and protections for women as exemplified in the 1967 Family Protection Law, which introduced many reforms pertaining to marriage, divorce, and the custody of children (resticting, for example, the traditional rights of men in cases of polygamy and arbitrary divorce). However, the shah's attention was focused not so much on the domestic agenda as on the economic, military, and geopolitical requirements for building what he believed would be the "Great Civilization" (Tamaddon-e Bozorg), a program that would lift Iran into the ranks of the most important countries in the world, on a par with a Japan or Germany.

THE SHAH AND THE WORLD

The roots of what now appears to have been a naïve and dangerous megalomania on the part of Mohammad-Reza Shah go back to at least the late 1950s, when he was anxious to prove to Washington that a strong Iranian military was essential not only to the perpetuation of his own rule but for Iran to be a reliable and effective regional ally in an age of instability and local conflicts. The need for such a regional power was made more credible by the 1956 Suez Crisis, the 1967 Arab-Israeli War, and Britain's announcement that it would withdraw its forces from Bahrain by 1971. The latter was of particular importance as it would leave the vitally important Persian Gulf without a Western guardian, and the United States could not take over this duty directly because of the problems its obvious ties to Israel would cause for Arab states.

Mohammad-Reza Shah seized the opportunity to take on the role of regional power for Iran and himself. This involved a three-point program. First, he engaged in an elaborate—and costly—process of image-building to portray himself as the natural successor of the great imperial Persian monarchs of the past. In October 1967, he staged an impressive coronation ceremony for himself and the Empress Farah at the Golestan Palace in Tehran. He had deliberately avoided a formal coronation until such time as he felt secure from domestic threats and free from foreign constraints. The message implied by the ceremony in 1967 was that with the vanquishing of the political opposition and the impending British withdrawal from the Gulf, that time had come. Four years later, an even more lavish celebration was held at Persepolis to commemorate the accession of Cyrus the Great and, with some historical exaggeration, 2,500 years of monarchy in Iran. The opulence and conspicuous consumption at this event—specially constructed tent pavilions and apartments for guests, food and chefs flown in from Paris, the finest china and crystal—were intended to impress the visiting dignitaries and heads of state with the grandeur of the shah's new Iran. These were but two of the most visible examples of his propaganda efforts; they also included measures such as the gratuitous introduction of a new calendar system which used the creation of the Persian Empire rather than the Islamic era as a beginning point, extensive gift-giving to foreign officials, support for educational and cultural efforts to increase foreign awareness of Iran, and so on.

Second, the shah sought to build up the size and strength of his military machine in order to give more weight to Iran's influence in the region. To do this, he attached himself enthusiastically to the ideas of the recently formulated Nixon Doctrine, which proposed that the United States, in the wake of the Vietnam fiasco, deal with regional crises through proxies rather than direct military involvement. The Nixon and Ford administrations readily endorsed the concept of having the shah take on the tasks of maintaining security and suppressing insurgencies in the Persian Gulf area. They were willing to allow the shah to acquire virtually unlimited quantities of any nonnuclear weapons in the American arsenal. Within a few years, the shah had built up what was on paper the fifth or sixth largest armed force in the world. In 1976, it had an estimated 3,000 tanks, 890 helicopter gunships, over 200 advanced fighter aircraft, the largest fleet of hovercraft in any country, 9,000 anti-tank missiles, and much more equipment either on hand or on order. This caused considerable anxiety on the part of his neighbors about his ultimate intentions as well as skepticism among critics in the United States who wondered whether the shah was being provided with a high-tech arsenal his country could not properly manage—in the words of one congressman, the equivalent of giving him a sledgehammer to crack a nut. In any case, evidence of the shah's intention to police the Gulf region was quite apparent. Not long after recognizing the independence of Bahrain, Iranian forces seized the strategic Abu Musa and Tunb islands (a major source of friction with Arab states ever since). In 1973, the shah sent troops to Oman to help suppress a Marxist-oriented insurgency there. He also gave tacit support to a Kurdish rebellion in order to pressure Iraq into signing the Algiers Accord of 1975, which redefined the boundary line on the Shatt al-Arab waterway and essentially recognized Iranian dominance in Gulf affairs.

Third, the shah secured the means to pay for his arms purchases and to fund the building of his "great civilization" at home. In 1971, he forced members of the consortium set up under the 1954 oil agreement to increase payments to Iran. In March 1973, he announced that the 1954 accord had been scrapped completely and full control over sale and production assumed by the NIOC. Later that year, he took advantage of the chaotic situation in the global oil market caused by the October war between Egypt, Syria, and Israel and the ensuing Arab oil embargo to push through an initiative giving the Organization of Petroleum Exporting Countries (OPEC) authority to set a common price for oil. As a result, oil that had been selling for less than $2 a barrel in 1971 went for almost $12 a barrel in 1973. This vastly increased the cost of petroleum for consumer nations and led to what has been described as the most sweeping transfer of capital from one set of nations to another in all of history. At its peak in 1975, thanks to the dramatic increases in both the cost per barrel and the amount of production, Iran was receiving $20 billion a year in oil revenues (as opposed to only $200 *million* a few years earlier). Ironically, public anger in the United States and other consumer nations at the economic difficulty this caused was not directed at Iran and the shah but at Arab countries that actually wanted to restrain prices. In fact, the shah's aggressive stance on oil prices had the active support of the Nixon administration, despite warnings by the Treasury Department and oil companies, since a substantial part of the increased revenues to Iran would be used to pay for Iranian arms purchases from the United States.

THE PATTERNS AND IDEOLOGY OF DISCONTENT

Political dissent had not disappeared during these years. It simply moved underground or was bottled up for want of any means of expression. It also remained fragmented and somewhat unorganized. The Tudeh Party went through an elaborate process of self-examination and critiquing of its performance. Apart from the ritual of organizing periodic strikes, the leftists remained ineffective and split into several rival factions with Marxist, Maoist, or other orientations. Some of these eventually formed guerilla organizations, modeled after the movements led by Che Guevara or other Third World insurrectionaries. The two most active of these groups were the Fedai-ye Khalq-e Iran, formed by the merger of two other factions in 1970, and the Mojahedin-e Khalq-e Iran, founded in 1965. Both had followings made up mostly of college students and a handful of professionals and intellectuals. The Fedai-ye Khalq was Marxist in origin and remained rigidly Marxist in ideology. The Mojahedin-e Khalq started out as a militant religious organization, but its leadership was attracted to Marxism-Leninism. As a result, it eventually developed into two factions, one emphasizing Islam and the other socialism. The primary goal of all these groups was to create an atmosphere conducive to revolution by carrying out terrorist attacks and urban warfare in order to shake public belief in the power of the state, and a few hundred of their members died in the course of such activities. Having crushed the Tudeh communist movement, SAVAK tended to concentrate its efforts on infiltrating and destroying these guerilla organizations.

Members of the former National Front attempted to regroup as the

National Resistance Movement, but they disagreed on many issues as well as questions of tactics and could maintain only a very loose coalition. They would periodically emerge at opportune moments to make various criticisms of the government and then retreat when confronted with repression by the police or SAVAK. By 1965, they had developed a relatively moderate and secular wing (called the Second National Front) and a more radical and religiously oriented wing (the Third National Front). The latter was increasingly influential and dominated in its outlook by a group known as the Liberation Movement. The Liberation Movement had been formed and led by two popular and highly respected men, both of whom had been staunch supporters of Mosaddeq: Mehdi Bazargan, a civil engineer, and Mahmoud Taleqani, a prominent member of the Shi'ite clergy in Tehran. Both were convinced that Islam was compatible with modernity and progressive social values and that it provided answers to the problems of modern societies. They also accepted, rather uncritically, the notion that clerical involvement in politics in Iran was desirable because of the supposed historical role of the clergy in imparting democratic and anti-imperialist values to the Iranian masses. The Liberation Movement was thus distinguished from other former National Front elements in two key respects: It openly held that the Pahlavi autocracy should be destroyed, not just reformed, and that religious support was essential to the success of any such movement in Iran. By the early 1970s, the Liberation Movement had articulated a clear policy calling for cooperation with the clergy and had identified with Ayatollah Khomeini as the most uncompromising opponent of the Pahlavi regime. It had also built up an extensive and very vocal base of support among the organizations of the large Iranian student population in Europe and the United States, where it was much easier to organize and to disseminate political literature than in Iran itself. As will be discussed in detail in the next chapter, the efforts of the Liberation Movement meshed with similar developments taking place in the circle of religious students and clerics associated with the exiled Khomeini.

Under the watchful eyes of SAVAK and the government censors, open expression of political dissent and criticism of the Pahlavi autocracy was virtually impossible. Nonetheless, in various guises, politics absolutely permeated the literature and popular culture of the late Pahlavi period. In terms of direct political discourse, attacks were not usually made on the Pahlavis directly but given in the form of critiques of Western culture and defenses of indigenous Iranian and Islamic values. The two intellectuals who were undoubtedly the most influential exponents of this approach were Jalal Al-e Ahmad (1923–1969) and Ali Shariati (1933–1977).

Al-e Ahmad was once a member of the Tudeh Party but abandoned it to join one of the leftist parties in the National Front. In addition to a number of works of fiction dealing with social issues affecting ordinary people, Al-e Ahmad wrote a treatise entitled *Gharbzadegi* (Afflicted by the West), which was widely read despite efforts to prohibit its publication. It can best be described, in the words of the Iranian political scientist Hamid Enayat, as a "tirade" against everything to do with the West, the Western civilization of "machines," and the pervasive Western influence in Iran. It was also a call for Iranians to escape the trap of Westernism into which they had fallen and to recover their own cultural identity. The message is curiously jarring since it comes in a book that cites Marx and Camus—and even the lyrics of Merle Travis!—as readily as Sadi. It also heaps scorn on many of the famous figures of Iran's premodern past and is highly ambivalent toward, among other things, the place of Islam and Shi'ite clerics in the defense against the disease of Westernism. Al-e Ahmad did, however, praise religious leaders like the conservative Fazl-Allah Nouri, whom he says was hung not for opposing the constitution but for demanding a government based on Islamic law. He also complained about clerics who had withdrawn tortoiselike into their shells and were not resisting the Western intrusion. In those respects, as in his sweeping dismissal of everything deemed Western, he did reflect important trends in popular Iranian thought.

Shariati was a teacher from Khorasan who won a scholarship to study sociology in France in 1960, where he was greatly influenced by the events of the Algerian Revolution and the ideas of French Marxism and socialism. After returning to Iran in 1965, he became a popular lecturer at an institution funded by the Liberation Movement and the author of a number of political pamphlets and books. Like Al-e Ahmad, Shariati was a nativist who championed the preservation of Iranian identity from foreign influences, but he attached more importance to the Shi'ite Islamic dimensions of that identity. He professed to disdain the materialistic "fallacies" of both capitalism and Marxism as alien and deficient philosophies and to find genuine inspiration for a better social order in Shi'ism. He distinguished, however between what he called "cultural" and "ideological" Shi'ism or, alternatively, "Safavid" and "true" Shi'ism. True, ideological Shi'ism was a militant and revolutionary spirit that would lead to a populist and egalitarian utopia; cultural, Safavid Shi'ism was a repressive invention of the ruling class, and the traditional clergy were its reactionary accomplices. He coupled this with highly idealized moral lessons based on stories of inspirational figures lifted from Shi'ite tradition, such as Abou Dharr, an ascetic and a fearless critic of the powerful and wealthy, or Fatema, the long-suffering daughter of the Prophet Mohammad.

Despite its emphatic if rather contrived "Shi'ite" character, Shariati's work, like Al-e Ahmad's, was infused with borrowings from European leftist intellectuals, Third World ideologues and apologists, and Marxist anti-imperialists. It primarily resembled an updated rehash of the ideas of Sultan Galiev, the Bolshevik activist from Central Asia, who had also held that there could be culture-specific, nationalistic forms of socialism and that an "Islamic" socialism should build on the values of the Muslim masses and focus its criticism instead on the practices of the traditional clergy. Shariati's work was often contradictory, opaque, ahistorical, and pretentious as well as extremely vague about the details of the paradise on earth revolutionary Shi'ism would establish. Nonetheless, his work was of fundamental importance in paving the way for an Islamic revolution in Iran. It found an enthusiastic and rapidly growing audience among young Iranians, especially students and the professional middle class. He was adopted as the chief ideologue of the Islamic wing of the Mojahedin-e Khalq. Much of Shariati's vocabulary, his themes, and his skillful manipulation of powerful religious icons and symbols, but not his core ideas and rejection of traditional Shi'ite "culture," would also be taken over by activist clerics for their own purposes.

THE REVOLUTION OF 1978–1979

The rapid changes that took place in Iran between 1971 and 1975 had placed great strain on the country and stimulated increasing opposition to Mohammad-Reza Shah and his policies. Like many of the architectural monuments in Iran, the edifice the shah had constructed had a dazzling façade but weak foundations and a shoddy structure. The impressive military might could intimidate Iraq or rebels in Oman, but it could not keep the streets of Tehran safe from terrorist attacks by urban guerillas. The program of industrial projects grew ever larger and more ambitious, but the infrastructure could not support them. In a country with vast energy resources and a long list of dam building projects, many villages had no electricity, and even the capital, Tehran, was routinely subjected to rolling blackouts. The influx of capital from oil revenues went for armaments and grandiose development schemes or simply disappeared as a result of what was suspected to be widespread graft and corruption. The sudden wealth, based on nothing more than the exploitation of a natural resource, created inflation and an unproductive, unbalanced, consumerist, import-oriented economy. The disparity between a small and fantastically wealthy elite and the masses of impoverished people was more noticeable than ever. Despite the promises of land reform and the White Revolution, agriculture was in decline, food imports up, peasants abandoning villages for overpopulated urban slums, illiteracy common, and social services inadequate. The shah's glamorous celebrations of monarchy and Iran's pre-Islamic past seemed an enormous waste of public funds and contributed to the sense that he was indifferent to the values and culture of his subjects. The influx of thousands of foreign military personnel, mostly American, and workers, usually in lucrative, high-profile positions, encouraged resentment and xenophobia as well as the feeling that the country was being operated for the benefit of others.

Between 1975 and 1978, two important developments intensified and focused political unrest and opposition to Mohammad-Reza Shah. First of all, there was an economic crisis, which by most accounts was rather badly mismanaged. Efforts to compensate for an economy overheated by the massive infusion of petro-dollars, runaway government spending, and spiraling inflation led to a marked downturn in economic growth and per capita income and an increase in unemployment. Wage earners and bazaar merchants were particularly hard hit by this. At the other end of the economic spectrum, efforts to control inflation through price controls and arrests of "profiteer" industrialists alienated wealthier entrepreneurs. This economic malaise was exacerbated by the astounding lack of confidence in or commitment to the existing system displayed by many of those who had profited most from it, as the rich transferred huge amounts of capital out of the country rather than investing it at home.

Second, there was increasing criticism abroad of the shah's record on human rights, which tended to confirm the worst Iranian suspicions about the activities of SAVAK and the security forces. The election of Jimmy Carter as president of the United States in 1976, with his vocal emphasis on the importance of human rights in international affairs, raised expectations of political liberalization among the Iranian middle and upper classes. The shah himself seems to have thought that the Carter administration would pressure him to do this and took some limited but unmistakable steps in that direction, dismissing Hoveida as prime minister, freeing political prisoners, and inviting the Red Cross to inspect Iranian prisons, which had been accused of practicing torture. The National Front coalition resumed activities, this time as the Union of National Front Forces, and its members began a campaign of writing letters and manifestos criticizing the government and calling for political reform. By late 1977, however, it was apparent that in the case of Iran geopolitical concerns had trumped human rights issues. The Carter administration continued to provide advanced weaponry to Iran, the State Department made only muted criticism of Iran's record on human rights, and Carter gave the shah a warm welcome on his visit to Washington (which thousands of Iranian protesters there did their best to disrupt). This transparent hypocrisy was like a slap in the face to the liberal opposition in Iran—a betrayal that seemed to confirm the conclusion that the regime would never be reformed and that hardened attitudes against it and the United States.

During a state visit to Iran at the end of 1977, President Jimmy Carter toasted Mohammad-Reza Shah with the extraordinarily ill-timed observation that his country was "an island of stability in a turbulent corner of the world," that it owed this to the shah's "enlightened leadership" and was "a tribute to the respect, admiration, and love" the Iranian people had for him. Little more than a week after Carter left Iran, thousands of religious students and their sympathizers held a rally in Qom which ended in a battle with police that left several dead. This was the beginning of a relentless yearlong storm of demonstrations, strikes, and riots across the country that ultimately drove the shah from Iran on 16 January 1979.

The spark that had ignited this process was an article published in a semi-official Tehran newspaper on 7 January 1978. Written under a pseudonym but obviously emanating from very high circles of the government, it bitterly attacked what it described as an unholy alliance between religious reactionaries and communist subversives. It went on to vilify in particular the Ayatollah Khomeini as everything from a British spy to a probable homosexual. What motivated this article is still not clear: It may have been a misguided response to accusations that the shah's government had been involved in the recent deaths of Ali Shariati and one of Khomeini's sons or simply a belated acknowledgment of the potent fusion of religious sensibilities with socialist ideals taking place among the intelligentsia. The effect of the article, however, was absolutely incendiary. The newspaper offices were attacked almost immediately, there were protests at the religious schools and in the bazaars, and the demonstration in Qom was organized the next day. Anger over the article galvanized not only Khomeini supporters but moderate clerics such as Ayatollah Shariatmadari and their followers.

In accordance with the Shi'ite custom of holding memorial services for the dead after forty days, Shariatmadari, along with other clerics and dissidents, called for prayers and ceremonies on February 18 in honor of those killed in Qom. The city where Shariatmadari had his largest constituency was Tabriz, and a massive demonstration there resulted in two days of rioting after one of the demonstrators was shot and killed by a police officer. The crowd turned its fury on the visible emblems of state power and foreign influence—liquor stores, theaters, hotels, banks, police stations, offices of the Revival Party. The local police were caught completely off guard, and the army had to be called in to put down the riots. It did so with a vengeance, and an unknown but large number of people were killed. This set the pattern for a series of provocative anti-shah demonstrations that materialized at regular intervals, in accordance with the forty-day memorials or religious holy days, during the first half of 1978, most of which produced still more martyrs for the cause.

While acting vigorously against demonstrators and opposition leaders, the government initiated some reforms to address the grievances they represented. These included both economic measures, such as reducing government expenditures and ending harassment of merchants for "profiteering," and political changes, ranging from promises of free elections to offers to deal with moderate religious leaders. Some of the economic changes adversely affected workers, and the number of industrial strikes increased over the summer of 1978, but the streets were generally quiet. The shah's effort at accommodation thus seemed to be working, and confidence grew that he would weather the storm. It was against this background that a business research group in Switzerland concluded that an "effective popular uprising" against the shah was "unlikely." Officials in the U.S. State Department reported that there was "no effective internal challenge" to the shah. As late as August 1978, the CIA similarly asserted that Iran was "not in a pre-revolutionary state" and that the shah's political opponents had "the capacity to be [no] more than troublesome." Over the next two months, three key events would dramatically change this situation and probably made the shah's position irretrievably lost.

On 19 August, the anniversary of the coup that had overthrown Mosaddeq, a fire broke out at the Rex Cinema in a poor district of Abadan.

Almost 400 people burned to death because the doors had been locked, reportedly to keep out gate-crashers, and the fire department was late in arriving and bungled extinguishing the flames. Public reaction to this tragedy provides perhaps the single best example of the convoluted, conspiratorial thinking that has so deeply affected recent Iranian history. Although suspects for the arson were arrested, the rumor spread almost instantaneously throughout the country that SAVAK had plotted the conflagration for its own nefarious purposes. The idea was that the religious opposition, which considered film-making contrary to Islamic values and had developed the habit of torching theaters showing foreign "pornographic" movies, would not attack an ordinary cinema showing an Iranian film in a neighborhood likely to be sympathetic to it. The fire must therefore have been set by SAVAK in the expectation that religious elements would be blamed and discredited. One might wonder, of course, why SAVAK, if it was so clever in its scheme to embarrass the religious opposition, would pick such an unlikely target as a run-down theater in an out of the way part of Abadan rather than an upscale cinema in Tehran. This seems to have generated yet another uncorroborated rumor that the fire had been set after the police had chased militant demonstrators into the theater. The difficulty that there was not a shred of evidence one way or another for any of this did not prevent the accusation from quickly gaining the status of an article of faith. It turned the funeral of the arson victims into riots, required the stationing of troops in Abadan, and provided the pretext for a resumption of the cycle of demonstrations. It also increased the probability of future acts of violence and militancy, since they would not be attributed to the likely perpetrators but to the agents of SAVAK.

The shah's response to the Abadan disaster was consistent with his approach to earlier crises: clean house of everyone even remotely connected with the embarrassment, including Prime Minister Jamshid Amouzegar and the head of SAVAK, General Nemat-Allah Naseri, and begin a new campaign of appeasement under the unlikely and unconvincing leadership of another close confidant, the former prime minister and head of the Pahlavi Foundation, Jafar Sharif Emami. As in earlier cases, too, the offer of a carrot was almost immediately ruined by the application of the stick. In the face of continuing protests and strikes, the shah declared martial law, banned demonstrations, ordered the arrest of several members of the National Front, and made the hard-line General Gholam-Ali Oveissi, known for his role in suppressing the disturbances of 1963, military governor of Tehran. Nonetheless, on 8 September, thereafter known as Black Friday, a massive demonstration was held in Jaleh Square in Tehran in defiance of the decree of martial law, and it turned exceptionally violent after marchers called for the ouster of the shah and the return of Ayatollah Khomeini. Reports of what happened differ, but it seems the army fired on demonstrators who refused to disperse, and guerillas in the crowd fought back. It was the bloodiest incident thus far, showed that an armed insurrection was a definite possibility, and made Sharif Emami's promises of change sound even more hollow.

By all accounts, one of the government's most serious blunders was pressuring Iraq either to harass Khomeini or to expel him from his sanctuary in Najaf. No doubt worried about the effect Khomeini and events in Iran might have on Iraq's own Shi'ite population, Saddam Hussein was willing to oblige. After Khomeini was refused entry into Kuwait, it was arranged, reportedly with the shah's express approval, that Khomeini take up residence in a suburb of Paris. One can only speculate about the rationale for sending Khomeini to France; but if the intent was to isolate him, the result was a fiasco. Communications between France and Iran were infinitely freer and more efficient for Khomeini than they would have been from Iraq. Many of the most doctrinaire and determined of the shah's opponents were already to be found among the Iranian expatriate and student populations in Europe and the United States, and they quickly formed a cadre of advisors and sympathizers around Khomeini in Paris that was far more dangerous than the pilgrims who had been visiting him in Najaf. The international press faced none of the restrictions and controls that would have limited its work in Iraq; hardly friends of the shah to begin with, reporters and media personalities were mesmerized by the exotic and mysterious Khomeini and his entourage, giving them extensive publicity and something less than the critical scrutiny they deserved.

It must be remembered that at least until August, Khomeini was but one of the religious figures associated with the protests. Shariatmadari had been more directly involved in the earlier demonstrations; Taleqani was probably better known and more appealing in intellectual outlook to some segments of the opposition. Several clerics, including Shariatmadari, outranked Khomeini in terms of their position in the Shi'ite hierarchy and were more moderate in their demands, primarily wanting a return to true constitutional government. Some informed observers believe that had the shah made a genuine accommodation with Shariatmadari early on, the overthrow of the monarchy might have been avoided. The cumulative effect of the Rex Cinema fire, Black Friday, and the removal of Khomeini to Paris was to give a much harsher and more militant edge to the opposition. As the consensus grew among the opposition that the only solution to the crisis was the removal of the shah, the position of Khomeini, who had consistently and emphatically insisted on this, as the natural leader of the movement was consolidated. Bazargan and the religious wing of the National Front were already behind Khomeini. On 5 November they were joined by the leader of the secular wing, Karim Sanjabi, who had come to Paris to pay homage to Khomeini. An agreement was reached by which members of the coalition pledged to make no compromise with the shah until the question of the monarchy was settled.

Also on 5 November, the most severe rioting to date took place in Tehran. The British Embassy was attacked, government offices ransacked, a statue of the shah at the University of Tehran pulled down, and large areas of the business district burned and looted. The next day, the shah made a televised speech announcing the formation of a military government under General Gholam-Reza Azhari, which implied a policy of cracking down on the opposition. Yet the shah was visibly shaken and actually praised the justice of the "revolutionary message," which he said he had heard and whose grievances he would address. Instead of arresting opponents and rioters, the government began putting into jail former officials who had been previously dismissed, notably Hoveida and the former head of SAVAK, Naseri. The opposition sensed that the shah was in fact already defeated and that it only remained to neutralize the army and allay the fears of the shah's foreign friends. In addition to stepping up strikes and demonstrations, they thus began to concentrate on subverting the military through appeals of friendship from demonstrators to common soldiers, encouragement of desertions, and contacts with some officers. They also began meeting with officials of the United States and other countries to nourish the impression that normal relations could continue even without the shah, and they continued the media campaign to win the sympathy of the public abroad.

Like many of the shah's other actions throughout the crisis, those in November 1978 were difficult to comprehend and virtually irrelevant. His constant mixing of the iron fist with the velvet glove approach communicated weakness and confusion as well as insincerity. His shuffling of personnel and arrest of longtime supporters and associates was matched by the release of hundreds of political prisoners, including prominent clerical opponents like Ayatollah Taleqani. Thus people who might have helped the shah languished in jail, where they would fall easy victims to retaliation after the revolution, while enemies were turned loose to fan the flames of the insurrection. Astonishingly, such obvious measures as stopping the salaries of bureaucrats, state employees, and workers in the national oil company, whose strikes were paralyzing the government and crippling the economy, were not taken. All in all, it was a remarkable lesson in how *not* to deal with mass political protest.

Many explanations for the shah's puzzling behavior have since been offered, apart from the usual assortment of conspiracy theories. It eventually became known that he was suffering from a terminal cancer, so depression or medication may have clouded his judgment. It is possible that his subordinates concealed the truth about the full magnitude of the disorders from him. His memoirs suggest that he was reluctant to tarnish his reputation in history by turning the full force of his military against his own people or to take drastic measures that would jeopardize the prospects of his son's accession to the throne. He also seems to have displayed the same fatalistic resignation as he had in 1953 and to have been increasingly convinced that his future would be determined in Washington and London rather than Tehran. He certainly, and probably wisely, did not want to take forceful action without a clear and unambiguous indication of approval from the United States.

The Carter administration, however, was as conflicted in its assessment of the crisis as was the shah and could give no such sign. The hefty geopolitical bet the United States had placed on the shah, the extensive transfer of advanced weapons to Iran, the substantial economic ties between the two countries, the large number of Americans in Iran, and the even larger number of Iranians in the United States all assured that American attention would be riveted on the crisis. Some officials wanted the shah to restore order with whatever force was necessary; others thought political concessions were required; some undoubtedly wanted to see the shah fall in order to vindicate their views about arms sales or the fate of tyrants who violated human rights. The many memoirs and accounts written by those involved, though full of contradictions and finger-pointing, make it clear enough that the United States was quite free in giving advice to the beleaguered shah, but its representatives spoke in contradictory tones, and no one was really willing to take the risk of being blamed for a bloodbath. A perfect example of American dithering and the mixed message it sent was that, even as it urged the shah to be firm and promised support for whatever decision he made, the human rights division of the State Department managed to hold up shipment of routine items for crowd control such as tear gas and rubber bullets until September 1978. Similarly, Carter phoned the shah after Black Friday, ostensibly to offer him support but at the same time "regretting" the loss of life and hoping that liberalization would continue. Such constant ambiguities could only have added to the shah's confusion, erratic behavior, fears of a conspiracy against him, and sense of abandonment.

In any case, the shah's options after November, like his support at home and abroad, were dwindling rapidly. The oil industry, and consequently government revenues, had been completely disrupted by strikes. The main bazaar of Tehran was closed for over a month. Electric service was often blacked out by strikes. Air and rail transport were undependable. Imported goods were left waiting at the borders when customs officials refused to work. The shah had little choice but to risk an all-out effort to use force to crush the opposition, throw in the towel and yield completely to the opposition, or put up with the disturbances and paralysis of the government and the economy indefinitely. The latter was not possible, and the shah could not choose between the other two, vacillating between half-hearted efforts at each. Faced with the approach of the emotionally charged Moharram holy days, the Azhari government announced a ban on all demonstrations. This was ignored, and on Ashura (10 December) Taleqani and Sanjabi led an estimated 2 million people through the streets of Tehran. Army troops began to defect in large numbers, others refused orders to fire on demonstrators, and some turned their weapons on their own officers and royalists. The loss of confidence by foreign countries in the shah's survival was palpable, and even American officials had begun to rationalize why his fall might not be such a calamity after all. It was no longer a question of if the shah would go, but when and how.

Looking for a way out, the shah approached Sanjabi, among others, about becoming prime minister, but Sanjabi stuck to the agreement made with Khomeini and refused to participate in any government until the shah abdicated. Finally, on 29 December, Shahpour Bakhtiar, another prominent member of the National Front, was persuaded to form a government; he was promptly expelled from the Front as a result. On 1 January 1979, the shah announced that he had decided to take a "vacation." After two weeks of prodding by Bakhtiar and American officials, he left Iran on 16 January. He had originally planned to go straight to the United States, but for some reason changed his plans and went to

Egypt instead. This fueled speculation that he was waiting for some sort of coup like that in 1953 and vastly complicated his eventual entry into the United States. With his departure, one phase of the country's ordeal came to an end, but there was great uncertainty as to what would replace his regime.

8

Khomeini and the Islamic Revolution

On 1 February 1979, Ayatollah Khomeini arrived triumphantly in Iran, with close to 3 million people lining the streets to cheer him. An object of fascination to all, he was still an enigma to many and an increasingly charismatic inspiration to others. Many expert observers and even members of the entourage around Khomeini were convinced that his role as an essentially symbolic leader of the revolutionary coalition had reached its conclusion. They fully expected that revolutionary fervor would subside, that Khomeini would gracefully revert to the normal pattern of a prestigious religious scholar offering only moral guidance to political leaders, and that the country would be governed by liberal, progressive members of the National Front or, alternatively, that one of the leftist movements might take control. In this respect, they underestimated Khomeini in at least three respects: He had a vision of the future of Iran that placed religious leaders at the very heart of political life, he had an organization dedicated to making that vision a reality, and he had the overwhelming support of the masses of people who had taken effective control of the streets. The Iranian Revolution was about to become the Islamic Revolution.

KHOMEINI AND KHOMEINISM

There is as yet no reliable, scholarly biography of Ayatollah Khomeini, and it will be difficult for one ever to be produced, especially in terms of his life before 1961. Many volumes have, of course, been written about him, but they tend to be based on hearsay and ex post facto reports that are inherently suspect. Similarly, diligent efforts have been made to assemble a corpus of virtually every word Khomeini ever wrote. This includes numerous poems, letters, and documents from his younger years, but they were not originally meant for publication, and their editorial history is largely unknown. Even some books published under his name were prepared by other hands and possibly modified in various ways. Likewise, there has been much debate about the extent to which his public statements and actions, before and after the revolution, were of his own making or were shaped by those around him. Figures in his innermost circle expressed totally contradictory interpretations of his views; he was very sensitive to mass opinion and quite capable of making tactical adjustments of his position when he encountered opposition; he constantly hedged seemingly conciliatory remarks with conditions and qualifications; he would frequently give support to first one faction and then another, presumably to keep any one of them from becoming too powerful; and he would promote and then abandon one associate after another. This makes it very difficult to know what he genuinely believed or intended to do, and it creates doubt as to whether he was leading or being led. This problem cannot be solved here, but it should be kept in mind while following the events that unfolded after his return to Iran.

Rouhollah Mousavi Khomeini was born on 24 September 1902 into a fairly well established family of clerics and landowners. His surname Mousavi indicated descent from one of the Shi'ite Imams (Mousa al-Kazim), and Khomeini that he was from the town of Khomein near Qom. His father was murdered a few months after Khomeini's birth (in a dispute with a rival family, but by "government agents" according to recent hagiography), and his mother died while he was still a teenager. His aunt and oldest brother were primarily responsible for his upbringing. He received a traditional religious education at schools in his home town, in Arak, and in Qom, where he eventually began offering classes himself and became a protégé of the grand ayatollah and chief *marja-e taqlid* of the time, Aqa-Hosayn Boroujerdi (1875–1961). Until the 1960s, Khomeini's life was spent in relative obscurity, and reports about him differ greatly. Some, for example, depict him as a born troublemaker and rabble-rouser, who could, for example, never resist an opportunity to incite a crowd to attack Bahais: Boroujerdi is supposed to have advised his followers to avoid choosing Khomeini as his successor since he would lead them up to their knees in blood. Others suggest that he was a quiet, modest professor of philosophy, surrounded by hordes of adoring students, who passed his time concentrating on mystical contemplation (*erfan*) and dabbling with poetry.

Perhaps the most revealing comments about Khomeini's formative years are the brief remarks he himself made in his 1989 "Message to the Clergy." There, he complained about "pseudo-pious, ossified, and backward" clerics who revered "stupidity," who were suspicious of "efficient . . . skillful and clever" scholars, and who, in accordance with "American Islam," divorced religion and politics. He pointedly noted that when he taught at the Fayziyye school in Qom, such people would wash out the jar from which his young son Mostafa had drunk—the implication being that since Khomeini taught a subject like philosophy he and his family were ritually impure. According to Khomeini, it was a period "when the influence of unaware pseudo-pious and illiterate simpletons was rampant," but nonetheless "some individuals" were able "to devote their lives and their dignity to saving Islam." Despite reports about Khomeini's fantastically popular classes, the fact is that his standing as a conventional religious scholar was never very great. His comments make clear how much this must have rankled him, just as his later actions showed the lengths to which he would go to attract support from other constituencies and to cut the ground out from under those against whom he nursed such a grudge: The greatest irony of his career is that he would change traditional Shi'ism as much as, if not more than, Iran itself. It is not difficult to guess why a distinguished fellow ayatollah, Tabatabai Qomi, would have concluded that Khomeini was "an egotist, a power hungry politician disguised in religious garb."

Various scholars have searched, without much success, for evidence of Khomeini's political acumen and zeal during the almost twenty years he stood in the shadow of the apolitical Boroujerdi. His first published work was *Kashf al-Asrar* (Unveiling of Secrets; ca. 1943), a pedestrian and uninspiring defense of traditional Shi'ite practices which, through some rather forced readings, has been interpreted as an early political attack on the Pahlavi monarchy. It was at most a criticism of the government's secular policies and can more profitably be read as a conventional plea for a return to traditional concepts of *din o dowlat*, with the state and religious leaders operating in harmony and mutual support. It did, however, reveal quite clearly his fear of foreign cultural influence and his basic commitment to traditional Islamic social values. He defended the veiling of women, attacked mixing girls and boys in coeducational schools, condemned the use of alcohol, insisted that music should be forbidden since it was conducive to "a mood of fornication and lust," and called for the imposition of the legal penalties (*hadd*) required by Islamic law, such as cutting off the hands of thieves. Accounts of Khomeini's life during the 1950s tend to be conspicuously silent about his role in the critical events of the Mosaddeq era, when he might be expected to have been politically active and anti-monarchist. Although still working for Boroujerdi, he appears to have established contacts with Kashani and the Fedaiyan-e Eslam and to have been involved in their efforts to undermine Mosaddeq by stirring up fear of the communists, an action that was essential to the success of the royalist cause.

It was only after Boroujerdi's death in March 1961 that Khomeini began to attain prominence and notoriety. He finally published the requisite work on *masael* (answers to juridical problems) necessary to be taken seriously as a senior religious scholar. Ultimately, though, it was not jurisprudence, or philosophy, or mysticism, or poetry that made Khomeini's reputation, but his seemingly abrupt turn to political activism during the events of 1962–1964. Khomeini was hardly the only religious leader to express his alarm at the direction Mohammad-Reza Shah's reforms were taking, but his voice was certainly the loudest and the most incendiary, as he launched scathing personal attacks on the shah and clamored that Islam itself was threatened by the insidious plots of Jews, Zionists, and Bahais. He also proved himself a master at appropriating long-established Shi'ite practices such as funeral commemorations and Moharram ceremonies as vehicles for agitation in support of his agenda, a tactic he would again put to good use in 1978–1979. After the fierce crackdown on protesters in 1963, and despite his own arrest, Khomeini continued to criticize the government. The fact that he was then almost alone among religious leaders in his vociferous condemnation of the status of forces agreement with the United States gave him a reputation for fearlessness and incorruptibility that could not be shaken. As had happened with previous cases of religious activism in Iran, it also tended to push the reactionary nature of his earlier opposition to land reform, the franchise for women, and minority rights into the background by emphasizing his anti-imperialist credentials.

By the time Khomeini was expelled from Iran in 1964, he had attracted a dedicated, intensely loyal, and well-organized group of followers. The historian Shaul Bakhash, for example, has studied the signatories of the various statements issued by Khomeini at that time and the network of Khomeini representatives in Iran and abroad; their names constitute a virtual who's who of the future political stars of revolutionary Iran: Ali Khamenei, Hasan-Ali Montazeri, Ali-Akbar Hashemi Rafsanjani, Ali Qoddousi, Mohammad-Reza Mahdavi Kani, Mohammad Yazdi, and so on. These supporters were invaluable in terms of continuing to collect funds on Khomeini's behalf and disseminating his teachings within Iran and among Iranian students abroad. Thus Khomeini was able to keep up a steady barrage of speeches, epistles, and manifestos expressing his opposition to virtually everything the Pahlavi regime did.

In Najaf, Khomeini was also able to continue to hold classes and give lectures. A series of them given in early 1970 took up the topic of guardianship (*velayat-e faqih*) in Islamic jurisprudence, reportedly in response to the position of the Grand Ayatollah Khoi that this concept had no political dimension. Notes of those discussions were apparently written up by one of Khomeini's students and published as *Hokoumat-e Eslami* (Islamic Government). Perhaps because of the way it was composed, the book has many odd features and is full of hyperbole, anecdote, emotion, sensationalism, superficial and wildly inaccurate generalizations, and raw prejudice. It is difficult to imagine anyone of Khomeini's background seriously maintaining, for example, such absurdities as the claim that "the *khoms* [a juridical term used by Shi'ites in the general sense of tax] of the bazaar of Baghdad" would be sufficient to support the sayyids (descendants of the Prophet Mohammad), religious schools, and "all the poor of the Islamic world." Anyone who approaches the book expecting to find coherent political philosophy and logical, factually informed scholarly argument is likely to be severely disappointed. Nonetheless, Khomeini does not seem to have disavowed any part of the text, it is in keeping with the simplistic but highly effective nature of most of his pronouncements, and it is certainly a blueprint for what he would do following the revolution.

According to Khomeini, Jews and imperialists had planted "agents" in religious and other educational institutions to propagate a "defective" view of Islam as an apolitical religion which "has no laws or ordinances pertaining to society" and "no particular form of government" since it is concerned "only with rules of ritual purity after menstruation and parturition." To the contrary, the Koran and the Sunna "contain all the laws and ordinances man needs"; what was lacking was a government to *implement* these laws. Like St. Augustine, Khomeini held that all existing governments were "a form of banditry," but instead of looking only to the city of God he maintained that a legitimate government on earth was both possible and necessary. At the same time, every government must have "an individual entrusted with the maintenance of its laws and institutions." That individual could not be a monarch, since Islam had supposedly invalidated monarchy and hereditary succession (a curious position for a Shi'ite, supported neither by centuries of history and tradition nor by the flimsy evidence Khomeini produced in defense of his dogma). Instead, Khomeini took up the venerable juridical concept of *velayat-e faqih*, normally applied in a very limited sense to the question of providing guardianship for orphans, and so on, and held that true Islamic government was the collective duty of the Islamic jurists (*foqaha*). In the event one "worthy individual" with knowledge of the law and justice succeeded in establishing such a government, he would "possess the same authority as the Most Noble Messenger" and it would be obligatory for people to obey him. In chillingly prophetic words, he emphasized that the just ruler must always "ignore personal feelings and interests" and remember that Islam "is prepared to subordinate individuals to the collective interest of society" and "has rooted out numerous groups that were a source of corruption and harm," such as the Jews of Medina whom the Prophet Mohammad "eliminated." Rather oddly, even as Khomeini argued that the *foqaha* constituted a kind of aristocracy of virtue and should be entrusted with the right to govern, he derided them for their love of mere ritual, personal piety, and juridical hairsplitting. He did not expect, he said, that "the gutless people who now sit in the religious centers" would ever create such a government. Instead, he appealed directly to Muslims everywhere to disseminate the idea of Islamic government, to refrain from assisting or cooperating with existing governments, and to create new, truly Islamic institutions.

The revolution of 1978–1979 naturally provided Khomeini with just such an opportunity to make his concept of *velayat-e faqih* a reality. Given the views expressed in *Hokoumat-e Eslami* and his public pronouncements, the widely held perception at the beginning of 1979 that he would do nothing of the kind seems utterly astounding today. It was not due so much to the use of *taqiyya* or deception on his part as to the typical postmodernist tendency to always see the best in Third World revolutionary movements: A dose of anti-Americanism and denunciation of the evils of capitalism tended to provide cover for a multitude of sins in the eyes of many. The superficial similarity of some of his rhetoric with that of the Ali Shariati–inspired Islamic socialists also predisposed them to believe that Khomeini was of their own mind and would be a useful icon for their movement. Under such circumstances, apparently, Khomeini's contemptuous remarks about an Islam confined to rules regarding "menstruation and parturition" were sufficient to blot out memory of his own book of *masael* on just such questions and to create the impression that he stood for a "progressive" Islam detached from its legalistic heritage. When he attacked the "harshness" of the shah for imposing a death penalty on drug traffickers, it was overlooked that he was only criticizing the shah, not the "harshness" itself, which he was actually defending. Even his frank statement that he did not seek an office such as prime minister but would "direct the nation" was uncritically accepted as evidence of his nonpolitical intentions. It did not take long for the process of stripping away such illusions to begin.

THE FALL OF THE BAKHTIAR REGENCY

Shahpour Bakhtiar, the shah's last appointee as prime minister, was a strong and capable man, and he acted in a principled way by trying to accommodate revolutionary demands within the framework of the existing constitution, but he was really in an impossible position. By breaking ranks with the rest of the National Front and accepting an appointment from the shah, he had forfeited the support of his natural allies and compromised his legitimacy. His gestures at embracing revolutionary demands served only to alienate potential supporters. Strikes, demonstrations, and street violence continued unabated; he had no control over most government ministries. His efforts in January 1979 to make a face-saving arrangement with opposition forces ran into the stone wall of Khomeini's refusal even to meet with him unless he would resign first. The very fact that he was willing to deal with Khomeini implied that Khomeini had some legitimate position of authority. His frantic and unsuccessful efforts to block Khomeini's return by closing Mehrabad airport left him looking weak and desperate. Astoundingly, his government even took steps to provide security for Khomeini and to transport him to and from a rally at Behesht-e Zahra cemetery at which he threatened to "punch the government in the mouth."

By early February, Bakhtiar's survival depended more than anything else on the willingness and ability of the Iranian military to support him. Since early January, General Robert Huyser had been active in Iran trying to provide American encouragement for military leaders to do just that, but the chances of success, never very great, were fast evaporating. Shortage of fuel (because of strikes in the oil industry) and desertions posed logistical difficulties, but the greatest problems were political. Given Iranian feelings about the Mosaddeq era, it is hard to see how any government that owed its existence to American backing through the military could have survived for long. In any case, even as Huyser was attempting to prop up military support for Bakhtiar, other American officials were working at cross purposes with him by dealing with the opposition. Meanwhile, the Khomeini forces continued to try to neutralize the military through a combination of discussions with officers, encouragement of deserters, and physical attacks on known military opponents.

Generals who might have been eager to stage a coup on behalf of the shah were much less enthusiastic about doing so for Bakhtiar. They had repeatedly warned Huyser, correctly as it turned out, that the shah's departure would lead to the disintegration of the military. Deeply resentful that, in their view, the United States had undercut the shah and thrown him out "like a dead mouse," worried that the revolution was leading to a communist takeover, and naturally fearful for their lives, there was little incentive for these generals to risk a civil war at that point in the game. Many suspected that the United States, Britain, and France were already in collusion with Khomeini, and it is highly probable that several of them were already making their own accommodations with either Khomeini or Bazargan. The actions (and subsequent fate) of two extremely important figures regarded as exceptionally close to the shah, the supreme commander, General Gharabaghi, and a top intelligence officer, Major General Fardoust, were especially curious and have raised many questions about their loyalties. There are a number of possible explanations for their behavior, but it is difficult not to wonder if they, as well as the shah, had concluded that if the Iranian people wanted Khomeini so badly they deserved to have him. Acceptance of Khomeini was not only useful in terms of personal survival, it could also be seen as the best way to conform to the shah's stated desire to avoid bloodshed and civil war. It was certainly a good bet to stave off the communists and a fitting way to repay America for its "support" during the crisis.

As early as 23 January, technicians (*homafars*) in the air force had begun to defect to the Khomeini side. The desertions increased and expanded to the navy and the army in the following days. On the night of 9 February, *homafars* at the important Doshan Tappeh air base near Tehran rioted and began fighting with troops from the Imperial Guards. Large numbers of leftist guerillas, Islamic revolutionaries, and military defectors rushed to assist the pro-Khomeini air force personnel. Others blocked convoys moving to the support of the Imperial Guard. The pro-Khomeini forces routed the Imperial Guard, seized the armory, and handed out the weapons to the crowd. Over the next day, attacks on other armories, factories, and police stations resulted in an estimated 300,000 firearms being captured and distributed among the insurgents. In effect, a popular revolutionary army had been created and was now a force to be reckoned with. On 11 February, the head of the army, General Badrai, was assassinated outside his headquarters, and numerous other high-ranking officers were seized and imprisoned. General Gharabaghi, who was conspicuously not arrested, then announced "the military's neutrality in the present political crisis" and ordered the troops back to the barracks. Incredibly, according to several reliable reports, officials of the Carter administration made inquiries to Huyser and others that night about the possibility of launching a coup—the most breathtaking example thus far of the unparalleled mix of hubris and stupidity that substituted for policy during the Iran crisis. By the next day, revolutionaries were in full control, and Bakhtiar went into hiding (eventually escaping to France). Sporadic fighting continued around the country, but by 16 February the remaining royalist forces were defeated everywhere.

THE BAZARGAN INTERLUDE

On 5 February, Khomeini and the semi-secret Islamic Revolutionary Council (IRC) had authorized the establishment of a provisional government to be headed by Mehdi Bazargan. Bazargan assumed the office of prime minister on 12 February and over the next few days appointed a cabinet composed almost entirely of members of his own Iran Freedom Movement (notably Ebrahim Yazdi) or the secular wing of the old National Front (such as Karim Sanjabi, Daryoush Forouhar, and Ahmad Madani). Clerics and leftists, so prominent in the revolution, were conspicuously absent in the new government, which seemed to be the fulfillment of predictions that liberal nationalist elements would take charge. Bazargan certainly wanted to reassure moderate elements and to come to an understanding with the United States, but he faced enormous obstacles.

The critical difficulty was that his government was neither the only nor the most important center of power in Iran. Bazargan's government had never been intended to be anything more than provisional and transitional, and it had little real control over anything of significance, not even its own ministries. By accepting appointment from Khomeini and the IRC, Bazargan had already effectively conceded that whatever legitimacy he had was derived from them. The real figure of authority continued, of course, to be Khomeini. Bazargan constantly had to defer to him in relation to key decisions and policies. Whether Khomeini genuinely supported the Bazargan government, as he claimed in frequent public statements, or simply viewed it as an expedient tactical necessity on the way to his ultimate goal is open to debate. An exasperated Bazargan professed that other, sinister elements were manipulating the "sensitive and good-hearted" Khomeini to undermine him. In any event, the end result was that Khomeini frequently intervened in ways that tended to foster other centers of power rather than to bolster Bazargan.

Bazargan also had to work in tandem with the reorganized and powerful IRC. Its membership was kept secret for a while, but eventually it was understood to be composed of seven clerics, six laymen, and two security advisors. The clerics included Mortaza Motahhari, a close friend of Khomeini and chair of the council; Mahmoud Taleqani, well known for his friendly relations with leftist groups; and five other clerical activists long associated with Khomeini: Mohammad-Reza Mahdavi Kani, Ali-Akbar Hashemi Rafsanjani, Mohammad-Javad Bahonar, Abd-al-Karim Mousavi Ardabili, and Mohammad Beheshti (later joined by Ali Khamenei). It was this last group that posed the biggest problem for Bazargan, as they formed a clique bent on pursuing its own agenda. They did so by forming their own parties (the most important being the Islamic Republican Party [IRP], of which all but Mahdavi Kani were founding members); associating themselves with the informal revolutionary organizations and militias that had come into being; and gaining control over the financial resources of the various "charitable" foundations that took over the confiscated properties of the former monarchy and its *taghouti* (devilish) associates. Indeed, as Bazargan struggled with one intractable problem after another, it became ever clearer that there was the equivalent of an alternate government within a government at work in the IRC. While Bazargan attempted to assert control over existing governmental institutions and to build legal bases for new ones, the clerical forces worked at cross purposes to him through their own judicial and vigilante groups. One event after another had the effect of strengthening this faction and its hold over the revolution.

First of all, whatever confidence Khomeini may have had in Bazargan was seriously undermined by the latter's ineffectiveness during the first few months of his administration. One of the basic tasks Khomeini had given Bazargan was the restoration of the economy and public order, which primarily entailed reining in the Marxists and guerilla organizations. To that end, Khomeini had called on the populace to stop attacking government buildings, to turn in weapons, and to obey Bazargan. The guerilla organizations, having come so far, were not about to cease their efforts to drive the revolution in the direction they preferred. While professing their loyalty to Khomeini, they rejected his appeal to give up their guns on the grounds that they were needed to "safeguard" the revolution. As if to emphasize the point, one group attacked the American Embassy in Tehran on 14 February and briefly held the staff captive. Even after Khomeini had described the Marxists in Iran as "evil" and "bandits," the Fedai-ye Khalq was able to hold a rally in Tehran attended by about 70,000 supporters. A second, and probably related, problem was a rash of attacks on prominent revolutionary figures. These included the assassinations of General Mohammad-Vali Qarani, security advisor to the IRC, on 23 April and of Ayatollah Motahhari, chair of the IRC, on 1 May. They were attributed to a shadowy terrorist group named Forqan, the specific orientation of which remains a mystery. There was also an outbreak of ethnic unrest in Kurdish, Arab, Turkoman, and, to a lesser extent, Baluchi areas. On 21 February, for example, Sheikh Ezz-al-Din Hosayni, a Sunni Kurdish leader in Mahabad, petitioned Bazargan for the formation of a largely autonomous regional government for Kurdistan, and fighting with government forces broke out in May. Arabs in Khuzistan, led by their ayatollah, Mohammad Taher Khaqani, demonstrated for autonomy in March and April and were fired on by government forces. Turkomans in Gorgan also organized and demanded various economic reforms and recognition of minority rights, clashing with government forces in March. The Bazargan government was relatively sympathetic to the demands of the ethnic minorities, and Ayatollah Taleqani tried to mediate settlements in Kurdistan and Gorgan.

As later events would show, Khomeini preferred a much tougher approach to dealing with all these problems. As early as 7 March, he was complaining about the "weakness" of the provisional government; if this was aimed at encouraging Bazargan to be more assertive, it had little effect. Suspicious of the army, Khomeini decided on 5 May to authorize the formation of the Revolutionary Guards (Pasdaran), an armed force capable of dealing with any threat to the revolution. Militia groups cultivated by the clerical faction in the Revolutionary Council and the IRP, such as the Hezbollahis organized by Hadi Ghaffari and the Mojahedin-e Enqelab run by Behzad Nabavi, were already in place to be adapted for this purpose. They were made up primarily of men from the lowest social classes and lumpenproletariat, absolutely loyal to Khomeini, and highly dependent on the financial rewards and status they derived from the revolution. Thanks to confiscated property and the creation of such institutions as the Crusade for Construction (Jehad-e Sazandegi) and the Foundation for the Oppressed (Bonyad-e Mostazafan), which had taken over the resources of the former Pahlavi Foundation, the IRC and IRP could recruit and fund such militias and paramilitary organizations, which could be depended on to provide gangs of knife- and club-wielding agitators to attack their political opponents. Now the Guards, drawn from the elite among these groups, acquired an institutionalized status alongside the army but essentially served as a kind of strike force for the IRC and IRP. They remained under the control not of the Bazargan government but rather of the IRC, with their organizers, notably Rafsanjani and Khamenei, drawn from the IRP. The Guards quickly went to work ruthlessly suppressing the ethnic dissidents. In mid-July, they abducted Ayatollah Khaqani and machine-gunned some of his supporters. Exhorted by Khomeini, they also launched a protracted campaign in Kurdistan in August, during which they summarily executed a large number of Kurdish rebels. Other activities were directed at harassing and intimidating political foes of the IRP, especially leftists, liberals, and critics of the concept of clerical rule.

From Bazargan's point of view, the credibility of his government hinged on gaining control over the hundreds of revolutionary "committees" (*komitehs*) and tribunals that had taken de facto control of police, judicial, and administrative activities in most cities. The committees harassed or arrested people, seized property, and occupied buildings at will. On 28 February, and numerous times thereafter, Bazargan complained that the interference of the committees would compel his government to resign. Khomeini's solution was not to abolish or even to discipline the committees, but to streamline and centralize them under the supervision of a clerical member of the IRC, Mahdavi Kani: They were in effect institutionalized and shielded from interference by Bazargan. The power and independence of the committees, backed by their own militia, were dramatically illustrated in mid-April when one of them arrested the sons of Ayatollah Taleqani. Taleqani renounced politics to protest the return of "dictatorship and despotism" and went into hiding, and Karim Sanjabi resigned his post as foreign minister in disgust. Although Taleqani and Khomeini were later reconciled, nothing was done to rein in the committees. Later that month, when Bazargan attempted to have the regular police take over the duties of some committees, Khomeini confirmed that the committees were necessary and should stay in place "until the authority of the government has been established." With the ayatollah's apparent blessing, they were thus able to continue to conduct what amounted to a purge of the military, the bureaucracy, and the educational institutions.

Much to Bazargan's dismay, a veritable reign of terror was also being instituted by a judiciary he did not authorize and which he could not restrain. The Tehran tribunal, headed by Hojjatoleslam Sadeq Khalkhali, a close associate of Khomeini who combined an improbably jovial and elf-like appearance with a seemingly insatiable appetite for blood, set the pattern for revolutionary justice by holding summary trials and executions. During the first few days of the Bazargan administration, at least eight generals were killed, including not only obvious targets like the former head of SAVAK (Naseri) but even one (Motamadi) whom Bazargan had just proposed to be the new head of the air force. The executions, unlike the trials, were highly publicized, with gruesome morgue photographs provided for the use of the press, which only seemed to whet the public desire for still more vengeance.

Mahdavi Kani justified the executions on the grounds that they were necessary "to purify society." Throughout March, tribunals all over the country followed this example and expanded the range of people put on trial from top agents of the shah's regime to those who "spread corruption on earth" or "fought God." In many instances, such vague charges were merely a pretext for settling old grievances, appropriating property, or dealing with political opponents. Some religious leaders, lawyers, and human rights groups complained about the tribunals, and on 14 March Bazargan described their actions as a "disgrace." He appealed to Khomeini, who once again responded by issuing directives that seemed to support Bazargan in theory but increased clerical authority in practice. He temporarily halted the trials while regulations to govern them were drafted, but he also confirmed the role of the IRC as a supervising agency of the tribunals. When the new guidelines and procedures were issued on 5 April, they gave the tribunals authority over almost any conceivable case from economic crimes to those against the people's "honor." Rights of defendants in trials were also severely curtailed. This touched off another wave of executions of dozens of people, including the former prime minister Amir Abbas Hoveida, air force general Amir Hosayn Rabii, Foreign Minister Abbas Ali Khalatbari, and SAVAK commander Hasan Pakravan. Even after Khomeini finally proclaimed the equivalent of a general amnesty in July, it did not apply to those accused of killing, torture, or "plundering" and was largely ignored in any case. The exact number of victims is uncertain but probably averaged one hundred a month between February and November 1979.

As a provisional government, the most basic task with which the Bazargan administration had been entrusted was the establishment of the legal foundations for a post-monarchist state. This specifically entailed holding a popular referendum to determine the form of government, the consequent drafting and submission for approval of a new constitution to replace the Constitution of 1906, and elections to fill the offices of the new state. In this regard, too, Bazargan found that he had very little room for discretionary action as he again had to work in tandem with the IRC and in accordance with Khomeini's dictates. Khomeini had already determined in advance that the only choice in the referendum would be to vote for or against the creation of an "Islamic Republic" to replace the monarchy. When various groups proposed alternatives such as "Democratic Islamic Republic," which would have implied a greater degree of popular sovereignty, Khomeini brushed them aside on the grounds that democracy (unlike republic!) was a Western rather than an "Islamic" concept. The voting took place over a two-day period, 30–31 March, and resulted, not surprisingly, in 98 percent of the more than 20 million voters agreeing that Iran should be an Islamic Republic.

Khomeini, the clerical faction in the IRC, the IRP, and the militias clearly understood there was more than just a name involved in this vote. They took it as an overwhelming indication of support for their program of an extensive Islamization of Iran in all respects. In May, Khomeini declared that those who wanted "to separate from Islam" were enemies of the revolution, as were those who did not believe clerics should be the political leaders. He encouraged the takeover of banks, insurance companies, factories, and other companies to augment the resources of the Bonyad-e Mostazafan. He also demanded greater IRC control of the national oil company and of the radio and television. On 23 July he banned the playing of music. He authorized renewed and merciless attacks on the ethnic minorities seeking autonomy. He began criticizing papers such as *Ayandegan*, which published articles he did not like, as "depraved" and "un-Islamic." New press laws were issued, and over forty newspapers were closed down in August, beginning with the occupation of the offices of *Ayandegan* by the Revolutionary Guards. The Guards also attacked the offices of the Fedai, Mojahedin, and Tudeh, as Khomeini vowed that "in a few hours" he could toss the leftists into the "rubbish bin of death." Gradually, and too late, the euphoria of revolution dissipated in the light of these events, and voices of protest against Khomeini and such actions began to be heard. In May, Ayatollah Shariatmadari openly questioned the wisdom of having clerics involved in politics. In June, Hedayat-Allah Matin Daftari (Mosaddeq's grandson) and his National Democratic Front criticized Khomeini for his repressive policies. By 6 September, even Ayatollah Taleqani, the one figure strong enough to be a credible alternative to Khomeini, was again warning of the danger that a religious despotism was being established. He died three days later, under circumstances that many have found extremely suspicious (some of the mourners at his funeral accused Beheshti of poisoning him and were attacked by Revolutionary Guards). The center of the political storm that was brewing was the issue of a new constitution.

DRAFTING THE CONSTITUTION

Work on a draft constitution for the Islamic Republic had begun at least as early as January, and a tentative text was published on 28 April, followed by a revised draft on 18 June. It was not markedly different from the 1906 constitution and gave only a very limited role to clerics. Surprisingly, Khomeini made no objections and even recommended submitting the proposed constitution to an immediate referendum. This has been taken as evidence that he was not yet thinking of putting his ideas about *velayat-e faqih* into practice. More likely, in his typically idealistic way of thinking, now that the "government of God" had been established with himself as its de facto custodian there was no need to worry over such trivial details as a constitution.

In any event, Khomeini could hardly have come up with a better ploy to give the proponents of clerical rule an opportunity to affect the process: Events in Iran had already done much to arouse the suspicions of the secularists, the leftists, the liberals, the ethnic minorities, and those who favored only limited religious influence in government. Led by Ayatollah Shariatmadari, they insisted that the constitution must be drafted by representatives of the people rather than drawn up by a secretive and self-appointed committee. After some sharp debate, Khomeini and Shariatmadari agreed that the proposed constitution should be reviewed by a seventy-three-member Assembly of Experts, to be elected on 3 August.

This had two important effects. First, Khomeini realized that there was sufficient opposition to the concept of *velayat-e faqih* that it could not be taken as a given and should be enshrined in a constitution, and he accordingly called on the clerics to take an activist role in the deliberations. Second, it allowed the IRP, now well organized, with much popular support, and more than willing to resort to violence and intimidation, to dominate the elections for the Assembly of Experts (marked by very low voter participation), winning over fifty of the seats. Under the shrewd and domineering guidance of Ayatollah Beheshti, the Assembly proceeded to revise the draft constitution drastically, incorporating the key ideas of Khomeini's *Hokoumat-e Eslami*, including a decisive and direct role for the clergy and the establishment of the all-powerful office of Faqih. Debate over these and other changes was heated, but the outcome and subsequent approval of the constitution became forgone conclusions thanks to the success of a brilliant diversionary tactic, the American Embassy hostage crisis.

THE HOSTAGE CRISIS

On 22 October 1979, after much bureaucratic wrangling, the United States admitted the former shah, then known to be dying of cancer, to the country for medical treatment. This created a firestorm of protests and demonstrations in Iran, which Khomeini fanned furiously. On 4 November a small group of students affiliated with the Islamic Associations of the University of Tehran and calling themselves "Followers of the Line of the Emam," led by Hojjatoleslam Mohammad Mousavi Khoeniha, took advantage of the situation to attack and seize control of the American Embassy in Tehran. The sixty-three staff members at the embassy were held hostage, and three others, including Bruce Laingen, the *chargé d'affaires*, who happened to be in a meeting at the Foreign Ministry, were detained there. The students pledged not to relinquish the embassy or release its personnel until the shah was returned to Iran for trial (thirteen hostages, blacks and some women, were released on 20 November in a transparent effort to manipulate American political opinion).

Although the embassy had been taken over briefly once before, and there had been consideration of the possibility that the admission of the shah to the United States would precipitate such an action, the initial impression was that the takeover of the embassy by this group of students had been a spontaneous gesture that had caught almost everyone by surprise. In many respects, however, it had unmistakable signs of careful forethought and planning: The Revolutionary Guards assigned to protect the building were nowhere to be found. The students took over the embassy quickly and efficiently. In what should have been an unfamiliar building, they knew exactly where to go to grab documents despite the frantic efforts of the staff to destroy them. (They also had the fanatic determination to put shredded papers back together piece by piece—and to use them selectively to discredit opponents.) Their efforts were also coordinated with a systematic effort to embarrass the Bazargan government and nip in the bud an effort to normalize relations between Iran and the United States. Khomeini had repeatedly and vehemently called for militant action against the United States and the "American-loving rotten brains" in Iran. The government media had been busy publicizing a meeting of Bazargan and Yazdi with Zbigniew Brzezinski in Algiers on 2 November, which now made it difficult for Bazargan to intervene on behalf of the hostages without appearing to be an American lackey.

In a futile effort to salvage its position, the Bazargan government unilaterally abrogated the military agreement between Iran and the United States, a move that was followed by the freezing of Iranian funds in U.S. banks. In a matter of days, however, it was clear that Bazargan would receive no support from Khomeini against the students, and he and his government finally gave up and resigned on 6 November. The fact that the students had been congratulated for their action by Khomeini, Beheshti, and Montazeri, and that Khomeini's son Ahmad scrambled over the embassy wall to join the hostage takers, removed any possibility of pretending that this was the action of individuals rather than the state itself.

Under an unprecedented and unrelenting glare of media attention, the melodrama of the hostages and their fate, which dragged on for 444 days, became the object of public fascination and galvanized passions in both the United States and Iran in ways that were difficult to control. In Washington, other capitals, and the United Nations, interminable debates went on about whether the United States should have admitted the shah, whether it should expel him or send him back to Iran for trial, whether it should "apologize" for its alleged misdeeds in the past or make some other bargain with the hostage takers—none of which had much to do with either the reasons for the takeover of the embassy or with resolving the crisis. Khomeini was no doubt highly suspicious of the United States; he had accused the CIA of being behind the Forqan assassinations, thought the United States was encouraging separatism among the ethnic minorities, and believed it was intriguing to stage a coup. He supported the taking of the hostages, however, out of sheer political calculation. In reality, as the historian Rouhollah Ramazani has noted, it was simply one more example of Iranians using foreigners in pursuit of a domestic political agenda.

SECURING THE CONSTITUTION

The controversial vote to include *velayat-e faqih* as part of the constitution had just been passed on 14 October, and there was sure to be bitter controversy over it. A disgusted Abbas Amir Entezam, Bazargan's deputy premier, had already persuaded Bazargan and a majority of the cabinet to call on Khomeini to suspend the Assembly because it was going beyond its mandate, an idea Khomeini had immediately rejected. The Assembly finished its work on 15 November, and a vote was scheduled on 2 December to approve the constitution. That would have to be followed by elections for the presidency and the Majles, which would again have entailed extensive debates and political divisiveness with an uncertain outcome. The anti-American furor conveniently served to give the coup de grâce to the Bazargan administration, to deflect public interest from debates over the new constitution to the rehashing of a litany of American misdeeds, real or imagined, in Iran, and to eliminate other critics and opponents in the political arena.

In short, by escalating the war against the Kurds and then by picking a fight with the "Great Satan," Khomeini and his cohorts artfully created the impression that the Islamic Republic was under siege, preempting effective dissent on the constitutional issues. By the time of the December referendum, most political leaders, including Bazargan, had opted to vote for the constitution, either out of spinelessness or the delusion that they should not compromise the ostensible struggle against "imperialism" that was under way. Most prominent critics had been driven into either hiding or exile. Several leaders who might have exerted a moderating influence, notably Ayatollahs Motahhari and Taleqani, had been killed or had died. The burden of leading the opposition to clerical rule and radicalism thus fell on the unlikely shoulders of the frail and essentially apolitical Ayatollah Mohammad Kazem Shariatmadari.

Shariatmadari, one of the successors to his mentor Boroujerdi, enjoyed a considerable following among the Azerbaijani Turks. He was backed by a political party rivaling the IRP, the Muslim People's Republican Party (MPRP), with the support of men like Hasan Nazih (who had resisted Beheshti's encroachment on the National Iranian Oil Company) and Rahmat-Allah Moqaddam Maraghai (one of the most outspoken critics of clerical rule at the Assembly deliberations). Shariatmadari had consistently supported the revolution but tried to keep it within bounds by avoiding violence and sudden change. He had spoken out against the summary trials and executions, he supported free expression and the rights of minorities, and he maintained that the clergy should have only the most limited, essentially advisory, role in government. On the eve of the referendum, he pointed out the essential contradiction between the constitution's promises of popular sovereignty and the dictatorial powers it gave to *velayat-e faqih* and indicated that he would boycott the referendum. Although this definitely had an impact on the turnout for the vote, it did not much affect the outcome: About 16 million people voted, and 99.5 percent approved the constitution.

In preparation for the upcoming presidential and parliamentary elections, the clerical forces then began to settle scores with their adversaries, beginning with Shariatmadari. On 5 December, a pro-Khomeini mob in Qom attacked a group of Azerbaijanis who had come to visit Shariatmadari (according to some reports the riot was cover for an effort to assassinate him). Khomeini then met with Shariatmadari and condemned the "plots" against him, but this had no discernable effect on the situation. Over the next several days severe fighting erupted in Tabriz, and Shariatmadari supporters seized the radio station and government buildings. Hasan Nazih, whom Khomeini had ousted as head of the NIOC after he resisted Beheshti's efforts to control it, appealed to the Azerbaijanis to help fight the "despotism" of the new constitution. Given the importance of Azerbaijan and the long history of Azerbaijani activism, this was potentially a serious threat, and Khomeini dealt with it in his typical fashion: soothing remarks and offers of compromises coupled with vehement denunciations of "rebellion against the rule of Islam," vicious *ad hominem* attacks on key Shariatmadari supporters, and the unleashing of thugs to express the "will of the people" through street violence.

On 13 December, a "reconciliation" rally produced a compromise according to which Shariatmadari secured more control over Azerbaijani affairs and promises to discuss amending the constitution. The accord quickly broke down, as Khomeini refused to recognize the representatives named by Shariatmadari to the constitutional committee (Nazih and Moqaddam Maraghai) and began claiming that events in Azerbaijan were being orchestrated by the United States. In what would become a

familiar tactic, the students at the American embassy produced documents showing that Moqaddam Maraghai had once met with U.S. officials and must therefore be a counter-revolutionary agent; orders for his
arrest were issued. Violent confrontation was simply not in Shariatmadari's nature, and on 5 January, with Revolutionary Guards threatening
his house in Qom, he made the fatal mistake of issuing a statement dis-
tancing himself from the MPRP, which the Khomeini faction was demanding should be disbanded. Khomeini immediately recognized and
pounced on this sign of weakness. Having successfully linked the Azerbaijani dissent to the struggle against America, and taking advantage of
the passions of the Moharram holy days (as well as the distractions
caused by the Soviet invasion of Afghanistan and U.N. Secretary General
Kurt Waldheim's visit to Iran to try to resolve the hostage crisis), the
Khomeini forces launched an all-out assault on the Shariatmadari supporters in Qom and Tabriz during the period 7–12 January. When the
Revolutionary Guards captured the MPRP headquarters in Tabriz and
executed eleven of its supporters, the struggle was effectively over.

THE PRESIDENTIAL ELECTION

All that now remained to confirm the new constitution and the triumph of *velayat-e faqih* and clerical rule was the holding of the presidential and parliamentary elections. Having been preoccupied with
Shariatmadari, the IRP was not fully prepared for the presidential election on 25 January 1980. Khomeini had made acceptance of Article 110
of the constitution a prerequisite for anyone to stand for election, which
eliminated candidates opposed to *velayat-e faqih*. Bazargan and other like-
minded potential candidates declined to run, apparently fearful that they
would be targeted for the kind of smearing by the discoveries of the
militant students at the American Embassy that had been applied to
Moqaddam Maraghai. Khomeini also disqualified candidates known to
have boycotted the constitutional elections, which ruled out the candidates of most leftist parties (notably Masoud Rajavi, a leader of the
Mojahedin-e Khalq). This should have smoothed the way for an IRP
victory, but there were two unexpected hitches. First, Khomeini barred
clerics from running, which removed the likely victor, Beheshti, from the
race. This, like Khomeini's desire to submit the draft constitution for
immediate approval, was quite surprising, and it is difficult to interpret
its motivation, although in light of subsequent events it appears to have
been a rather cunning tactical move. This meant that the IRP had to field

a proxy candidate, which it did in the person of Jalal-al-Din Farsi. Late in the process, it became known that his citizenship was in question since his father was an Afghan, and he had to withdraw. His replacement, Hasan Habibi, was a virtual unknown and had no time to mount an effective campaign.

There were thus only two other notable candidates left, Ahmad Madani and Abu'l-Hasan Bani Sadr. Madani was backed by Bazargan and the National Front, which essentially guaranteed that the leftists and their other opponents would unite for the moment behind Bani Sadr. A rather eccentric and unpredictable character, Bani Sadr was the son of an ayatollah and had spent a good part of his life in France. His writings, primarily on the concept of "Islamic economics," reflected the eclectic blend of socialist ideals and Islamic metaphors popularized by Ali Shariati and made him acceptable to groups like the Mojahedin, while his family background helped him to enter the circle of advisors around Khomeini in Paris. Khomeini was reportedly very fond of him; he was among those who had accompanied Khomeini on the return flight from Paris, and he was made a member of the IRC. As might be expected, he won the presidential election in a landslide, obtaining 75 percent of the votes (over 10 million, compared to Madani's 2 million and Habibi's less than 1 million). Khomeini confirmed him as president on 4 February and designated him as commander-in-chief of the military on 19 February.

By the start of the Iranian new year in March, Khomeini was confident enough in the establishment of the new regime to declare that it would be a year of "order and security." This proved to be one of his least prophetic statements.

9

The Khomeini Era

However much the establishment of the Islamic Republic, the approval of the constitution, and the conclusion of presidential elections may have encouraged the feeling in spring 1980 that the revolution was about to settle down into the "year of order and security," events were leading in a very different direction. Iran was on the verge of a decade of continued upheaval and struggle, dominated throughout by the inexorable presence of the Ayatollah Khomeini.

THE BANI SADR PRESIDENCY

Bani Sadr's electoral triumph raised great expectations of what he could accomplish, not least of all in his own mind. He quickly proposed to end the hostage crisis, assert his control over the Revolutionary Guards and government agencies, deal with the minority problem, and introduce numerous social and economic reforms. In actuality, his situation was not at all unlike that which had confronted Bazargan. With Kurdistan and the American hostages, he was saddled with tough problems that needed to be solved through compromises which would discredit him if he failed and be used to attack him if he succeeded. He was a lay leader, not a cleric, and could not expect to control the clerical forces. Moreover, the IRP saw Bani Sadr's election by such a large margin in relation to their own candidate as an embarrassment and was determined to cut him down to size. However much Khomeini may have liked him, he repeatedly failed to support Bani Sadr and made statements that undermined him just as he had with Bazargan.

The limits of what Bani Sadr could do became apparent in a matter of days. With the constitution approved and the new Islamic government established, the hostages had a rapidly diminishing value and were a major liability for the government. The problem for Bani Sadr and his foreign minister, Sadeq Qotbzadeh, was how to get rid of them without seeming weak or being outflanked by other political rivals. For its part, the Carter administration was going as far as it could in giving face-saving concessions to the Iranians without exposing itself to charges of unmitigated appeasement. On 6 February 1980, Bani Sadr began criticizing the students as "children" trying to maintain a government within a government, and by 14 February he was confident enough to say that the hostages could be released within hours of the United States meeting certain conditions. On 23 February, however, Khomeini essentially took the matter out of his hands by stating that the Majles would decide what to do with the hostages after it was constituted, a process that would not be completed until May. In March, Bani Sadr attempted to have custody of the hostages transferred to the IRC. However, a hardcore faction among the students refused to turn them over or to allow a United Nations delegation to visit them. Again, Khomeini did nothing to support Bani Sadr and clearly wanted to prolong the crisis until he himself decided the time was propitious to end it.

With its hopes for a deal dashed, the Carter administration was coming under intolerable political pressure to act. Neither the shah's departure for Panama on 15 December and thence to Egypt on 23 March, nor the elaborate intrigues of Qotbzadeh with American officials had done anything to ameliorate the crisis. On 7 April, the United States finally made a formal break of diplomatic relations with Iran, and, on 17 April, it initiated an economic blockade. Then, on the night of 24 April, it launched an effort to rescue the hostages through a clandestine military operation. It ended in utter disaster: a key helicopter broke down, security was compromised when an Iranian bus passed by the landing site, and a transport plane collided with a helicopter, creating a huge explosion and killing eight American servicemen. Taken at face value, the rescue operation would seem to have been a desperate and hare-brained scheme that would have resulted in the almost certain death of the hostages. It was suspected in Iran, however, that the rescue attempt was actually intended to be coordinated with a coup attempt by royalist and pro-American elements in the Iranian military and, at a minimum, must have had support from elements within the Iranian air force. In that case, it might have made more sense, but poor planning and execution doomed it to failure. The fiasco was a gift to Khomeini; in the atmosphere of suspicion it created, his forces were able to carry out a much more thorough purge of the military and government bureaucracies and build up their own security apparatus. For the United States, about the only option left was to wait until the political climate in Iran changed.

The hostage crisis was not the only political setback for Bani Sadr. He did no better than Bazargan at asserting control over the revolutionary committees, tribunals, militias, and foundations, which remained either forces unto themselves or in the hands of clerical stalwarts like Beheshti and Mahdavi Kani. Significantly, his nominee to be commander of the Revolutionary Guards, one of the few appointments he, as commander-in-chief of the military, could make unilaterally, lasted barely a month before being replaced by a man under the influence of the IRP. The national media came under the control of Mohammad Khoeniha, the clerical leader of the students at the American Embassy, who used his position to continue the selective leak of documents from the embassy to discredit political opponents of the IRP.

As had happened with Bazargan, Bani Sadr's efforts to co-opt some of these rivals by cooperating with them or incorporating them into his government backfired, sometimes disastrously. One of his worst mistakes was calling on Khalkhali to head a crackdown on drug trafficking. Khalkhali and his henchmen quickly went far beyond that mandate to launch another gruesome wave of executions, with hundreds of victims ranging from former government officials to prostitutes and petty criminals to political opponents. After Khomeini complained on 18 April about Western influence in higher education, Hezbollah and other gangs attacked universities and colleges throughout the country. Bani Sadr, in an apparent attempt to control this movement, joined in the occupation of the University of Tehran on 22 April. He succeeded only in discrediting himself and helping bring about the "cultural revolution" that closed the country's universities for two years. Throughout June and July, the purges of government bureaucracies and the military continued, despite Bani Sadr's efforts to halt them.

Things only got worse for Bani Sadr after the Majles elections. Candidates affiliated with him won just a few seats, and several potential allies were either barred from running, disqualified after being elected, or too afraid to actually come to Tehran and sit in the Majles. Even Khomeini's older brother suggested that the elections had been rigged, but Khomeini himself declared them fair and approved the results. The new Majles convened on 28 May and, after taking its time getting organized, elected a leading member of the IRP, Hashemi Rafsanjani, as its speaker on 20 July.

The next step should have been for the Majles to approve Bani Sadr's choice for prime minister. Instead, it rejected the candidates he proposed and forced him to accept Mohammad-Ali Rajai, a man he detested, for the office. It was an outrageous and humiliating affront to Bani Sadr, but one that speaks volumes about the nature of the IRP. Rajai came from a poor family in Qazvin and can best be described as a career thug who could be trusted to do whatever dirty work his masters in the IRP desired. After the revolution, he had made a name for himself by using his band of armed supporters to loot institutions like the former American School in Tehran and distribute the largesse to the urban poor. That and his feeble credentials as a former high school teacher enabled him to worm his way up to be minister of education, where he distinguished himself by such policies as making sure boys and girls were kept separate in the educational system, revising the curriculum to remove "un-Islamic" elements that might impart even a vague awareness of the rest of the world, and dismissing some 20,000 teachers. He was a perfect symbol of the power base on which the IRP rested, the methods it used, and the upward mobility and material rewards it offered in return for the support of some of the basest elements in society. Bani Sadr and Rajai fought over virtually every issue and could never even agree on the appointment of ministers to a cabinet.

By fall, with the IRP clearly in control of the Majles and the prime minister's office, the American hostages had lost their value to their captors and were becoming a liability. After the abortive rescue effort, they were scattered throughout the country under sometimes appalling conditions, which made them difficult to use for propaganda anymore. The possibility that one might die or be killed raised the risk of military retaliation. The death of Mohammad-Reza Shah in Cairo on 27 July made demands for his extradition or trial irrelevant. The Iranians had sensed and taken full advantage of weakness in Carter, but they were much less eager for a confrontation with his likely successor, Ronald Reagan. The outbreak of the war with Iraq (discussed later) would provide another incentive for ending the crisis. Most important, as the key actors behind their capture acknowledged, every conceivable political benefit of holding them had been extracted, and the IRP was ready in September 1980 to start serious haggling over the price for their release.

On 12 September, Khomeini announced four conditions for the release of the hostages, all extremely modest in contrast to prior demands: return of the shah's wealth to Iran, cancellation of American financial claims on Iran, release of frozen Iranian assets, and a pledge of nonintervention in Iranian affairs. With Algeria acting as intermediary, negotiations for the release of the hostages began; Bani Sadr was essentially out of the loop, as Rajai and his minister of state, Behzad Nabavi, were now in charge. The main obstacle to a speedy resolution seems to have been the absolute contempt in which hardcore elements in the IRP held Jimmy Carter and their desire to hold out until they could savor his defeat in the American elections. Along with some politicians who also wanted to make things difficult for Rajai and Nabavi, they managed to drag out the process, even though this sharply reduced their leverage in the negotiations. It took until 19 January 1981 before the Algiers Agreement for the release of the hostages was accepted. It was a complicated arrangement, but essentially the hostages would be released in return for the usual diplomatic chatter about the United States not interfering in Iran's internal affairs. Beyond that the United States would release the frozen Iranian assets—but only after withholding some $7.7 billion to cover various American and international claims against Iran, so that Iran actually got only about $2.3 billion back. In a final slap at the unfortunate Carter, the release of the hostages was delayed until the very moment of Reagan's inauguration on 20 January 1981.

The hostage crisis may have succeeded in its purpose insofar as it provided cover for the establishment of an IRP-dominated regime and stole the anti-imperialist thunder from its leftist opponents, but in other ways it was highly counterproductive for Iran. However much temporarily rubbing the American nose in the dirt may have delighted some people, it had not done much to inspire Islamic revolution elsewhere. To the contrary, Iran was becoming increasingly isolated in world affairs, and many Muslims were shocked by the violent and irresponsible nature of the new government. At the same time, the crisis virtually assured the election of Ronald Reagan and worked wonders in terms of reawakening an American willingness to assert its power in pursuit of its interests. It both hardened Iranian dislike for the United States and made it very difficult for any American administration to sell any rapprochement with Iran to the American public. In the end, Iran had very little to show for its efforts beyond retrieving a small fraction of its own money. Twenty years later, memory of this incident remains a significant factor in limiting relations between the two countries.

THE IRAN-IRAQ WAR AND THE FALL OF BANI SADR

On 22 September 1980, in a well-planned but poorly executed attack, Iraqi forces bombed Iranian airfields and invaded Iran at several points along its sparsely defended border, from Kurdistan in the north to Khuzistan in the south. This was the opening salvo in a bitter war that would last for almost eight years and that would claim hundreds of thousands of lives and cost tens of billions of dollars.

Ostensibly, the war was over Iraqi claims that Iran had violated some provisions of the 1975 Algiers Accord, which had recognized the *thalweg* (main navigation channel) of the Shatt al-Arab waterway as the border between the two countries. Iraq had resented this agreement, which it had accepted as the price for getting Mohammad-Reza Shah to end his support for Kurdish rebels in Iraq, and started clamoring for its revision shortly after the revolution (October 1979). On 17 September, Saddam Hussein, the Iraqi president, had declared the agreement abrogated in view of continued Iranian interference in Iraqi affairs. The implication that the war was an international dispute involving demarcation of borders, however, gives it an aura of legitimacy it hardly deserves. The boundary question was at best camouflage for other, much deeper, problems. In a sense the conflict was but one more expression of the complex relationship between Mesopotamia and the Iranian highlands that can be traced back to antiquity, but this too tends only to dignify a wasteful war that was fought and prolonged primarily because of fear, ideology, emotion, and crass political opportunism on both sides, as well as the cynical, almost inexplicable, meddling of outside powers.

There were many common interests that might, perhaps should, have drawn revolutionary Iran and Iraq closer together: anti-imperialism; animosity toward Israel; the need to maximize petroleum profits; and the desire to be strong, progressive, important nations. Had the leftist opponents of the shah come to power, as many thought they would, such a scenario is conceivable, but no such harmony between a staunchly secular, nationalist, Baathist Iraq and an Islamic Iran was likely. Throughout 1980, tensions rose with numerous border clashes between Iraq and Iran and a barrage of charges and countercharges in the propaganda of the two countries as each gave aid and comfort to the other's enemies.

The duty to spread the Islamic Revolution throughout the world was enshrined in the preamble to the Iranian constitution, and Saddam Hussein was genuinely concerned that Iran would export its revolution by stirring up trouble among the Iraqi Shi'ite population. One of the top Shi'ite leaders in Iraq, Ayatollah Mohammad-Baqer Sadr, was closely associated with Khomeini and had pointedly congratulated him on the success of the revolution. After attempts to assassinate Tariq Aziz and other Baathist officials in Iraq in April 1980, Saddam retaliated by expelling thousands of Iranian residents, rounding up and killing a large number of Shi'ite militants, and executing Sadr. At the same time, the disturbances among the Arab minority in Iran, concentrated in Khuzistan with its vast oil resources, and their fierce repression raised the prospect that the province was ripe for "liberation" and reunion with the greater Arab motherland. Finally, there had long been friction between the civilian and military wings of the Baath Party, and Saddam Hussein liked to keep the army, the most likely source of any successful challenge to his rule, as busy as possible with other matters. As a target of opportunity, Iran seemed particularly vulnerable, with its military ties to the . United States destroyed, its increasing international isolation because of the hostage crisis and the excesses of the revolutionary terror campaign, its army purged and under suspicion, and signs of internal discord appearing.

If, however, the Iraqis thought that Iran would crumble or that they could achieve some minor but quick and cheap victory, they badly miscalculated. In the first days of the war, Iraqi forces captured several Iranian cities and brought others under siege or artillery barrage, but the Iranian navy and air force struck back at targets in Iraq with surprising success. When the UN Security Council called for a cease-fire on 28 September, the Iraqis, recognizing they were in for more of a fight than they had anticipated, indicated a willingness to consider it, but Iran flatly rejected it. Neither the Khuzistani Arabs nor the Kurds showed any indication of wanting to help the Iraqis; volunteers from all over the country rushed to help on the front; and the purge of the Iranian military was halted. On 13 October, Khomeini confirmed Bani Sadr as head of the Supreme Defense Council. Saddam Hussein stepped up propaganda for the war, describing it as another Qadesiyya, as a liberation of Arab territory that would be a first step toward reclaiming Palestine, and as a battle on behalf of Saudi Arabia, Kuwait, and the other Gulf states against Iranian adventurism. His forces enjoyed a few more victories, notably the capture of Khorramshahr, and occupied roughly 10,000 square miles of Iranian territory, but at a very heavy cost. They failed, however, to take other strategic targets such as Susangerd and Dezful during campaigns at the end of November. By January, the Iranians were able to mount a counteroffensive in Khuzistan, but it did not achieve much. With the onset of winter and the rainy season, the war had essentially reached a stalemate.

The panic among the Iranian leadership during the early days of the war had produced some rare moments of political cooperation, but they did not last long. The great fear of the IRP was that Bani Sadr might be able to parlay some success in the war or revival of the professional army into a vehicle for breaking its hold on the revolution. As soon as it became clear that Iranian defenses would not collapse and that the Iraqis could be stopped, feuding between Bani Sadr and Rajai resumed. Bani Sadr did in fact attempt to cultivate an image of himself as an energetic and dedicated wartime leader and to forge a coalition of anti-IRP forces. In October, he urged Khomeini to dismiss Rajai and his entire cabinet on the grounds that they were undermining the war effort. He spent long periods of time touring the fronts; he helped plan the (unsuccessful) January 1981 counteroffensive; he derided the lack of expertise and the interference of Rajai and the clerics in military affairs; he charged officials of the IRP (notably Beheshti, Rafsanjani, Khamenei, and Nabavi) with corruption, especially in transactions for arms purchases; he criticized the deal that had been struck for the release of the American hostages as far inferior to what he could have obtained earlier and implied that it amounted to "high treason"; he made speeches and sponsored newspaper articles reviving the charges that the IRP was despotic and repressive; he accused the judiciary and prison authorities of using torture. For its part, the IRP fought right back, suggesting that it was Bani Sadr who was militarily incompetent and that the Revolutionary Guards, not the regular army under Bani Sadr, were really carrying the brunt of the war effort; claiming that Bani Sadr was giving away state secrets in his speeches; temporarily arresting his former colleague Qotbzadeh a day after he made comments critical of the IRP on television; cracking down on what was left of the National Front; unleashing the militias to disrupt opposition rallies and to pillage the offices of critical newspapers; and accusing the Bani Sadr supporters of plotting against Khomeini himself. Both sides sought to cultivate Khomeini's support; he issued several statements trying to resolve the quarrels and on 4 February implored the politicians to stop fighting "like scorpions."

After the convening of a reconciliation meeting sponsored by Khomeini in March, the IRP began to turn the full force of its control of the judiciary, the militias, the media, and the Majles against Bani Sadr. It launched an investigation of Bani Sadr's handling of a demonstration on the University of Tehran campus and implied that he might face charges as a result of having made "inflammatory remarks" in contravention of the March reconciliation meeting. It restricted his access to radio and television and banned newspapers that supported him. Its most effective tactic was having the Majles pass laws stripping Bani Sadr of his constitutional powers and then labeling him a tyrant for refusing to accept them. This had the desired effect on Khomeini: On 27 May he (of all people!) warned Bani Sadr against disobeying the Majles and instituting a "cult of personality." On 10 June, he removed Bani Sadr as military commander. Bani Sadr apparently believed that either the army or the populace would come to his support. Instead, the army reaffirmed its intention to stay out of politics. The Mojahedin and the National Front attempted to stage demonstrations in favor of Bani Sadr but were routed by Hezbollah gangs. Around 12 June, Bani Sadr went into hiding, and on 16 June the Majles decided to begin impeachment proceedings. On 21 June, the Majles declared Bani Sadr incompetent to govern and ordered his arrest; Khomeini formally removed him from office the next day. Despite an intense hunt for him, Bani Sadr managed to escape and arrived in Paris on 29 July, accompanied by the leader of the Mojahedin, Masoud Rajavi.

THE IRP IN POWER

For several months after the fall of Bani Sadr, Iranians seemed to be fighting each other more than the Iraqis who had invaded their country. Faced with the inexorable rise to power of the IRP and the increasing number of arrests and executions of their supporters, the Bani Sadr and Rajavi forces put together a National Council of Resistance and essentially called on their supporters to wage war against the IRP. On 28 June, the IRP had convened a top secret meeting of party leaders to decide on a replacement for Bani Sadr and other matters of political strategy. While it was under way, a bomb blast in an adjoining building brought down the roof of the conference hall, killing at least 72 IRP officials, including several members of the Majles, ministers of the cabinet, and the party's secretary and guiding light, Ayatollah Beheshti. The bombing was immediately blamed on the Mojahedin, although many suspicions have been raised by the curious coincidence that Rafsanjani and Rajai left the building minutes before the explosion and several members opposed to Beheshti's policies had stayed away.

Although its leadership had been decimated, the IRP attempted to regroup, with Ayatollah Mousavi Ardabili taking over Beheshti's duties as chief of the judiciary and Ayatollah Bahonar becoming head of the party. On 9 July, it named Rajai as its candidate for the presidency; he was elected on 26 July, with the IRP doing everything possible, including having the voting age lowered and getting some candidates to withdraw, to ensure that he received a larger vote than Bani Sadr had. Rajai named Bahonar as his prime minister. Then, on 30 August, another bomb explosion, this time at a meeting of the National Security Council in the prime minister's office, killed Rajai, Bahonar, and the head of the national police, Houshang Dastjerdi. A few days later the prosecutor general, Ali Qoddousi, was killed by yet another bomb.

The Majles immediately named Ayatollah Mahdavi Kani as Bahonar's replacement, prompting Khomeini to observe that the speed of the decision showed that Iran was "the most stable country in the world." The IRP selected Hojjatoleslam Ali Khamenei as its candidate for president, the first cleric allowed to seek the office. He was duly elected on 5 October and sworn in on 13 October. Only two days later, Mahdavi Kani resigned as prime minister and was subsequently removed as head of the Ministry of the Interior. He was the head of a non-IRP clerical faction, the Combatant Clergy of Tehran, which was opposed to Khamenei on many issues, and he had briefly considered running against Khamenei for the presidency. Khamenei nominated Ali Akbar Velayati as his successor, but the Majles rejected him; they finally agreed on Mir Hosayn Mousavi at the end of October. With Khamenei as president, Mousavi as prime minister, and Rafsanjani as speaker of the Majles, a semblance of stability was restored to the IRP-dominated government.

Whether or not the Mojahedin were responsible for the July and August bombings, there is no doubt they had stepped up attacks on IRP officials, Revolutionary Guards, and government offices in Iran and abroad. In September, they initiated what amounted to armed insurgency in the streets of Tehran and other cities, apparently hoping to spark another revolution. They were crushed, and the government retaliated by arresting and executing suspected Mojahedin members as well as instituting effective new security measures. Already by 24 August, the minister of justice had boasted that over 700 people had been executed in two months, and that number would soon swell into the thousands. According to press reports in mid-September, executions averaged one hundred per day. On 8 February 1982, government forces succeeded in raiding a house where the top Mojahedin leaders in Iran were staying; among those killed were Rajavi's wife and Mousa Khiabani, the tactical commander. The Mojahedin were able to keep up isolated street battles and to carry out assassinations for several years, but their effort to overthrow the IRP-had clearly failed.

Although the Mojahedin-e Khalq represented the most determined and dangerous threat to the government, the IRP did not confine its efforts at eliminating rivals to them alone. On 8 April, Sadeq Qotbzadeh was arrested for a second time and charged, along with almost 200 other alleged conspirators, with plotting to kill Khomeini and overthrow the government. Some seventy military officers accused of involvement were executed on 16 August. Qotbzadeh was given a televised hearing in order to extract a public confession; he was then tried secretly and executed on 15 September.

This incident was also used as part of an orchestrated campaign of vengeance against one of Khomeini's main clerical rivals, Ayatollah Shariatmadari. Qotbzadeh had supposedly told Shariatmadari about the plot, and the latter was charged with not informing the government about it. Meanwhile, Mohammad Khoeniha produced routine communiqués from the American Embassy and other documents (largely falsified or taken out of context) that supposedly proved that Shariatmadari had been in collusion with the shah and the United States. The IRP would hardly have wanted to set an example by executing a high-ranking member of the clergy, but there were other ways of dealing with the problem Shariatmadari posed for the regime. His religious school in Qom was raided, and, on 20 April, various religious authorities declared him unfit to be a Grand Ayatollah. This was a most unusual, if not absolutely unprecedented, action, but one in keeping with Khomeini's call to "knock off the turbans" of apolitical clerics and which was soon applied to many other lower ranking clerics. The man who had interceded to help save Khomeini from execution in the shah's prison, but who now had the temerity to criticize a constitution giving Khomeini dictatorial power, was thus repaid by being placed under house arrest and, later, by being denied proper medical treatment, which was probably responsible for hastening his death in 1985.

Finally, the IRP turned on the Tudeh, once one of the strongest and most credible communist parties in the entire Middle East. Since the beginning of 1979, under the leadership of Nouraddin Kianouri (and presumably following instructions from Moscow to the letter), the Tudeh had scarcely been able to contain its enthusiasm for Khomeini and gushed praise of him at every opportunity. Even after Revolutionary Guards had attacked its party headquarters, banned its newspaper, and arrested members of its central committee, the Tudeh continued to support the clerical government. It participated in the vote for the constitution, provided intelligence on the activities of other leftist groups, attacked Bani Sadr as a mentally ill traitor, and encouraged the crackdown on the Mojahedin. The IRP welcomed the support of the Tudeh in its confrontations with other groups, but it never trusted the party and by 1983 felt it no longer served any useful purpose. Kianouri was arrested on espionage charges in February. The party was outlawed in May and its members arrested en masse, with several of the leaders being executed.

THE "IMPOSED WAR"

Iraq had failed to take any advantage of the political turmoil in Iran. In January 1981, the Revolutionary Guards were augmented by a militia called the Vahid-e Basij-e Mostazafan as the first step in creating what Khomeini called an "Army of Twenty Million" men and women to assure the victory of the Islamic Republic. These paramilitary groups began to take the lead in pressing the war, with the purged and demoralized regular army reduced to something of a directing and support role. Although poorly trained and equipped, the Basij, mostly young boys and older men who volunteered for the effort, had their religious passions stirred up by the clergy, who exhorted them to participate in campaigns given religiously symbolic code-names such as the Road to Jerusalem (Tariq-e Qods) or Certain Victory (Fath-e Mobin). They were also assured that the government would provide for them and their families through the Martyrs Foundation should they be killed or wounded. Willing to engage in human wave assaults or to clear mine fields by walking through them, they were repeatedly able to surprise, confuse, and overwhelm the Iraqi forces.

In September 1981, the Iranians broke the siege of Abadan and drove Iraqi forces back across the Karun River. In March 1982, just before the New Year holiday, the Revolutionary Guards and Basij launched a surprise attack on Iraqi positions near Dezful and Shush, inflicting heavy casualties and forcing the Iraqis back almost to the border. Iraq immediately began signaling that it was ready to withdraw its troops and end the conflict; Iran responded with a new offensive in April and May that pushed the Iraqis back even further. By 24 May, Iranian forces had recaptured Khorramshahr, and riots began to break out in Shi'ite cities in Iraq. The Iraqis appeared defeated, and various Arab states and Organization of the Islamic Conference appealed for the fighting to stop. On 9 June, the Iraqi Revolutionary Command Council indicated that it was willing to accept a cease-fire; on 20 June Saddam Hussein confirmed that Iraqi forces were willing to withdraw from Iranian territory by the end of the month.

There was a very different mood in Iran. The clerics had now taken full control of the war effort as well as the government, and they had many incentives not only to welcome the war but to do everything possible to prolong it. The internal political crisis had passed, and the economy was beginning to improve thanks to increased oil revenues. From his stay in Iraq, Khomeini had developed utter disdain for the Baathists and an intense personal hatred of Saddam Hussein. He did not see them as having provided him with sanctuary in exile but as willing collaborators of the shah in confining and oppressing him. Iraq had clearly proclaimed its hostility toward the Iranian revolution, first by cooperating with monarchists like Bakhtiar and General Oveissi, then by launching its invasion, and finally by its sympathy for the Mojahedin. It was another of the satanic forces in the world and had to be resisted at all costs. Iran even went so far as to organize a kind of puppet government in exile, the Supreme Council of the Islamic Revolution of Iraq, headed by a top Iraqi Shi'ite leader living in Iran.

Moreover, Khomeini was well aware of the larger implications their possible triumph in the war would have; control over Iraq had historically always been a critical element in making Iran a great power. Not only might it bring the great Shi'ite shrines under Iranian authority, it would vastly increase Iranian prestige and influence throughout the region and the world. Khomeini openly speculated that if Iraq could be joined to Iran, the other Gulf countries would align themselves accordingly. He had already taken steps to have Khoeniha and the Hajj Organization use the Muslim pilgrimage to Mecca as a vehicle for Iranian propaganda and to increase efforts to stir up Shi'ite populations in Kuwait, Bahrain, and Lebanon. Far from wanting to halt the war, Khomeini saw the spring victories as a vehicle to propel the Islamic Revolution abroad and to continue to stifle dissent at home.

Although some officials urged caution, Khomeini's views prevailed at a meeting of the Iranian Supreme Defense Council in June, which decided to carry the war into Iraq and to set a very high price for any cease-fire, including huge reparations for war damage and the "punishment" (i.e., removal) of Saddam Hussein. On 12 July, the United Nations Security Council, fearing an escalation of the war, passed Resolution 514, calling for a cease-fire and withdrawal of forces to the international boundaries. The Iranian reply came the next day when it launched its Ramazan-e Mobarak campaign, pushing into Iraq and threatening the city of Basra. The fighting was very intense and involved large numbers of troops on both sides; after two weeks, however, the Iraqis blunted the offensive and gained back all but a small portion of the territory the Iranians had overrun. This time it was the Iranians who underestimated their adversary. The Iraqis had learned from earlier mistakes, and the political leaders placed more trust in the judgment of their military leaders. They were also receiving American satellite intelligence about Iranian troop movements from Saudi Arabia and supplies of advanced weaponry from France. Saddam Hussein's position as head of state remained secure, and the Iraqi Shi'ites appeared no more interested in helping the Iranians than the Khuzistani Arabs had been willing to help the Iraqis. When the Iranians resorted to shelling Basra, the Iraqis replied by attacking their shipping and oil installations.

Nervous about the expansion of the war, Saudi Arabia proposed a peace plan at the Arab League meeting in Fez in September 1982 which included a cease-fire and payment of $70 billion in reparations to Iran, which the Gulf Arab states would finance. Saddam Hussein announced his support for the plan, but Iran rejected it. By doing so, it missed an opportunity to settle the war on very advantageous terms, just as it squandered the opportunity for a better deal in resolving the earlier hostage crisis. On 1 October, it began another campaign, aimed this time at Baghdad itself. This also failed after resulting in very heavy casualties. The indecisive pattern of offensives and counteroffensives continued for the better part of a year. They also seemed to get larger and bloodier, especially in February 1984, with an assault on the Majnoon Islands and an effort to take Qurna and cut the Baghdad-Basra highway. The Iranians threw about 300,000 troops into the campaign, and the Iraqis had to resort to the use of poison gas to drive them back.

Faced with relentless pressure from the Iranians on the ground, the Iraqis decided to step up attacks on oil installations and shipping to Iran. This "tanker war" had several advantages. By this point, the Iranian air force was virtually grounded because of a lack of spare parts, so there was minimal threat of retaliation. The Iraqi air force was still in good shape and had acquired Exocet missiles from France. Ships were much easier to hit than heavily defended installations such as the loading station at Kharg Island. Moreover, Iraqi oil went by pipeline to neutral ports, so it did not have to worry about protecting its own shipments. If Iran did attack ships from Kuwait or Saudi Arabia or other countries carrying Iraqi oil or supplies to or from neutral ports, it risked further alienating those countries and internationalizing the war (as indeed it eventually did).

One of the reasons the Iraqis had concentrated their air force on Iranian shipping was that the two sides had agreed to a United Nations–brokered agreement not to attack major population centers. This accord broke down in March 1985 as the "war of the cities" began. Iraqi aircraft began bombing Tehran and cities all over Iran. The purpose, as an Iraqi general frankly admitted, was to take the war to the Iranian people in the hope that they would rebel and demand an end to the fighting. This was not without risks, however, as Iranian artillery resumed shelling Basra, and Iran had acquired surface-to-surface missiles, which it fired at Iraqi cities. A major Iranian offensive that same month was repulsed. By this point the strains of the conflict were beginning to tell in Iran, and the issue of the war became entangled more and more in the politics of the Islamic Republic.

SOCIAL AND ECONOMIC DEBATES

The political history of the Islamic Republic during the period of the First Majles (1980–1984) was dominated by the struggles of the IRP to assert its dominance, to remove Bani Sadr from office, and to crush the leftist opposition. Although the IRP succeeded in eliminating all its rivals and tolerated only Bazargan's Freedom Movement as a token opposition party, it was itself composed of groups with quite different views on economic and social issues. Shi'ite clerics represent and derive authority from constituencies which recognize them, and the constituencies of the clerics in the government of the Islamic Republic ranged from the "barefooted" and "oppressed" lower-classes to the traditional bazaar merchants to workers and the professional middle classes. Inevitably, they would have disagreements on the role of the state in the economy, private property, and the nature and enforcement of "Islamic" values. Somewhat muted at first, these became much more noticeable as efforts were made to translate the platitudes and promises of revolutionary rhetoric into concrete policies. By the end of the Second Majles (1984–1988), and under the strains of the war with Iraq, they had hardened into factional politics and taken on an institutional dimension. It is not possible in the space available here to discuss this process in detail, but a general overview of some of its dynamics may be suggested.

In terms of the economy, the revolutionary era had begun with a vast expansion of the public sector. The Revolutionary Council had led the way with nationalization of industries, banks, and other businesses. At the same time, the establishment of the various charitable foundations such as the Bonyad-e Mostazafan (Foundation for the Oppressed) created a kind of informal welfare state within a state. A system of rationing and subsidies for goods in short supply, price controls, redistribution of confiscated property, and direct financial rewards all helped sustain the loyalty of the lower classes to the revolution. There were also many local and spontaneous efforts by workers to take control of factories and by villagers to appropriate land.

There was thus an expectation that the Islamic Republic would continue to disperse money and property to the "oppressed," and a substantial group of clerics strongly supported the idea of an Islamic socialism that entailed obliteration of class distinctions, an egalitarian redistribution of wealth, and state control over vast areas of the economy. However, respect for private property was deeply entrenched in traditional Islamic law, and many clerics, major landowners themselves, had no desire to see this disrupted. They were typically aligned with the bazaar merchants, who favored a freer, largely private economy and did not like government interventions to restrict prices in the name of helping the poor or to limit imports in order to discourage dependence on foreign countries. This difference in ideological orientation was amplified because of the way the new Iranian constitution had created multiple centers of power and authority: The economic "radicals" were strong in the Majles, but the conservatives were strong in the Council of Guardians. Thus in 1982, the Majles passed a bill to nationalize all foreign trade, but it was promptly vetoed by the Council of Guardians as unconstitutional and contrary to Islam. The same year, the Majles passed a land reform bill, only to have it rejected by the Council of Guardians in January 1983. After 1984, however, economic difficulties mounted rapidly. In addition to the costs of the war itself, the economy suffered from slumping oil prices, material shortages, inflation, increasingly expensive social programs, excessive government spending, low rates of investment and production, and the difficulties of raising new taxes. The over-riding concern was not to threaten the stability of the social welfare net that supported the lower-class minions of the regime; the question was whether that could be done by maintaining extensive etatist policies or whether to try to increase overall prosperity by returning to a largely privatized economy. As the economic crisis worsened, it forced a shift in the debate toward the side of the economic realists and pragmatists, but it was extremely difficult to reach consensus on effective policies.

On social issues, the political alignment was somewhat different. Many, but certainly not all, economic radicals wanted to present a "progressive" type of Islam and tended to argue for reinterpretations of traditional practices and less strict enforcement of religious conformity. The conservative clergy and bazaar elements were generally much more inclined to support established values and interpretations. Whereas the popular militias and organizations tended to favor the "radicals" on economic issues, they were more inclined to the conservative clergy and bazaar elements on issues of enforcing Islamic values in society. This was the basis for the "cultural revolution" of 1980–1982, when a wholesale effort was made to Islamize society by closing universities, putting more Islamic content in the school curriculum, replacing existing civil law with law based on Islamic jurisprudence, creating a "Bureau for Combating Corruption" to stamp out petty vices and enforce Islamic mores, and so on. There was a brief relaxation of this with Khomeini's "December Decree" in 1982, which promised a "judicial revolution to protect the dignity and honor of individuals." The universities were gradually reopened, it was made easier to travel abroad, Iranians who had fled the country were invited to return home, and so on. However, by 1984, the drive for ridding the country of foreign cultural influences was back at work, and the vigilante and anti-vice squads as active as ever. To a degree, debates over these issues were coming to be more between groups in and out of government than within the governing party itself.

Undoubtedly the most contentious aspect of the social debate pertained to the status of women. Women's groups had already been alarmed in March 1980 by moves to do away with the Family Protection Law, to segregate women in schools, and to require dress in the workplace according to "Islamic standards." Sensitive to public opinion at a critical moment in the revolution, Khomeini had made a tactical retreat in the face of protest demonstrations by women. In 1981, however, the question was revived with the passage of an Islamic Dress Law, which required the use of strict *hejab* (veiling), by women at work and in public. It was vigorously enforced by the vigilante and militia groups. This of course was but one of many subtle and not so subtle pressures brought to bear on women in order to limit their role in public life and enforce a traditional patriarchal system. Other problems faced by women in the new social order included clerical support for polygamy, the practice of temporary marriage (*mota* or *sigheh*), child marriage, arranged marriage, easy divorce for men and difficult divorce for women, and so on. The state even intervened in matters of women's reproductive rights, first by limiting birth control in order to increase the population for the struggle against Iraq and "imperialism," and then, faced with the consequences of a spiraling population, making birth control almost a mandatory duty. While conservatives have frequently maintained that women should be barred from judgeships and certain public offices, no one has challenged the right to vote guaranteed women under the republican constitution. As efforts to coerce women into conforming with conservative Islamic values increased, women began exercising that right with considerable effect.

The interplay of these and other forces is not always easy to detect or to follow, but the combination of the war, deterioration of the economy, and rising social discontent certainly increased tensions within the IRP. After bitter debates over budgets and the role of the Council of Guardians, the 1984 Majles elections somewhat increased the representation of the economic radicals and definitely brought the economic debates to the fore. There was a move to replace Mousavi as prime minister with one of the chief radicals, Khoeniha, but Khomeini intervened to keep Mousavi in office, apparently to prevent an appearance of disunity. In the 1985 presidential elections, Bazargan attempted to force the IRP to deal with the problems caused by the war but was barred from running by the Council of Guardians. Khamenei was reelected president but by a much smaller vote than previously. He again moved to remove Mousavi, but Khomeini continued to support the latter. In June 1986, Rafsanjani openly acknowledged that two "powerful factions" had developed within the IRP, and these were related to differences between pragmatists and idealists over continuing the war, moving toward a less confrontational position in world affairs, and economic policies. On 2 June 1987, the IRP was formally dissolved.

THE END OF THE WAR

In February 1986, Iran staged another major offensive that succeeded in crossing the Shatt-al-Arab waterway and capturing the Faw peninsula. In his New Year's speech, Khomeini rashly proclaimed that the "Year of Victory" was at hand. He and Mohsen Rezai, commander of the Revolutionary Guards, called for a full mobilization and effort to win the war. Any plans for celebration, however, were definitely premature. First of all, Iraq used its superior air power to step up attacks on Iranian oil installations, shipping, and economic infrastructure. This had the effect of reducing both the amount of oil for export and the refining capacity to meet domestic needs. At one point, Iran actually had to import refined petroleum and introduce rationing of gasoline. Coupled with a sharp drop in oil prices, increasing public debt, inflation, and shortages of imported goods, the economic effect of the war was becoming severe and starting to have its impact on the political climate.

Then, in November 1986, news about secret arms deals between Iranian and American officials, with Israelis as intermediaries, became public. Khomeini and Rafsanjani were able to hide their embarrassment behind propaganda that this represented a victory for Iran since its adversary had come crawling back trying "to establish relations and making apologies." For the Reagan administration, "Irangate" was an unmitigated disaster. By offering arms for the release of hostages, it had made a mockery of its publicly stated policy of not dealing with terrorists (and only encouraged the taking of still more hostages to replace those who were released). It shook the faith of friendly Arab countries in American willingness to stand by them and help contain the Iranian revolution. It made the United States a laughingstock in the eyes of allies it had been pressuring not to supply weapons to Iran. In the long run, however, this was also bad news for Iran since the only way for American policy to redeem itself in public opinion was by taking a much tougher stance against Iran. Iran's installation of Silkworm missiles capable of attacking American warships in the Straits of Hormuz and its mining of the Persian Gulf to inflict damage on ships carrying goods for Iraq provided a perfect pretext for such action. This played directly into Saddam Hussein's plans for bringing the war to an end by internationalizing it.

In addition to increasing its diplomatic and economic pressure on Iran, the United States agreed on 7 March 1987 to protect Kuwaiti tankers against Iranian attack by reflagging and escorting them. At the same time, Saudi Arabia became much more hostile toward Iran because of political demonstrations in Mecca it stirred up and which turned violent during the Muslim pilgrimage in July 1987. For all practical purposes, an Iraq–Kuwait–Saudi Arabia–United States alliance against Iran had come into being. Many other countries also thought it was time for Iran to end its intransigence and bring the war to a close. On 20 July 1987, with strong support from both the United States and the Soviet Union, the UN Security Council passed Resolution 598 calling for a cease-fire. It was accepted by Iraq but received no response from Iran. Meanwhile, the United States and other countries sent minesweepers and other military vessels to the Persian Gulf. On 21 September, American forces destroyed an Iranian ship said to have been laying mines. On 8 October, they destroyed three Iranian patrol boats near Farsi Island. On 19 October, they destroyed two Iranian oil platforms in retaliation for a Silkworm attack on an American-flagged supertanker in Kuwaiti waters. In April 1988, they attacked Iranian oil rigs, frigates, and a missile boat. Then, on 3 July, the American cruiser *Vincennes*, shortly after having sunk two Iranian speedboats that had been used to fire on American helicopters, mistakenly shot down a civilian Iranian airliner on a routine flight from Bandar Abbas to Dubai, killing 290 people.

In Iran, pressures to end the war were building rapidly. On 3 June, not long after Iraq had retaken Faw and the Majnoon Islands, Khomeini transferred command of the armed forces from Khamenei to Rafsanjani. Rafsanjani was emerging as the leader of a pragmatist faction that recognized that the war was no longer sustainable. The economy was on the verge of collapse and might require drastic cuts in the social benefits on which the regime's core constituency depended; enthusiasm for the war had dissipated; Iran's military equipment was being depleted while Iraq was freshly rearmed; the United States was now clearly determined Iraq should prevail and escalating its actions against Iran; and Iran risked having a settlement imposed on it if it continued to defy Security Council calls for a cease-fire. The downing of the airliner by the *Vincennes* was apparently the last straw: The Iranians thought there would be an international uproar over the incident; instead there was a generally apathetic dismissal of it as merely an accident of war. Nothing showed more starkly how isolated Iran had become in the international community. Backed by President Khamenei, the Assembly of Experts, leaders of the Majles, ministers, and military and economic advisors, Rafsanjani told Khomeini that there really was no choice but to agree to Resolution 598. Reluctantly, Khomeini agreed, informing the nation on 20 July that it was a decision "more deadly than poison" for him to accept but which was necessary "to save the revolution."

The actual implementation of the cease-fire, disentanglement of troops, and exchange of prisoners would take much longer to complete. However, the war was over, and with it an era of revolutionary zeal.

10

The Era of Reconstruction

In the period between his grudging acceptance of the cease-fire with Iraq in July 1988 and his death on 3 June 1989, the Imam Khomeini made or endorsed a number of proposals that would be of the most profound significance for the future development of the Islamic Republic of Iran. These set the stage for the ascension of the diumvirate of Khamenei as Faqih and Rafsanjani as president, followed by the commencement of the "era of reconstruction." Years later, however, the consequences of these decisions were still being felt, while many of the problems of the postwar era remained unresolved.

THE OUSTING OF MONTAZERI

As Khomeini's health was markedly deteriorating, one of the most pressing issues to be settled was the question of his successor as Faqih. Since the early years of the republic, it had been apparent that Ayatollah Hosayn-Ali Montazeri was in effect the heir apparent. His revolutionary credentials seemed solid: He was one of the circle of Khomeini's former students; he had been active in the 1963 protests; he had served as Khomeini's personal representative in Iran during a period of his exile; he had been arrested during the crackdown on the clergy in 1975; he was elected president of the Assembly of Experts when it was formed; he headed the Organization of Militant Clergy; he supported the export of the revolution to other countries and had agreed with the demand for the overthrow and trial of Saddam Hussein as a condition for ending the war with Iraq; he was extremely vocal in his support for the Palestinians and his denunciation of Zionism. He had also attained appropriately high religious status, being generally recognized in 1980 as a "Grand Ayatollah" (*ayatollah-e ozma*). He had been given the prestigious post of leader of the Friday prayers (*emam jomeh*) in Qom; his picture appeared alongside Khomeini's in public buildings; he received extensive television coverage and held frequent press interviews; and he often met with official foreign dignitaries visiting Iran.

In retrospect, however, it is clear that Montazeri also had a number of powerful adversaries who either distrusted or disliked him. As early as 1982–1983, the Assembly of Experts had met to consider the succession question, receiving a sealed copy of Khomeini's will (which they may or may not have read at that time). Significantly, the deliberations concluded without endorsing Montazeri and by merely adopting procedures to be followed in the event of Khomeini's death. The reasons for this are open to debate. Some may have concluded that Montazeri lacked the charisma and popular appeal necessary to serve as Faqih; others may have been alarmed by his association with the "radical" or idealistic wing of the revolution. Conservatives may have been particularly wary because of Montazeri's close friendship with the late Ayatollah Taleqani, well known for his leftist sympathies, and because of his involvement in a dispute over the publication of a controversial book on the martyrdom of Imam Hosayn which had led, according to the historian Ervand Abrahamian, to the murder of a conservative cleric in Isfahan. In any case, it was not until 1985 that the Assembly of Experts confirmed Montazeri; even then, the decision was not immediately made public but was leaked by one of Montazeri's supporters.

By the late 1980s, Montazeri had made numerous political enemies and was gradually falling into disfavor with Khomeini as well. Among other things, he was involved, directly or indirectly, in the revelations of the secret dealings among Iran, Israel, and the United States that produced the Irangate fiasco. It was Mehdi Hashemi, the brother of Montazeri's son-in-law and an agent of the organization run by Montazeri to support militant Islamicist groups abroad, who was thought to be responsible for leaking the embarrassing information about clandestine meetings between American, Israeli, and Iranian officials. In light of subsequent developments, it is not clear whether this was done primarily to stop the cooperation of the erstwhile enemies, to expose the hypocrisy of those involved, or both. In any case, it did not sit well with the politicians burned by the episode, including Khamenei, Rafsanjani, Mehdi Karroubi, and Velayati. Hashemi, whom Montazeri refused to denounce, and a number of others were eventually arrested on charges of "counter-revolutionary activities" and executed in 1987; this appears to be the main basis for charges that Montazeri was giving aid and comfort to enemies of the Islamic Republic. Montazeri was also quite critical of Mousavi, whose reappointment as prime minister Khomeini had gone out of his way to support, and he expressed his views in public as well as in private. He called for a frank and open assessment of the revolution's failures, he argued that those responsible for the fiasco in the war with Iraq should be held accountable (he himself seems to have favored a more aggressive approach and probably a continuation of the war), he protested directly to Khomeini the continued execution of political dissidents, and he no longer advocated the active export of revolution. Instead, he argued that Iran should simply serve as an example other countries would want to emulate, and that the best way to do that was by reducing state interference in the economy, lifting censorship and other barriers to free speech, and encouraging the expression of competing political ideas.

In February 1989, Khomeini began making not-so-veiled verbal attacks on Montazeri for "ineptitude." A special message that month to the clergy (*rouhaniyat*) made frequent allusions to Khomeini having, on the advice of others, mistakenly placed his confidence in people who did not deserve it. In it, Khomeini also derided the "pseudo-pious," those who wanted to remove the clergy from politics, those who favored "American Islam," and those who were inclined to the "liberals." He affirmed that he believed in traditional jurisprudence (*feqh*), but that matters previously decided could be reinterpreted in the light of time and place and considerations of politics, economics, and society. Indeed, Khomeini now argued that it was essential for an authoritative jurist (*mojtahed*) to be a "skillful manager" and to understand "the methodology of confronting the deceptions emanating from the existing world order," that is, economics, politics, and "the strengths and weaknesses of the capitalist and communist blocs." It subsequently became clear that these arguments were critical in discrediting Montazeri and smoothing the way for his replacement. On 27 March, Khomeini called a special meeting of the Assembly of Experts to discuss the matter, after which he sent a letter to Montazeri essentially accepting his resignation in advance. Montazeri immediately acquiesced, gave up his office, and returned to teaching at his religious school in Qom, where he was kept under virtual house arrest.

REVISION OF THE CONSTITUTION

Not long after Montazeri's forced resignation, on 25 April 1989, Khomeini directed President Khamenei to undertake a review and revision of the country's constitution. To this end, a special committee was established, with twenty members appointed by Khomeini himself and the remainder elected by the Majles. Khomeini indicated a number of problems the committee should address, the most crucial being the selection and authority of the Faqih and the distribution of power in the executive branch. The review committee did not complete its work until after Khomeini's death, but it seems to have been following the basic outline of ideas he had endorsed.

Aside from the now urgent matter of arrangements for Khomeini's succession, there were many reasons why a review of the constitution was needed. Complex and often ambiguous or contradictory in design, it had been extremely difficult to implement. It presupposed that the various branches of government would operate in harmony; in fact they were frequently at odds, with the president working against the prime minister, or the Council of Guardians vetoing legislation passed by the Majles. Khomeini had the prestige to intervene to break an impasse when necessary, but it was by no means certain that his successor would be able to do so. In an effort to deal with this problem, Khomeini had established an "Expediency Council" on 6 February 1988 to resolve differences between the Majles and the Council of Guardians, but it had not been very effective and had been criticized by Montazeri as unconstitutional. The committee solved this by adding Article 112 to the constitution. It confirmed the institutionalization of the Expediency Council, with members to be appointed by the Faqih. It was intended to serve as an advisory body for the Faqih, to formulate long-term policies for the government, and to arbitrate in cases where legislation passed by the Majles was rejected by the Council of Guardians.

There was also agreement that the original constitution had dispersed the power of the executive branch too widely. The rift between Bani Sadr and Rajai had shown from the start how easy it was for the president, prime minister, and Majles to come into conflict. Even under the best of circumstances, the prime minister, appointed by the president but confirmed by the Majles, was in the awkward position of trying to serve two masters. This had been a major factor in the ineffectiveness of the Mousavi ministry. The committee thus recommended that the office of prime minister be abolished; at the same time, the office of president was to be greatly strengthened. The president was recognized as second only to the Faqih in authority, and he was to have executive control of all matters except those directly related to the office of Faqih.

Among the numerous articles the committee either added or revised, the most important applied to the office of Faqih itself. The original constitution had specified that the representative of the Twelfth Imam (i.e., the supreme authority) would be "an honest, virtuous, well-informed, courageous, efficient administrator and religious jurist, enjoying the confidence of the majority of the people." It further allowed that if no one person who fit these qualifications could be found, a "leadership council" of three to five qualified candidates could exercise this authority. The revised constitution stipulated that there should be a single Faqih only, and that preference should be given to a candidate on the basis of "public support" or knowledge of "social and political issues" as well as Islamic jurisprudence. At the same time, the powers of the office of Faqih were spelled out more precisely. It has been argued that defining the Faqih's prerogatives was tantamount to limiting them, but they still left him in an extremely if not absolutely strong position. He would be supreme commander of the armed forces and could declare war or make peace; he was authorized to call for referenda; he controlled appointments to the Council of Guardians, the judiciary, the military and security forces, and the state radio and television networks; and he worked with the Expediency Council to set general policies and arbitrate differences between different branches of government. While the powers now assigned to the Faqih were not as far-ranging as those exercised by Khomeini, they still made him the true head of state, with effective control over all the ultimate levers of power and coercion.

The committee that drafted these reforms was dominated by two key political figures, President Khamenei and Speaker of the Majles Rafsanjani. Immediately after Khomeini's death, the Assembly of Experts, acting on the basis of the as yet unapproved revisions to the constitution, named Khamenei as the new Faqih on 5 June. Since Khamenei could not be both Faqih and president, the Council of Guardians authorized elections to be held earlier than planned, at the end of July. Rafsanjani, with only one token opponent, won overwhelmingly (15,537,394 to 650,000).

The constitutional amendments were also approved with the degree of unanimity that characterized most Iranian elections.

KHAMENEI AND THE OFFICE OF FAQIH

To all appearances, the revision of the constitution and arrangements for succession to Khomeini represented an elaborate deal between the two strongest politicians in the country for a division of power between them and the means to push through their agendas. In the interest of short-term tactical and political gains, however, they introduced new elements with potentially far-reaching implications which, in some respects, turned the early values of the Islamic Republic upside down.

The original idea of *velayat-e faqih* was that the most prestigious of the high-ranking Shi'ite clerics, one of the "sources of imitation" (*marja-e taqlid*), would become leader. The problem after Khomeini's death was that none of the surviving senior clerics had endorsed the concept of *velayat-e faqih*, and some had openly rejected it. When chosen by the Assembly of Experts, Khamenei's credentials as a religious scholar were very weak and far inferior to those of several other clerics—at the time of his appointment he was not even recognized as an ayatollah, although he was speedily granted this title in view of his sudden apotheosis to the most elevated office in the land. His real strengths were his long political career, his influence with the Revolutionary Guards and other militias and vigilante groups, and his hold over the affluent Bonyad-e Mostazafan (run by his brother-in-law Mohsen Rafiqdoust). With his selection, it became quite clear why Khomeini had suddenly insisted on the importance of political acumen rather than pure religious scholarship and why the new constitution emphasized the criteria of knowledge of "social and political issues" for appointment as Faqih. Khomeini had highlighted the distinction between clergy whose status is primarily based on knowledge of religious law and those who are distinguished by knowledge about socioeconomic and political issues, and he indicated that rule should be entrusted to the latter. This was an altogether different proposition from the premise of the doctrine of *velayat-e faqih* that supreme authority belonged to the most distinguished jurist.

Moreover, in addition to increasing the importance of political credentials for selection as Faqih, Khomeini had also taken extraordinary steps to confirm the authority of the office. In January 1988, he had suddenly declared that the authority of the Faqih was absolute and that the duty to preserve the Islamic Republic took precedence over all others. The state, in the person of the Faqih, could literally do whatever it felt was needed, even if this meant going against well-established religious law or the objections of senior jurists. The argument, rather absurdly, was that in order to "save" Islam, the Faqih had the authority to supercede it! It was tantamount to arguing that the state had Godlike infallibility, and the Faqih greater authority than the Prophets and Imams (at least one group critical of the theory quickly pointed out that this was terribly close to the grave sin of *shirk*, as it usurped the unique sovereignty of God).

The motivation for emphasizing this dogma was almost certainly political expediency, with a view to buttressing the authority of the office of Faqih against any challenges after Khomeini's death. Coyly delivered as an ostensible rebuke to Khamenei, who had suggested that the government was constrained by the requirements of the *sharia* (traditional religious law), it was in effect a way of ensuring that the office Khamenei would inherit retained as much prestige and power as possible: The lower the stature of the person holding the position, the more exalted the office itself should be. Yet the audacity in suggesting that a middling cleric such as Khamenei, selected for political, not religious, qualities, could wield such power was staggering. By radically elevating political above religious concerns, this astonishing doctrine threatened to jettison centuries of Shi'ite tradition on the nature of clerical authority, to alienate Shi'ite communities outside Iran, and ultimately to split the religious establishment in Iran itself.

Khamenei was not foolhardy enough to press the point too far. For several years, he kept a relatively low profile, concentrating on projects such as reform of the seminary system at Qom and only gradually asserting his ultimate authority over Rafsanjani. There was a transparent effort to promote Khamenei as a grand ayatollah after the death of the senior cleric Ayatollah Mohammad-Reza Golpayegani in 1993, but it failed to marshal much support and was flatly rejected by much of the clerical establishment in Qom. Indeed, Khamenei's efforts even to influence the choice of Golpayegani's successor were rebuffed. The problem of the disparity between Khamenei's religious stature and that of old rivals like Montazeri, or that of distinguished critics of the concept of *velayat-e faqih* such as Grand Ayatollah Rouhani, would not go away. As a result, there has been increasing use of the Special Court for Clergy, a judicial entity created in 1987 and which operates in great secrecy, to intimidate high-ranking clerics who might pose a threat to Khamenei. Gangs of Ansar-e Hezbollah have also frequently attacked the offices and followers of ayatollahs who have criticized Khamenei or suggested limits on the office of Faqih. The full consequences of this shift in the concept and ideology of *velayat-e faqih*, and the stark contrast between the theory of the office and its occupant, have undoubtedly contributed to simmering internal disputes and competition between and among the religious and political elites which have yet to be played out fully.

THE RUSHDIE CONTROVERSY

At the very time Khomeini was handing Khamenei and Rafsanjani the tools they would need to consolidate their positions and to push their programs, the need to break Iran's isolation and renew economic ties foremost among them, he took another action that cut the ground out from under them. In September 1988, Salman Rushdie, a British citizen and a nominal Muslim, published a rather tedious and mediocre novel, *The Satanic Verses*, which left to its own merits would probably have passed into obscurity rather rapidly. The book took its title from an incident mentioned frequently in early Islamic histories and commentaries on the Koran, according to which the Prophet Mohammad had once accepted as a revelation some verses authorizing veneration of some pagan goddesses (the "daughters of Allah") but later rejected them as having been sent as a temptation by the devil. In one section of the book, a character had a surrealistic dream about "Mahound" (a derogatory name for Mohammad in medieval polemics) that seemed to allude in crude and embarrassing ways to many famous people and events from the time of the Prophet. It immediately became the object of a public furor, especially in Indo-Muslim communities, where the book was deemed obscene and blasphemous (and an example of the dangers cultural assimilation posed to Muslims living abroad). Their demonstrations against the book, which often turned violent, began in India and Pakistan and culminated in a much-publicized burning of the book in Bradford, England, in January 1989. These demonstrations must have been carefully organized and directed, considering that the book had not been translated into any foreign language and had only limited circulation.

The matter was also brought to the attention of Khomeini, reportedly by his son Ahmad, the chief prosecutor, Khoeniha, and the minister of the interior, Mohtashemi. On 14 February 1989, Khomeini issued a *fatva*, or authoritative juridical opinion, on the controversy. On the basis of the widely accepted legal principle that apostasy from Islam is a capital offense, Khomeini wrote to "inform the proud Muslim people of the world that the author of *The Satanic Verses*, which is against Islam, the Prophet, and the Koran, and all those involved in its publication who were aware of its content, are sentenced to death. . . . I call on all zealous Muslims to execute them quickly, wherever they find them. . . . Whoever is killed [trying to do so] will be regarded as a martyr." In response, hundreds of Iranians marched outside the British Embassy in Tehran; the foreign minister, Velayati, threatened to close cultural centers of countries that allowed publication of the book; the deputy speaker of the Majles, Karroubi, claimed that Rushdie and those "who think in the same way" deserved "death, annihilation, and eternal hell"; and Hassan Sanei, head of the "charitable" 15th Khordad Foundation, promised as much as a $2.6 million reward to anyone who succeeded in killing Rushdie.

With the extensive international press coverage they received, the *fatva* and the sensational and inflammatory remarks that ensued did incalculable damage to the image of the Islamic Republic abroad and undermined generations of efforts to emphasize the humane and tolerant aspects of Islam as a religion. As some Muslims noted, the *fatva* itself was rather dubious: Could the content of a work of fiction, the dream of a fictional character at that, be taken as proof of the apostasy of the author? Did not Islamic law require that anyone accused of apostasy be given a chance to repent? Did Islamic law require the punishment to be inflicted on one who resided in territory ruled by non-Muslims? Could a death sentence be imposed on the nominally Sunni author by a Shi'ite jurist or on those involved in the book's publication if they themselves were not Muslims?

In actuality, Khomeini was not primarily concerned with either the state of foreign opinion or the finer points of Islamic jurisprudence. His *fatva* was inspired by politics as much as, if not more than, anything else. As he explained in his "Message to the Clergy," the publication of Rushdie's book was God's way of shocking Muslims out of their "complacency." It was part of a plot by Zionism, Britain, and the United States, "the world devourers' effort to annihilate Islam"; it was evidence of the dangers of "foreign infiltration of Islamic culture." Above all, it revealed the error of those who "go seeking to establish extensive ties [with other countries], because the enemy may think that we have become so dependent and attach so much importance to their existence that we would quietly condone insults to our beliefs and religious sanctities." It was an example to "those who . . . warn that we must embark on a revision of our policies, principles, and diplomacy and that we have blundered and must not repeat previous mistakes; those who still believe that extremist slogans or war will cause the West and the East to be pessimistic about us, and that ultimately all this has led to the isolation of the country; those who believe that if we act in a pragmatic way they will reciprocate humanely and will mutually respect nations, Islam, and Muslims."

In other words, the Rushdie controversy, like the earlier American hostage crisis, allowed Khomeini to seize on a spectacular, highly publicized, emotional issue in order to rejuvenate his image as a leader of militant Islam, to buttress his position among Indo-Muslims, and to divert attention from matters he was not quite so eager to discuss, such as the fiasco of the Iran-Iraq War. It also demolished efforts that were under way to improve relations with the United Kingdom, threw an obstacle in the way of relations with other European countries, and in general seemed to challenge the most basic policy assumptions of the very people whose consolidation of power Khomeini had backed. As had happened so often before, Khomeini showed a remarkable propensity for straddling the political fence.

THE "ERA OF RECONSTRUCTION"

As the Khamenei-Rafsanjani era began, there could be no doubt that Iran faced formidable problems, especially in terms of the economy. In addition to its awful human costs, the war with Iraq had done tremendous damage to the country's infrastructure. Between 50 and 80 cities had been affected, and up to 4,000 villages damaged or destroyed. Over 300,000 homes were likewise damaged or destroyed, and close to 2 million people displaced. Electrical, transportation, and telecommunication facilities had been repeatedly attacked. The country's main port, Khorramshahr, had been utterly destroyed. Close to a thousand industries had been wrecked, and thanks to the oil war, the Abadan refinery, the Kharg Island loading facilities, and many other oil and gas installations were in shambles. It was estimated that the total economic cost of the war to Iran approached $1 trillion. Per capita income had dropped at least 40 percent since the revolution, and the war created shortages in many key commodities. In short, the nation was thoroughly exhausted by a decade of austerity and hardship.

The war alone, however, was not to blame for all of the country's difficulties. However much Khomeini and the revolutionaries might have wanted to believe that Islam provided a perfect system with a perfect solution to every problem, the ruthlessly realistic world of economics had little use for slogans and platitudes. "Islamic economics" was proving to be a chimera, and fundamental differences among various factions on the most basic issues, such as the rights of private property and the role of the public sector, had prevented the government from producing any coherent and practical economic plan. As Jahangir Amuzegar, the economist and former minister under Mohammad-Reza Shah, has pointed out, the Islamic Republic had failed to deliver on one promise after another, notably to reduce dependence on oil revenues or, most embarrassing of all for a government that had excoriated the Pahlavi monarchy for its supposed neglect of agriculture, to make the country self-sufficient in food production (agricultural output had stagnated and the country was more dependent than before on imports of wheat and other commodities). Moreover, problems such as inflation, unemployment, deficit spending, and even crime and drug addiction were worse than ever.

The election to the presidency of Rafsanjani, who had begun to cultivate an image of himself as a progressive leader in the mold of the great 19th century statesman Amir Kabir (whom he admired and whose biography he had written), was widely perceived as a victory for a realistic and pragmatic approach to dealing with the country's severe problems. He naturally did not presume to reject the values and objectives of the Islamic Revolution in any way, but he insisted that tactical adjustments potentially at variance with them were necessary to avoid a crisis that would threaten the very existence of the Islamic Republic. He thus placed the utmost importance on economic issues and made no secret of his preference for technocrats over ideologues. At a petroleum conference in Isfahan in 1991, for example, his foreign minister announced that "economic considerations overshadow political priorities," and Rafsanjani himself urged that "cooperation . . . replace confrontation" in world affairs. This was the basis for his program of economic adjustment (*tadil-e eqtesadi*), a restructuring of the economy often compared to *perestroika* in the Soviet Union.

As spelled out in his first and second five year plans, Rafsanjani's goals were to repair damage from the war, improve the overall infrastructure, and increase production and economic growth. This could only be achieved, however, by stimulating private and foreign investment, expanding the role of the private sector, and limiting government expenditures—in other words, by returning to an essentially privatized, globalized, and free market system. Many specific measures were devised or implemented to meet these objectives. The Tehran stock exchange was revived. Shares in enterprises owned by the National Iranian Industries Organization were sold. Various government assets such as mines were privatized. Revenues from taxation were to be increased. Free trade zones were set up on Kish and Qeshm islands in the Persian Gulf. Construction projects for roads, dams, factories, and other public works were undertaken. Expatriate Iranians, with their significant technical expertise and capital, were encouraged to return home. The currency was devalued to conform to the true exchange rate on the open market. Incentives were offered to promote the export of goods. A program to promote birth control was instituted in order to bring the exploding population growth rate under control. It was also quickly realized that this economic program would inevitably require some outside involvement, and barriers to foreign investment and enterprise in Iran were lowered or abandoned.

During the period 1991–1992, the Kuwait crisis and the Gulf War also tended to reinforce many of Rafsanjani's policies. Iran strongly condemned the Iraqi invasion and supported Kuwaiti sovereignty, including the restoration of the Sabah sheikhdom, yet made it clear that it would not seek to use force itself in the conflict. This was in marked contrast to earlier years, when Iran's belligerent tone had caused great anxiety in Kuwait, Bahrain, Saudi Arabia, and the Gulf Emirates. In general, this lent credibility to Iran's portrayal of itself as a moderate, stabilizing power in the region. This facilitated the restoration of relations with a number of Arab states which had been broken off during the Iran-Iraq War. Iraq, however, was hardly convinced that Iran would not take advantage of the situation and, as the Allied noose tightened, undertook a number of desperate gestures to placate its old adversary. Iraq essentially gave up everything it had gained in the war and more: It reversed its position on the demarcation of the border in the Shatt al-Arab and again accepted the terms of the 1975 Algiers Agreement; it also fully accepted the terms of Security Council Resolution 598. The international animosity toward Iraq also led to its being formally declared the aggressor in the Iran-Iraq War and thus liable to pay reparations. In the short term, the war was thus a positive development for Iran, but it did pose some significant long-term problems. No matter how relieved Iran might be to see the Iraqi military machine devastated, it could hardly be pleased with the vastly increased American presence in the Gulf, which showed no signs of receding. The war also accelerated the process of Arab-Israeli reconciliation, which Iran had no interest in supporting and many reasons, both ideological and strategic, to oppose.

By 1992, significant economic progress had been made in many areas, helped greatly by a temporary jump in oil prices due to the Gulf War, but the economic crisis had not passed and much remained to be done. Anxious to secure approval for his program and to facilitate its implementation, Rafsanjani, with Khamenei's support, attempted to rid the government of as many rivals and opponents as possible. None of the applications to form political parties, as authorized by the 1981 Parties Law (and which was supposed to be put into practice after the war), were approved. In addition, Rafsanjani arranged to have the Council of Guardians administer a competency exam in jurisprudence to candidates for the Assembly of Experts. This was followed by close scrutiny of those applying to run for the Majles, which resulted in more than a thousand of the 3,150 candidates being eliminated. The people with "difficult attitudes" who were disqualified tended to belong to an informal grouping of politicians known as the Combatant Clerics Society (Majma-ye Rouhaniyan-e Mobarez; MRM) and were typically champions of exporting the revolution, Third Worldism, and a highly socialized, etatist vision of the economy—all things Rafsanjani was trying to restrain. Among those pushed out in what amounted to a purge were such prominent revolutionary firebrands as Sadeq Khalkhali, Behzad Nabavi, Mehdi Karroubi, Ali-Akbar Mohtashemi, and Mohammad Khoeniha. Not surprisingly, the Fourth Majles was initially perceived as being stuffed with Rafsanjani supporters and thus another victory for the "pragmatists" and "moderates." In actuality, the voting for the Majles had reflected an anti-incumbency and anti–status quo sentiment. It also had the effect of strengthening the position of the main rival of the MRM, a conservative, bazaar-backed group known as the Combative Clergy of Tehran Association (Jamaa-ye Rouhaniyan-e Mobarez-e Tehran; JRM), one of whose leaders, Hojjatoleslam Nateq Nouri, was elected speaker. Throughout the 1992–1996 period, the JRM steadily increased its hold on the government, apparently winning the support of Khamenei and gaining control of the extremely important ministries of intelligence, culture and Islamic guidance, and the interior as well as the state media.

In sum, the Fourth Majles definitely did not guarantee smooth sailing for Rafsanjani, and the presidential election of 1993 did not strengthen his hand. He won a second term against token opposition, but only 56 percent of the electorate bothered to vote, and 35 percent of those voted against Rafsanjani. Inevitably, factionalism and heated political debate developed in unpredictable ways and made for many odd coalitions. Rafsanjani faced difficulties in almost any direction he wanted to move: Limiting imports worried the important bazaar merchants; imposing new taxes was attacked as a burden for the "oppressed," and the government had to be content with simply collecting existing taxes more efficiently; ending government subsidies for basic goods would anger the lower classes who constituted the bedrock foundation of support for the revolutionary government; increased investment and borrowing from abroad aroused xenophobic sentiments and were contrary to specific provisions of the constitution. The MRM essentially boycotted the elections for the Fifth Majles in 1996, which proved to be especially nasty and eventually left the JRM in a stronger position.

As oil prices slumped, Iran's foreign debt skyrocketed from about $9 billion in 1991 to as much as $34 billion in 1993; this, coupled with continued deficit spending, resulted in inflation of 30 percent and more. Dropping the artificially maintained official exchange rate of 70 rials to the dollar led to an immediate devaluation of the currency to 1,540 rials to the dollar in 1993, and that had increased to over 7,000 rials to the dollar by 1995. Increased costs and drastic reductions in real income severely affected the standard of living for many social classes. An early sign of trouble was an outbreak of riots by workers in several large cities in 1992, which the government ruthlessly repressed. There were additional violent disturbances across the country in 1994 and 1995, from Tabriz and Qazvin in the northwest to Zahedan in the southeast. It was thus increasingly apparent that there were considerable social and political costs to Rafsanjani's program of reconstruction, and the level of discontent in the country by the end of his second term was dangerously high.

In foreign policy, Rafsanjani had to face an increasingly hostile United States. Angered by Iran's implacable opposition toward the Arab-Israeli peace process and by its support for "terrorist" groups such as Hamas and Hezbollah, and concerned about reports regarding Iran's arms acquisitions and apparent efforts to acquire "weapons of mass destruction," the Clinton administration announced a policy of "dual containment" in May 1993 aimed at cordoning off both Iraq and Iran. In the case of Iran, the barriers were mostly in the form of economic sanctions, which did have the potential to hurt in view of the country's economic crisis. However, few American allies accepted this approach, and even American companies continued to do business with Iran. After Conoco announced a $1 billion contract to develop offshore Iranian oil, the Clinton administration, under pressure from Congress and the pro-Israeli lobby, announced a total economic embargo on Iran in April 1995.

To the chagrin of American businesses, trade between the United States and Iran, which had climbed back since the revolution to over $700 million a year, plunged to virtually nil. The containment strategy was carried to an entirely new level in 1996, with the passage of the Iran-Libya Sanctions Act, which threatened economic penalties even for foreign companies that made certain types of investments in Iran. This annoyed European countries, which were anxious to take advantage of opportunities for more economic ties with Iran and had been arguing that a policy of "engagement" and "critical dialogue" would better serve to influence Iranian behavior. In the end the act proved rather toothless, since it was almost immediately challenged by a French, Russian, and Malaysian consortium that signed a deal to exploit Iran's vast reserves of natural gas, and the Clinton administration eventually decided not to pursue the matter.

Even in the case of Europe, however, Rafsanjani's plans to improve relations ran into trouble. In addition to the continuing embarrassment of the Rushdie *fatva*, there was the problem of the Iranian government's predilection for hunting down and killing its opponents on foreign soil. There had been any number of these incidents, including the savage murder near Paris of Shahpour Bakhtiar, the last prime minister of the Pahlavi period, in 1991. It was a much less high-profile case in a country which had been Iran's favorite trading partner, however, that caused the most trouble: In 1992, four Kurdish dissidents were killed at the Mykonos Restaurant in Berlin. The German investigations led directly to high officials of the Iranian government, and one, Minister of Intelligence Ali Fallahian, was actually indicted in the case and a warrant for his arrest issued. Fallahian was accused of issuing orders for the murders on 17 September 1992 on behalf of a committee that included both Khamenei and Rafsanjani. When the court heard the case in 1996, the infuriated Iranian government denounced the trial as "political," and the foreign minister, Velayati, threatened to sue the German government for "insult[ing] our values." Some clerics clamored for a Rushdie-style death warrant against the German prosecutor in the case. On 10 April 1997, the German court nonetheless confirmed that the highest authorities of the Islamic Republic, including both Khamenei and Rafsanjani, were directly responsible for the assassinations. Germany then had little choice but to recall its ambassador, who was followed by the ambassadors of other European Union countries in a gesture of solidarity. They sought to restore relations a month later, but this hit a brick wall when Khamenei refused to accept the return of the German ambassador. The other countries thus declined to send their ambassadors back, and the policy of "critical dialogue" was abandoned.

CULTURAL DEVELOPMENTS

What history will likely remember as the brightest spot of the Rafsanjani decade will be in the field of cultural achievements. As would be expected, religious studies flourished, and scholarship on previously neglected topics in fields from history to literature increased, particularly in terms of editions of texts and historiographical reinterpretation of earlier periods of Iranian history. Many excellent new scholarly, literary, and popular journals appeared both in Iran and among expatriate Iranian communities. Some of the most impressive accomplishments, however, were in the realm of cinema. This was rather surprising given the hostility of revolutionary leaders to film both on religious grounds and as a vehicle for the penetration of foreign cultural elements; theaters had been a favorite target of revolutionary violence. The Islamic government had little use for film for anything except propaganda and imposed a censorship regime that was far more rigorous and extensive than anything the Pahlavi rulers had imposed. Film-makers were smothered by bureaucracy and scrutinized at every step of production not only in terms of the political content of their work but also for its compatibility with Islamic values. The generally spartan economic environment and shortage of material supplies also limited what film producers and directors could do.

Adversity, however, has often served to stimulate cultural creativity in Iran, causing it to bubble up in unexpected ways, and several talented directors were able to turn these handicaps into assets that became essential features of their cinematic style. Films used little known or nonprofessional actors; they emphasized story and character development over effects and technical wizardry; they cultivated a simple, almost documentary-like, presentation that reduced the need for elaborate sets, costumes, and the other paraphernalia that characterize Hollywood movies. Many of the directors supported the revolution and shared its values, and this was reflected in their interest in the lives, problems, and essential dignity of ordinary people, the poor, and the oppressed. The best of such films were drenched in Iranian local culture and yet told stories that were captivating and universal in their appeal.

In the mid-1980s, the government began to recognize the immense value of films not only for internal propaganda but for polishing the rather tarnished image of Iran abroad. With the establishment of the Farabi Cinema Foundation and other measures, the government became financially more supportive of film-making. Rafsanjani's new minister of culture and Islamic guidance, Mohammad Khatami, also relaxed the strict controls over the content of films. This led to a remarkable outburst of brilliant film-making, and Iranian movies began to win international acclaim at one film festival after another.

The quintessential figure of Iranian revolutionary cinema was undoubtedly Mohsen Makhmalbaf. As a young man, he had been arrested for an attack on a police officer and thrown into one of the shah's prisons, where he claimed he was tortured and fully expected to be killed. Released after the revolution, which opened previously closed doors of opportunity to many people like him, he turned to film-making. His early films portrayed the lowest classes of Iranian society, usually placed in desperate situations where they had to confront corruption, oppression, and exploitation by those who take advantage of the misfortune of others. *The Cyclist* (1989), for example, dealt with the plight of an Afghan refugee frantically trying to get money to pay for medical treatment for his wife by agreeing to ride a bicycle continuously for a week. Although he was once a supporter of the revolution, Makhmalbaf's films often skirted the limits of what the censors would allow. Perhaps his most controversial work was *A Moment of Innocence* (1995), in which Makhmalbaf recreated the incident that had landed him in prison, astonishingly choosing to cast as himself the very police officer he had attacked, and ending with an exchange of guns and knives for flowers and bread. In other films such as *Once upon a Time, Cinema* (1992) and *Gabbeh* (1996), Makhmalbaf further blurred the line between fiction and documentary, pursued his interest in visual imagery and unusual camera work, and offered homage to the idea of cinema.

Established directors from the pre-revolutionary era also resumed work and created new masterpieces. Dariush Mehrjui, whose classic *The Cow* (1970) has repeatedly been called the best film ever made in Iran, continued his relentless exploration of suffering, oppression, and alienation and also tackled the sensitive question of gender relations and the place of women in Iranian society. Another director and writer who won fresh acclaim was Abbas Kiarostami, whose terse, simple, and understated films used a distinct and instantly recognizable approach to cinematography. He delighted in erasing distinctions between the world of the film and the real world, and he would leave much unsaid or not depicted in order to involve the viewer more deeply in the film. His work typically reflected a passion for the truly precious moments of life; an interest in capturing the innate goodness and dignity of ordinary people, often caught up in some disaster; the portrayal of events from the perspective of a child; and a fascination with the rich ethnic and geographical diversity of Iran (his films frequently feature Turks, Kurds, Afghans, and other ethnic minorities). These qualities were apparent in his trilogy of films dealing with the village of Koker in northeastern Iran and the effects of the devastating 1990 earthquake that killed 50,000 people in that region. His *Taste of Cherry*, which follows the wandering of a middle-aged man contemplating suicide as he drives around Tehran looking for someone willing to bury him if he succeeds or to rescue him if he has a change of heart, won the Palme d'Or at the 1997 Cannes Film Festival and made Kiarostami one of the most celebrated directors in the contemporary world of cinema.

THE 1997 PRESIDENTIAL ELECTION

After eight years in office, Rafsanjani was no longer eligible to run for the presidency of the republic, and efforts to amend the constitution yet again to allow him to stand for a third term failed. So that he did not have to leave the political scene entirely, Khamenei named him head of the Expediency Council, the agency that had been created to resolve conflicts between different branches of the government, a position ideally suited for giving Rafsanjani a way to continue to exert an influence on political developments.

The vacancy created by Rafsanjani's departure prompted a great deal of interest in the 1997 presidential election, which was further fueled by discontent over the continued poor state of the economy and the desire of many to relax the austere and rather stifling social environment in the country. Over 200 candidates applied to run for president. As usual, these were screened by the Council of Guardians in order to weed out those deemed unqualified or undesirable for one reason or another. None of the nine women who applied were accepted; neither were opposition candidates such as Ebrahim Yazdi, despite the prominent role he had played in the early days of the revolution. This reduced the field to four contenders: Ali-Akbar Nateq Nouri, Mohammad Khatami, Mohammad Reyshahri, and Reza Zavarei. Zavarei, a lawyer and the only noncleric in the race, and Reyshahri, an ultraconservative ayatollah and a former prosecutor general (1989–1993) who had been very active in the jailing and execution of those suspected of royalist or leftist sentiments, were not particularly strong candidates and were probably in the race just to provide some token opposition.

Nateq Nouri, a member of the activist clergy since 1963 who had fled Iran in 1971, had served in several minor posts after the revolution, was elected to the Majles in 1986, and became its speaker after the triumph of the JRM in 1992, a position that often put him at odds with Rafsanjani (he almost lost his seat in the Majles in 1996 to Rafsanjani's daughter). Nateq Nouri was all but openly endorsed by Khamenei and was widely perceived as the establishment's candidate of choice, receiving an inordinate amount of attention from the government-controlled television and radio. The commander of the Revolutionary Guards actually issued written orders to vote for Nateq Nouri, and it was also evident that other groups such as the Basij and Ansar-e Hezbollah were behind him. Pre-election polls thus indicated that over 60 percent of the public (and almost 100 percent of his own supporters) fully expected Nateq Nouri to win, but ironically and more presciently the same polls suggested that only 40 percent or less of the electorate actually intended to vote for him.

The wild card in the race was Khatami. Apparently encouraged by his one-time mentor Rafsanjani, the pro-Rafsanjani "Servants of Reconstruction," and political personalities among the MRM with whom he had long been associated, Khatami entered the race somewhat reluctantly and only after receiving assurances from Khamenei, a longtime friend of the Khatami family, that his candidacy would be accepted. While not exactly an unknown, he was hardly one of the more prominent members of the political elite or "old guard" of the revolution composed largely of Khomeini's former students. After his religious studies in Isfahan, Qom, and Tehran, Khatami had become active in the 1970s as a leader of the Association of Muslim Students in Isfahan and was reportedly friendly with Khomeini's son Ahmad and his colleague Ayatollah Montazeri. After the revolution, he took Ayatollah Beheshti's place as director of the Islamic Center in Hamburg, was elected to the Majles in 1980, and held various minor positions mostly having to do with culture and propaganda. Most notably, Rafsanjani selected him in 1989 to be minister of culture and Islamic guidance in his new "cabinet of construction." Khatami was apparently quite popular, receiving the highest number of positive votes by any member of the cabinet during the process of confirmation by the Majles, and he won many friends among intellectuals for his relaxation of controls over the press and the cinema. However, he had the misfortune of being in charge of a ministry that was caught up in a particularly bitter controversy when the Special Court for Clergy arrested Hojjatoleslam Abolfazl Mousavian because of views he had expressed in his newspaper, *Khorasan*. When Khatami's ministry attempted to defend Mousavian, pointing out that the Special Court was acting in contravention of the constitution and the press laws, the Court asserted that its religious authority superceded any such considerations and placed Mousavian under virtual house arrest in Qom. Khatami was then criticized for being too lenient in his administration of the ministry. He was dismissed in 1992 and sent off to run the National Library.

The electorate quickly came to regard Khatami as the only one of the four candidates who was something of an outsider and thus an alternative to the political, social, and economic status quo, despite indications that he was in reality the candidate preferred by Rafsanjani and on good terms with Khamenei. In the vigorously contested campaigning that ensued, Khatami definitely caught the public imagination and rose rapidly in popularity. He cultivated an amiable, populist image, touring the country by bus and mixing with ordinary people. His allusions to guarding against "superstition and fanaticism" and the need for the "rule of law" were widely accepted as code-words implying support for a relaxation of interference by religious leaders in private life and the creation of a more humane and responsive government. Nateq Nouri's attacks on Khatami, claiming that he was soft on the United States or too permissive in his social thinking, simply confirmed this impression.

By the time of the election in May 1997, the best hope for the Nateq Nouri supporters was that no candidate would receive a majority, so that he might prevail in a later runoff. As it turned out, Khatami won outright in an astonishing landslide: A record number of voters (29.7 million, 94 percent of those eligible) went to the polls, so many that voting hours in many places had to be extended. Khatami received 20.7 million votes (69 percent), and analysis of the voting patterns revealed how the changing demography of Iran had worked in his favor. He was very popular in large cities such as Tehran and Hamadan, and women and young people in particular had voted in large numbers for him. In contrast, the apparent candidate of the old establishment, Nateq Nouri, received only 7 million votes.

These surprising results seemed to confirm that a new chapter in the political history of the Islamic Republic was about to begin.

11

Contemporary Iran

Given the restrictions on who could run for the presidency in Iran, it was difficult to judge whether the election of Khatami represented a vote for him, a vote for values he was supposed to reflect, an expression of economic dissatisfaction, or a vote of protest against the system itself. Nonetheless, the sheer magnitude of Khatami's victory raised expectations among his supporters about the extent of the reforms he would introduce and at the same time created alarm among his opponents that the level of discontent reflected in the vote would lead him to jeopardize fundamental principles of the revolution. It became clear that the Nateq Nouri camp would not yield ground to Khatami without putting up stiff resistance, and that Khatami would have enormous difficulty translating the hopes he had aroused during the election into reality, if indeed that was his objective. Iran settled into an uneasy and protracted political struggle, the outcome of which remains uncertain.

KHATAMI AND THE REFORMISTS

In his inaugural address and subsequent speeches, Khatami emphasized that religion should not be an obstacle to freedom, including the freedom to question authority; that the state as well as the people were obliged to respect the rule of law; that the dignity and rights of individuals should be protected; that societies must be materially prosperous for religious values to flourish; and that "dialogue among civilizations," rather than confrontation, was essential in the contemporary world. The cabinet of ministers he presented and, to the surprise of many, persuaded the Majles to approve included several ministers regarded as outspoken reformists, notably Abd-Allah Nouri, a sharp critic and rival of Nateq Nouri, and Ata-Allah Mohajerani, who had publicly advocated a rapprochement with the United States and who was widely respected by writers as an advocate of intellectual freedom.

Khatami also prevailed on Khamenei to dismiss the powerful commander of the Revolutionary Guards, Mohsen Rezai, who had openly backed Nateq Nouri during the election, and he declined to reappoint the notorious Ali Fallahian as minister of intelligence. He appointed a woman as one of his vice-presidents, indicating recognition of both the role women had played in his election and the importance of women's issues in his agenda. He relaxed controls over the print media, and a number of newspapers began to criticize aspects of Iranian government and society openly and frankly. He continued to tour the country in a simple entourage, meeting with workers and talking to ordinary citizens. He spoke out on behalf of the Kurds and other minorities. There were moves toward allowing the formation of political parties. This had been authorized in 1988, but none of the first thirty applications to do so had been approved. In late 1997, he raised the issue of rapprochement with the United States and agreed to be interviewed for an American television network in January 1998. He encouraged the renewal of cultural contacts between Americans and Iranians, which led to exchange visits by American and Iranian wrestling teams and seemed to be reflected in the good-natured uproar of publicity surrounding the meeting of the American and Iranian soccer teams at the World Cup matches in France.

Modest as they were, Khatami's policies were sufficient to provoke a very harsh response from those worried about where they might be leading, the so-called hard-liners, who were still firmly entrenched in both the Majles and the judiciary and who had plenty of support among the paramilitary groups and the Revolutionary Guards. In addition to Nateq Nouri, who was still speaker of the Majles, the leaders of the opposition to Khatami and the reformists included Mohammad Yazdi, the head of the judiciary; Ahmad Jannati, the secretary of the Council of Guardians; and Ali Meshkini, chairman of the Assembly of Experts. All were thought to be close to and supported by Khamenei. Rather than attack

Khatami directly, the initial strategy of the opposition was to go after some of his most prominent allies and supporters as well as other advocates of reform or critics of clerical government. The struggle unfolded in electoral politics, the courts, and an apparent campaign of violence and intimidation.

On the political front, the Council of Guardians intervened extensively in the elections for the Assembly of Experts held in October 1998 by throwing out over 200 of the 396 clerics who applied to run for the 86-member assembly. The election, marked by an apathetic turnout, resulted in a victory for those perceived as hard-liners. By way of response, Khatami used a largely ignored provision of the constitution to organize elections for local councils, which were held on 26 February. In that case, there were over 300,000 candidates for some 200,000 positions; it was impossible for the Council of Guardians to do much to control who could run or otherwise manipulate the elections. In contrast to the voting for the assembly, that for the councils attracted many people to the polls to participate in what was probably the most freely contested election in the history of the Islamic Republic. Independents and pro-Khatami candidates did quite well, especially in Tehran. Khatami's opponents attempted to fight back by disqualifying several of the reformists elected to the Tehran council, but this fizzled when the rejected council members were confirmed by both Khatami and Khamenei.

In April 1998, in private talks subsequently leaked by the reformist press, the new commander of the Revolutionary Guards, Yahya Rahim Safavi, supposedly warned Khamenei about the trouble being unleashed by "hypocrite" clergy calling for liberalization and advised "beheading" and "cutting out the tongues" of some of the dissident writers. Although he subsequently claimed his comments had been taken out of context and deliberately misrepresented, he made no secret of his belief that one of the main functions of the Guards was to "safeguard" the revolution against internal "cultural" and "ideological" threats. It was also quite clear that Revolutionary Guards, Basij, Ansar-e Hezbollah, and other vigilante groups had repeatedly raided newspaper offices and attacked pro-Khatami and pro-reformist demonstrators. This was accompanied by judicial attacks to force the closure of newspapers identified as reformist and the arrest of their journalists. Khatami made a speech on 28 July calling for protection of the rights of the press, but three days later the head of the courts, Mohammad Yazdi, insisted that the press was abusing its freedom. He was backed up on 15 September by Khamenei, who called on officials to take action against such papers. A wave of legal closures then ensued, including shutting down *Tous*, the most pro-Khatami and pro-reformist newspaper. Amazingly, Khatami's own Ministry of Culture and its liberal minister, Mohajerani, supported the closure and revoked the paper's license.

Against this background, a particularly ominous development, which has led to perhaps the murkiest controversy thus far in the Khatami era, was what seemed to be a pattern of mysterious deaths of writers, journalists, scholars, and intellectuals thought to be critical of the Islamic Republic. During the first year and a half of Khatami's presidency, at least nine dissident writers or activists were murdered, died under suspicious circumstances, or disappeared. Many others were attacked, harassed, or arrested. In an especially important and gruesome case, Daryoush Forouhar and his wife were found dead at their home in Tehran on 22 November 1998, having been stabbed repeatedly and according to several reports left in pools of blood with daggers in their hearts and the bodies facing Mecca. The seventy-year-old Forouhar, minister of labor in the Bazargan government, had become one of the most vocal critics of the Islamic Republic and led the technically illegal but tolerated Iran National Party, a secularist group. The murders were all the more puzzling since it was known that the intelligence service kept the Forouhar house under surveillance. Two days later the body of Majid Sharif, a journalist who had disappeared, was discovered. On 3 December, the poet Mohammad Mokhtari disappeared; he was found a week later in the Tehran morgue, apparently having been beaten and strangled. On 13 December, another writer, Mohammad-Jafar Pouyandeh, was also found strangled. These events prompted a group of prominent intellectuals to write an open letter to Khatami and Khamenei demanding a prompt investigation and arrest of those responsible for the murders.

In the aftermath of the Forouhar killings, Khatami denounced the murders as a "repulsive crime" and pledged to bring the killers to justice, setting up a special task force for this purpose. In mid-September some suspects in the case were arrested, and government officials hinted that the murders would be blamed on the Mojahedin or some other dissident group. Khamenei himself made a widely publicized speech blaming the crimes on "foreign agents" and "plots." However, former president Bani Sadr, in exile in France, claimed that he had evidence that Yazdi and Jannati, with the backing of Khamenei himself, were behind the killings. The very next day, in a shocking turn of events, Khatami's own Ministry of Intelligence admitted that "some of the irresponsible colleagues of this Ministry with deviatory thoughts acting on their own and without doubt as surreptitious agents and in the interests of aliens perpetrated these crimes." What had long been suspected was now openly admitted, leaving the uncomfortable impression that the Islamic Republic was resorting to the very same tactics that it had chastised its Pahlavi predecessor for using. The feeble attempt to deflect blame to "aliens" was utterly unconvincing, and it was equally implausible that underlings would have taken such a bold action without higher approval. In the subsequent public uproar, Ayatollah Montazeri and others called for a thorough investigation and purge of the Ministry of Intelligence. The obvious question was who was ultimately responsible for authorizing the killings, but it proved very difficult to answer.

In mid-January there were reports, impossible to confirm, that Khamenei summoned Khatami to a meeting at which Yazdi, Nateq Nouri, and Savafi excoriated the president for his handling of the matter, intimidated him by having the meeting surrounded by security forces, and ultimately presented him with an ultimatum: Either end the matter by concluding that the Forouhar murders were the work of a small renegade group or else face being removed from office. On 18 January, with the issuance of a report that effectively absolved the Ministry of Intelligence of guilt, Khamenei urged disputes over the investigations to cease, and he subsequently dropped repeated hints that the matter would best be forgotten. In the end, the minister in charge, Qorban-Ali Dorri Najafabadi, was forced to resign and was replaced by Ali Younessi. Some reports claimed that Khatami had been forced to appoint Najafabadi by Khamenei, who defended the ministry and urged Najafabadi to stay in office, and that his removal was thus a victory for the moderates. However, it is not at all obvious why Khamenei would have wanted Najafabadi, who had no previous involvement in intelligence matters. Moreover, his replacement, Younessi, was a longtime prosecutor and protégé of Reyshahri, and his pledges at his confirmation hearing in the Majles to strengthen the Ministry of Intelligence and make it "an ambush for the enemies and ill-wishers of the system" can hardly have served to reassure dissidents.

In April, Khatami once more confirmed his determination to root out "gangs that operate in society under the cover of religion," but at the end of 1999 the question of who ultimately authorized the murders had still not been answered. Investigations were conducted in absolute secrecy, and repeated requests for international observers to monitor the case went unheeded. Although ten suspects in the murders had been arrested, their identification was not forthcoming. Only after one, Said

Emami, a deputy minister said to be the mastermind, allegedly commit-ted suicide while in detention at Evin Prison, were names released, and then only for four of the ten. The minister of culture and Islamic guid-ance, Mohajerani, admitted that the "suicide" of the chief suspect was highly suspicious; although a taped confession by Emami was eventually turned over to the Majles, it remains uncertain that the judicial proceed-ings regarding the case will ever be made public. At last report, the investigation seemed to be settling on the story indicated in the supposed ultimatum: Emami was a rogue agent in the employ of American and Israeli intelligence services.

The campaign against the reformists was also carried on in the courts and the Majles, and it was there that Khatami's own calls for the "rule of law" served to limit his ability to intervene. Throughout 1998 and into 1999, many reformists were called in for questioning or targeted for pros-ecution under the ambiguous press laws or for other legal violations, and at least a dozen independent-minded newspapers were forced to close. One of the most prominent victims of this judicial offensive was Gholam-Hossein Karbaschi, the mayor of Tehran. Karbaschi, a Rafsanjani protégé who was very popular because of the public works he had un-dertaken in the capital, was a chief architect of Khatami's election cam-paign. In April 1998, he was arrested on the orders of the head of the judiciary, Mohammad Yazdi, and charged with financial improprieties. Despite the widespread perception that the trial was politically inspired, Karbaschi was convicted that July, fined, barred from politics, and ulti-mately sent to jail. In May 1999, Khatami and Rafsanjani issued messages regretting the sentence, but Khamenei, the only official who could grant a pardon, confirmed the decision after a request from numerous mem-bers of the Majles for his opinion. (Karbaschi was later given early release from prison.) Emboldened by this success, the anti-Khatami faction also targeted Abd–Allah Nouri, the minister of the interior, who had spoken out in support of Karbaschi, successfully bringing impeachment pro-ceedings against him in June 1998. He was later arrested, convicted, and sentenced to five years in jail for articles published in his newspaper, *Khordad*, but this strategy backfired when he managed to turn his trial into a showcase for questioning the legitimacy of the Special Court and only made him an icon for the reformist movement. The hard-liners failed in a subsequent attempt to impeach Mohajerani, the minister of culture. They did, however, resume the attack on him in February 2000, blaming him for the publication of a cartoon lampooning the controver-sial conservative cleric Ayatollah Mohammad-Taqi Mesbah Yazdi and holding demonstrations calling for his resignation and even his execution. The cartoon had appeared in the newspaper *Azad* in response to Mesbah Yazdi's accusations that a CIA agent had arrived in Tehran with a suitcase full of cash to fund pro-reform journalists.

Adding to the general atmosphere of tension and uncertainty, and a further indicator of the pressures building up in the society, was a string of attacks within Iran by various terrorist factions. Raids from Mojahedin bases in Iraq into Iran became almost routine throughout 1998 and 1999, and the Mojahedin assassinated two high-profile Iranian officials, Asad-Allah Lajevardi, the former governor of Evin Prison, in August 1998 and General Ali Sayyad Shirazi, Khamenei's military advisor, in April 1999. There were also reports that an attack on Ali Razini, the head of the judiciary in Tehran, and a plot to assassinate all the top officials of the government had been planned by a previously unknown and shadowy group known as Mahdaviyat. Early press reports indicated that the group was based in Mashhad and believed that all true authority belonged to the Hidden Imam and was trying to hasten his advent. This suggested that the Hojjatiyya group, which had similar ideas and was strong in Khorasan, might be reviving its oppositional activities.

The tense conflict between the various factions finally boiled over during the summer of 1999. On 8 July, students at the University of Tehran demonstrated against the closure of the pro-Khatami newspaper *Salam*. That night, members of the Ansar-e Hezbollah, with at least the tacit support of the Revolutionary Guards and police, attacked a dormitory, beating up students and setting fire to their rooms. Thousands of students and protesters then took to the streets of Tehran, and there were frequent clashes between groups of demonstrators and vigilantes from the Ansar-e Hezbollah and Basij. Over the next six days, the demonstrations turned into increasingly violent riots and spread to at least eight cities, including Hamadan, Isfahan, Mashhad, Tabriz, and Yazd. In Tehran, crowds attacked banks, the offices of the conservative newspapers *Keyhan* and *Jomhour-e Eslami*, and the Ministry of Intelligence. They shouted insults at the Ansar-e Hezbollah and Basij, demanded the firing of the chief of police, Hedayat Lotfian, and at times called openly for Khamenei to step down as Faqih (a very provocative act since it was technically illegal even to criticize him). It was not clear whether, as some maintained, the students were joined in their protests by other alienated groups in what represented a virtual revolution manqué, or rather were infiltrated by agents provocateurs who wanted to discredit the students by associating them with lawlessness and anti-Khamenei sentiments.

At first, Khamenei speculated that the demonstrations were a scheme against Iran financed by the United States, while Khatami encouraged the "lively, energetic, and active" students. As later revealed, the commanders of the Revolutionary Guards sent a blunt letter to Khatami on 12 July informing him that "our patience is at an end" and that they would not "show any more tolerance." In view of similar situations in Iran's recent past, these events must have seemed very much like the prelude to a coup, and by 14 July, the day of a large pro-Khamenei counter-demonstration, Khatami was decidedly backing away from the demonstrators, calling the protests "a deviation which will be repressed with force and determination." The crisis thus wound down bizarrely, with Khamenei shedding tears of concern for his poor "children" at the universities, and Khatami, whom the students thought they were supporting, saying they had "evil aims" and were a threat to national security.

In any case, order was restored, and the government media identified three individuals as the ringleaders behind the trouble: Heshmatollah Tabarzadi (a curious character who has been suspected of being a pawn of the Ministry of Intelligence used to infiltrate the student movement), Manouchehr Mohammadi, and Gholamreza Mohajerinejad. Mohammadi was displayed on television, apparently beaten and drugged, confessing to having met with a "counter-revolutionary" in Turkey. Many other students had to face revolutionary justice for their actions; press reports indicated that well over a thousand had been sent to Evin Prison, and there were calls for them to be tried as *mohareb* (one who wars against God), a capital offense. As of this writing, prosecutions had begun of low-ranking police officials involved in the raid on the dormitory, but a parliamentary inquiry had exonerated Lotfian and placed part of the responsibility for the violence on the students. Few of the students had been released, and at least one remained under threat of a death sentence.

The very real prospect in July of a bloody civil war if not a revolution did appear to have had a sobering effect on all concerned. The remaining student leaders kept a low profile and worked to secure support from senior members of the clergy in Qom. In addition to restraining the Revolutionary Guards and Basij, Khamenei went out of his way to praise Khatami in his speeches and sermons. He also acted to defuse a furor that had developed over the arrest of four students at Amir Kabir University of Technology for having written a play deemed blasphemous. Some clerics called for their execution, an idea Khamenei rejected (two of the students were nonetheless sentenced in November 1999 to three years in jail). Khamenei also engineered some changes in official personnel, the implications of which are not yet fully clear. On 17 July, it was announced that Khamenei's brother-in-law, Mohsen Rafiqdoust, was leaving his post as head of the Bonyad-e Mostazafan to take over the police forces. In August, Khamenei removed the arch-conservative Mohammad Yazdi as head of the judiciary and replaced him with Mahmoud Hashemi Shahroudi. In December, the Majles gave Hashemi Shahroudi sweeping authority to set aside court verdicts that he found contrary to Islamic law. For his part, Khatami left his various liberal allies caught up in the courts to their fate and concentrated instead on matters related to the economy and to foreign policy, allowing the domestic issues to follow their own course. The main lesson of summer 1999 thus seemed to be that the clerical forces, whatever their internal divisions, would not hesitate to close ranks and do whatever was necessary to head off any potential threat to the existing political system.

ECONOMY AND FOREIGN POLICY UNDER KHATAMI

Khatami was very slow in coming forward with a program to deal with the economic crisis in Iran, which continued to worsen. During the first two years of his administration, real growth fell to about 1 percent; investment in industry declined by 40 percent; unemployment was probably close to 20 percent; the value of the rial dropped, reaching 8,000 to the dollar before turning around; and Iran had difficulty paying its foreign debts. The country remained heavily dependent on oil for about 80 percent of export revenues and 90 percent of government revenues. Only the discovery of a large new oil field and a substantial rebound in oil prices by late 1999 provided much in the way of relief.

The Khatami government was made up of a rather odd coalition of MRM supporters and Rafsanjani technocrats. They have never seen eye-to-eye on economic issues, and this basic contradiction was reflected yet again in the five year plan Khatami finally put forward for the period 2000–2004. As Khatami explained, the plan was a compromise between economic realities and "political and spiritual" needs. On the one hand, it was a rehash of Rafsanjani's plans to reduce government bureaucracy, stimulate investment, devalue the currency, lower subsidies, and privatize the economy. On the other hand, it continued to pursue elusive and unrealistic goals in terms of increasing non-oil exports and becoming self-sufficient in agriculture and promised such etatist and welfarist policies as benefits for the "oppressed," "economic egalitarianism through the elimination of class differences," and "strengthening intellectual and practical values of the Islamic Revolution and putting up effective resistance to alien cultures." Perhaps the most blatant conflict was between the plan's absolutely essential need to attract foreign investment, despite the ideological and constitutional problems that created, and its simultaneous call for "prevention of foreign domination in the process of attracting foreign resources."

Khatami, much like his predecessors, presented no clear, consistent solution to the problems of debt and deficit spending nor the will to tackle sensitive problems such as ending subsidies, raising tax revenues, or controlling the powerful foundations. One of his advisors frankly admitted that simply to stay in place, given the large number of young people entering the workplace, the Iranian economy needed to grow at 6.5 percent a year but could barely manage even 1 percent. An indication of the defeatism, pessimism, and potential for future problems inherent in this situation was that Khatami's plan envisaged continued rates of perhaps 20 percent inflation and 13 percent unemployment. Foreign capital was thus absolutely essential for Khatami's economic program to have any chance of success, and that in turn required the creation of a climate conducive to such investment. It was in this respect that Khatami enjoyed perhaps his most striking successes.

The Khatami government continued Rafsanjani's efforts to strengthen relations between Iran and various Arab and Islamic countries. Khatami repeatedly stated that "elimination of tension" and promotion of peace and stability were the foundation of his policy. An early sign that this message was becoming effective was marked by the Organization of the Islamic Conference (OIC) summit held in Tehran in early December 1997. Despite efforts by the United States to discourage participation by organizing a rival economic meeting in Qatar, virtually all of the fifty-five members attended the summit, including such close U.S. allies as Kuwait, Jordan, Saudi Arabia, Egypt, and Turkey. Even such regular adversaries of Iran as Iraq and the Palestine Liberation Organization (PLO) participated, with an Iraqi vice-president and Yasser Arafat accepting invitations from Khatami to come to Tehran. The opening statements at the summit sent rather contradictory messages, with Khamenei preaching about "Western materialistic civilization . . . directing everyone toward materialism while money, gluttony and carnal desires are made the greatest aspirations" and Khatami speaking of reconciliation, mutual respect, and understanding. There were also attempts to use the summit to make strong denunciations of Israel, Turkey, and the Taleban in Afghanistan, but the final statement mostly confined itself to vague criticism of "expansionism" and "state terrorism" and calls for respect for "the dignity and rights of Islamic women" and "interaction, dialogue and understanding among cultures and religions."

Most delegates came away with the impression that there was a new spirit of restraint and moderation in Iran. The summit was followed by a definite thaw in Saudi-Iranian relations, which represented a radical change from the days when Khomeini, in his last will and testament, had excoriated King Fahd and "the baseless and superstitious cult of Wahhabism" practiced in Saudi Arabia. After many years of tension, the two countries had been drawn closer together by a desire to stabilize the Persian Gulf area and the need for a mutually beneficial oil policy. A formal cooperation agreement was signed in May 1998, which was made in "a spirit of friendship and mutual respect and understanding" and pledged to foster a wide range of commercial, technical, and cultural activities. It was more, however, than just a statement on bilateral relations. Prince Saud al-Faisal noted that it would have a positive impact on the whole region; it essentially confirmed the role Saudi Arabia had been playing as an intermediary between Iran and the Gulf Cooperation Council, trying to persuade the latter that Iran's former policies of subversion and aggression had been abandoned. The Iranian occupation of the Abu Musa and Tunb islands remained of some concern to the United Arab Emirates, but only the government of Abu Dhabi seemed to press the issue. The Saudis also helped facilitate a dramatic improvement in relations with Egypt. This seemed to be heading toward a full restoration of ties, but ran into a problem when some factions in Iran objected vociferously to Egypt's condition that a street in Tehran named in honor of Khaled al-Islambouli, the assassin of Anwar Sadat, be renamed.

On the other hand, Iran continued to face a number of challenges in its own region, and certain aspects of its behavior were not changing in any fundamental way. Tensions with Iraq remained very high as Iraq seemed to be stepping up its support for Mojahedin activities. For its part, Iran increased its cooperation with the Supreme Council of the Islamic Revolution in Iraq (SCIRI), mobilized forces and carried out training exercises near the Iraqi border, and made missile and ground attacks on Mojahedin training bases inside Iraq. Reports disagreed on whether assassinations of Shi'ite clerics in Iraq were the work of Iraqis eliminating pro-Iranian leaders, or the SCIRI removing clerics hostile to the idea of *velayat-e faqih*. After the success of the Sunni Taleban and the rout of pro-

Iranian forces, tensions also increased between Iran and Afghanistan. In September 1998, when a number of Iranian "diplomats" were murdered in Mazar-e Sharif, Iran mobilized troops on its eastern border, and it appeared for a moment that war might actually break out. Despite Arafat's appearance at the OIC summit, Iran remained highly critical of the PLO and its involvement in the American-backed peace process with Israel. There was no indication that Iran had relaxed its support for groups such as Hamas, Hezbollah, or Islamic Jihad.

Perhaps the most interesting development was the harsh criticism by Iran of Turkey at the OIC summit, which resulted in the early departure of Turkey's delegate, Suleyman Demirel, who had received a personal invitation from Rafsanjani to attend. Although relations between Turkey and Iran since the revolution had usually been correct if not always cordial, there were several reasons they were beginning to deteriorate. Iran could hardly fail to be suspicious of a country as staunchly secular and pro-American as Turkey, and it was especially perturbed by the close military ties developing between Turkey and Israel. In addition, there was the matter of the route for a pipeline to carry oil from the Central Asian republics and Azerbaijan. Turkey and the United States were particularly anxious for this Caspian pipeline to run to the Turkish port of Ceyhan in order to avoid using a simpler route from the Caspian to the Persian Gulf which would have to cross Iranian territory. This presented Iran with the prospect of facing in the next century a coalition of strong, prosperous, secular, pro-American, Turkish-speaking states to its north, a development that could hardly fail to have implications for the status of Iran's own Turkish minorities. For its part, Turkey had reason to suspect Iranian involvement with Kurdish guerilias and Islamist groups in Turkey; there were even rumors of Iranian involvement in the assassination of a prominent Turkish secularist, the journalist Ahmad Taner Kislali. The Turkish government had a particularly sharp response to Iran's criticism of its handling of the controversy caused when a female member of the Virtue Party wanted to take her seat in Parliament wearing Islamist garb. Tensions between the two countries became quite noticeable in 1999. Iranian officials objected strongly to comments by the Turkish prime minister, Bulent Ecevit, supporting the student protests that summer. In the televised student "confession," it was Turkey where his supposed "counter-revolutionary" contacts were supposed to have taken place. Also in late July, the Iranians claimed that the Turkish air force, in apparent pursuit of Kurdish rebels, had bombed one of its outposts at Piranshahr; they demanded compensation and "reserved the right to respond." Turkish military officials denied that there had been any violation of Iranian air space and suggested that the Iranians were attempting to divert attention from the student protest. Another diplomatic mini-tempest erupted after the parliamentary elections, when Ecevit expressed the hope that the reformist victory meant Iran would reduce its support for Islamist groups abroad, an idea the Iranian foreign ministry promptly denounced as interference in Iran's "internal affairs" (a standard it had hardly applied to itself in commenting earlier on Turkish politics).

To revive relations with Western countries, the Khatami government needed to show not only that Iran was improving its record on human rights issues but also that American perceptions of it as a "rogue nation" that needed to be "contained" were wrong. In response to charges that it sponsored international terrorism, Khatami argued that Iran was in fact "the worst victim of terrorism in the present time," pointing to the continued attacks and assassinations by Mojahedin-e Khalq forces and incidents such as the murder of the Iranian diplomats in Mazar-e Sharif. The Iranian government even issued statements deploring the bombing of American embassies in Africa and some minor terrorist attacks on American targets in Pakistan. At the same time, Khatami was careful to note that Iran did not consider attacks on occupying forces (e.g., Hezbollah or Hamas attacks on Israeli forces in Lebanon or Palestine) to be terrorism. The Khatami government also began to play up the progressive nature of Islam in Iran, particularly in regard to women's issues, by contrasting it with the activities of the Taleban in Afghanistan. Similarly, it drew attention to Iran's vigorous efforts at controlling the international traffic in illegal drugs (and the growing drug addiction problem in Iran) by suppressing the smuggling of heroin from Afghanistan and Pakistan.

Western European countries, displeased by Washington's efforts to hamper their commercial relations with Iran, were quick to accept these arguments and hail Khatami as a reasonable and progressive world leader with whom they could do business. In June 1998, Italian prime minister Romano Prodi visited Tehran and discussed the Rushdie case and other human rights issues with Khatami. On 9 March 1999, Khatami began a three-day visit to Italy—the first official trip to Europe by an Iranian head of state since the revolution. When Mohajerani visited Italy in November 1999, the president of the Chamber of Deputies, Luciano Violante, went so far as to describe the Islamic Republic of Iran as a "center of democracy and stability." Khatami's next triumph was an official visit to France in October 1999. The French took draconian measures to prevent any disruption of the visit by the Mojahedin or other Iranian dissidents, and even found a way to accommodate Khatami's demand that no wine be served at the state banquet (which was dropped in favor of a "reception" with nonalcoholic drinks only). The spectacle of the socialist, liberal, anticlerical custodians of the French Republic yielding to this bit of effrontery enabled Khamenei to declare that Khatami's European diplomacy was acceptable since it "took place from a position of strength." Both visits were paralleled by new and substantial commercial agreements, including an oil deal with France's Elf Aquitaine and Italy's AGIP worth an estimated $1 billion. It should be noted, however, that Italian and French opinion was not entirely comfortable with this new relationship. Numerous members of the Italian parliament protested Khatami's visit, and a group of prominent French intellectuals published an open letter criticizing the reception being given to the leader of a government that was still essentially repressive in nature.

At the outset of Khatami's presidency, the *fatva* condemning Salman Rushdie remained the greatest obstacle to restoring relations with the United Kingdom. It was very difficult for Khatami's government to distance itself from the *fatva* without seeming to compromise the dogma of Khomeini's infallibility so basic to the Islamic Republic. Finally, on September 22, in an interview with Western reporters, Khatami renewed his call for a "dialogue of civilizations" and indicated with some irritation that Khomeini had just given "his opinion" as an Islamic jurist in the *fatva* condemning Rushdie and that as far as Iran was concerned the case was "completely finished." It would not renounce the *fatva*, but neither would it act on it. This was precisely the development Khomeini had warned about in his 1989 message to the clergy when he said that he was afraid in ten years' time someone "occupying the seat of judgment" would say that it was necessary to see if the *fatva* "was in accordance with diplomatic regulations" in order to accommodate "the Common Market and the Western countries." Not surprisingly, the mere hint of compromise on the *fatva* created a storm of protest. Numerous clerics, including Grand Ayatollahs Mohammad Fazel Lankarani and Nouri Hamadani and even Khamenei's personal representative Ayatollah Hossein Mazahiri, emphasized that the *fatva* was absolutely irrevocable and its fulfillment was an obligatory duty "for every Muslim until the day of resurrection." Then, in the fall of 1998, at a meeting at the UN between the foreign ministers of the United Kingdom and Iran, Robin Cook expressed Her Majesty's regret for the offense to Muslims caused by Rushdie's book, and Kharrazi explicitly indicated that "the government of the

Islamic Republic of Iran has no intention, nor is it going to take any action whatsoever to threaten the life of the author of the *Satanic Verses* or anybody associated with his work, nor will it encourage or assist anybody to do so. Accordingly the government disassociates itself from any reward which has been offered in this regard and does not support it." Although newspapers like *Keyhan, Jomhour-e Eslami,* and *Resalat* continued to exhort the government to carry out the decree, a majority of the Majles confirmed the validity of the *fatva,* the offer of a reward was confirmed, and even the man named to be the ambassador to Britain said the *fatva* was "irrevocable," Kharrazi's statement was accepted as sufficient for the United Kingdom to justify upgrading its relations with Iran. They were fully restored at the ambassadorial level, for the first time since the revolution, in May 1999. British trade delegations, members of Parliament, and Robin Cook were soon queuing up for visits to Iran.

Because of its highly symbolic significance, the issue of American-Iranian relations arose early in Khatami's presidency and received much publicity in the foreign press. While there would certainly have been advantages to both sides in normalizing relations, the fact of the matter was that elements in both governments had always found an adversarial relationship far more useful to their agendas. Khamenei and other officials vehemently rejected any relaxation in Iran's attitude toward the United States, and large celebrations were held to mark the twentieth anniversary of the takeover of the embassy. By late 1999, the idea of a rapprochement with the United States was essentially dead, largely because the issue was so emotional and politicized on both sides.

Indeed, it is doubtful that Khatami ever attached as much importance to this question as speculation in the press implied. When pressed on the issue during the election, he had said that restoration of relations with the United States was "beyond logic," and it was difficult to see much more than rhetoric distinguishing Nateq Nouri's admonitions to beware of the "blood-sucking American wolf" and Khatami's warnings against "global arrogance" and American "hegemony." Moreover, one of Khatami's core constituencies included the former student militants who had held the hostages at the American Embassy in Tehran, a fact his critics have been quick to use against him. There was marked embarrassment when a reporter realized that Masoumeh Ebtekar, the vaunted "U.S. educated" former representative of Iran at the Beijing Women's Conference, whom Khatami had named as a vice-president, and who was also clearly intended to serve as the emblem of Khatami's progressive views on women's issues, was the notorious "Mary" who had acted as spokesperson for the hostage holders. One of the richest ironies of the Khatami era has been watching these former militants in the uncomfortable position of defending better relations with Washington while the conservative press derided them as "simple minded individuals" who were trying to "push back any responsibility they had during the revolutionary seizure of the spy den" in a "cheap move."

To the United States and other critics of Iran, it was not at all obvious that the situation had changed sufficiently to warrant reintegration of Iran into the world's diplomatic and economic system. The issue of whether Iran was pursuing acquisition of weapons of mass destruction was still held up as a major concern, although without access to highly technical and classified information it is impossible to judge how serious a problem this actually might be. Beyond that, there was the politically sensitive and virtually insurmountable issue of Iran's hostility toward Israel. Khatami's much heralded broadcast interview was not exactly reassuring to the American audience either. His scholarly style of discourse, which worked so well in Iran, sounded like a patronizing lecture; he was defensive on the issue of the hostage crisis; he took the opportunity to denounce American support for the "racist terrorist regime" in Israel; and he offered nothing more tangible in the way of improved relations than a freer exchange of scholars, artists, journalists, and tourists. On the whole the interview appeared to be aimed more at allaying fears in Iran about an imminent restoration of relations with the United States than opening up any serious dialogue between the governments of the two countries. Even the exchange of wrestling teams was marred by a flap over displaying the American flag in Iran and a problem at passport control when the members of the visiting Iranian team were photographed and fingerprinted at the Chicago airport upon entering the United States, which Iranians could hardly fail to interpret as an intentional snub.

At the same time, the rapid expansion of Iranian diplomatic and commercial ties with European countries, and Iran's improved relations with Arab countries, showed that the American policy of "containment" was collapsing. As so often in the past, the U.S. government found it difficult to come up with a coherent and consistent alternative since policy makers spoke with divided voices. In October 1999, in response to a more conciliatory attitude on the part of the Clinton administration, twenty-eight senators, led by Robert Torricelli and Christopher Bond, urged Secretary of State Madeleine Albright to consider recognizing the Mojahedin as a legitimate "resistance movement" and claimed that Iranian support for terrorist movements and suppression of human rights remained unchanged. In November 1999, President Clinton reversed direction, renewed the policy of economic sanctions against Iran, and agreed to review the question of enforcing the provisions of the Iran-Libya Sanctions Act in light of a recently concluded oil deal with Iran by Royal Dutch Shell.

Khatami's accomplishments in improving Iran's image abroad and its relations with European countries were thus quite significant, but in this field, too, his domestic opponents did not let him go unchallenged. One tactic was for vigilante bands to attack visiting tourists or official guests, especially if they were thought to be Americans, which undercut Khatami's efforts to promote "people to people" contacts. Another was to use highly charged and sensitive court cases to put the government into embarrassing situations. Because of the fallout from the Mykonos killings court case and the continued presence of Mojahedin offices on its soil, Germany was still in disfavor with certain circles in Iran and had seen its trade relationship decline precipitously. A new obstacle was added by the arrest of Helmut Hofer, a German businessman in Mashhad accused of having had a sexual relationship with a Muslim woman, a crime that carried the threat of a death penalty. By spring 2000, however, some progress had been made in resolving this case, and Germany was joining the parade of nations sending diplomats to visit Iran. Far more sensational and potentially devastating in its effects on relations between Iran and European countries was the arrest in June 1999 of thirteen Iranian Jews on charges of spying for Israel. In November, Lionel Jospin, the French prime minister, warned Iran that it would risk its reintegration into the international community if the Jews were executed and called on Khatami to help exonerate them. However, Jannati and other conservatives were adamant that they should receive the death penalty regardless of the impact that might have on Western opinion. Despite repeated entreaties from various governments, Khatami was only able to suggest that they would receive a "fair trial."

THE 2000 PARLIAMENTARY ELECTIONS

In February 2000, the much anticipated elections for the Sixth Majles, viewed as a potentially decisive test of strength between the reformists and their opponents, were held. It had been widely expected that the Council of Guardians would again use its authority to block reformist candidates from running. Instead, it rejected only a relatively small number of candidates, mostly those who were unfamiliar or who had taken positions clearly in defiance of the key ideological dogmas of the Islamic Republic. The Council may have hoped that under the voting system used in Iran a large number of reformists would split their vote and enable some conservatives to qualify for runoff elections, or they may simply have reconciled themselves to the inevitable.

As it turned out, candidates associated with reformist slates did much better than expected, not only in Tehran but in smaller cities and the countryside. In the case of Tehran, the two most popular candidates by far were Khatami's brother, Mohammad-Reza, and the wife of Mohajer-ani, Jamileh Kadivar. Rafsanjani, the former president and political powerhouse who had so carefully positioned himself as a centrist, suffered the humiliation of being forced into a runoff or squeaking by on the thinnest of margins (depending on the results of the recount of a recount, which was ordered to try to dispel perceptions of vote fraud on his behalf). No conservatives were elected. Outside Tehran, the reformist victory was not so complete but still quite overwhelming. In the runoff elections in May, reformist candidates continued to win in large numbers. It thus appeared that they would not only control the new Majles but have an absolute majority capable of pushing for radical change. These results could only be interpreted as a popular repudiation of the conservatives and much of the pre-Khatami political establishment as well as a sign of support for Khatami's administration.

As the magnitude of the reformist electoral victory became apparent, the mood of the conservative opposition seemed to range from shock to a grim determination to fight back. Abandoning the moderate tone that had characterized earlier pronouncements, Khamenei sharply criticized the pro-reform newspapers and insinuated that the reformers were either out to subvert the values of the Islamic Revolution or serving the interests of foreign powers. By the end of April, virtually every reform newspaper had been closed down, and even the newly elected Mohammad-Reza Khatami faced the threat of legal action for his journalistic activities. The Council of Guardians began to disqualify candidates elected to the new Majles and, amid allegations of vote fraud, held up certification of the entire slate of delegates from Tehran. Mohajerani, the *bête noire* of the conservatives, was accused of meeting secretly with foreign diplomats, in what was obviously intended as another campaign to embarrass him into resigning from Khatami's cabinet or to lay the groundwork for his impeachment. On March 12, there was an attempt to assassinate one of Khatami's closet advisors, Saeed Hajjarian, that left him hospitalized and in a coma—an ominous sign of the potential for violence as political positions in Iran hardened. The response of Khatami and his administration to these developments continued to be muted, ostensibly because of fear the conservatives were trying to provoke a crisis that would provide them with an excuse to impose some kind of martial law and halt the seating of the new Majles.

CONCLUSION

Scholars, analysts, and journalists in and outside of Iran largely failed to comprehend either the nature or the direction of the Islamic Revolution when it occurred. Since then, many of them have confidently and repeatedly predicted the imminent demise of the Islamic regime whenever it faces a crisis, or its transformation into a "moderate" or "pragmatic" government with every reshuffling of its personnel. This has been due to their determination to make the facts of the Iranian case fit into preconceived models of revolutions and revolutionary behavior, and they have invariably been proven wrong. In particular, the notion that such events lead eventually and inevitably to triumphs for the progressive forces of liberalism and democracy is not easily abandoned, and the temptation to apply such a interpretation to current events remains overwhelming. The recent presidential and parliamentary elections in Iran have again aroused, more strongly than ever before, the belief—or the hope—that such change is at hand. There remain many reasons, however, to be both cautious and skeptical.

First of all, the notion that the current conflict in Iran is between moderate reformists and hidebound religious reactionaries is a very convenient one both for some Iranian politicians and for countries anxious to normalize their ties with Iran. It disguises many unpleasant realities and is often used, especially by the popular press, in ways that border on the ludicrous. Less than ten years ago, it was Khamenei and Rafsanjani who were being praised as moderates and pragmatists for having ousted doctrinaire MRM "radicals" from Iranian politics. Today it is by and large those very same "radicals" who have been transformed into the leading "moderates" and "reformists," with Rafsanjani and especially Khamenei becoming "hard-liners." While many of the "hard-liners" have conservative views on social issues, their criticism of corruption and their support of private property and economic reform have often caused them to be viewed as the real "moderates" and "reformers." The political struggles in Iran are ideological, institutional, generational, and even personal, but they rarely fit into such simplistic categories.

When one looks closely at the "reformists," especially the members of the MRM who have jumped on Khatami's bandwagon, there is very little in their record that would suggest a deep commitment to "reformist" or "liberal" values at home or abroad. To the contrary, they have been characterized by extreme and unrealistic views on a number of social, economic, and especially geopolitical issues, where they seem driven by a hunger for publicity, shallow ideological pretensions, and a wildly inflated and exaggerated sense of self-importance for themselves and the place of Iran in world affairs. For example, three leaders of the MRM and outspoken supporters of Khatami are Mohammad Mousavi Khoeniha, Ali-Akbar Mohtashemi, and Hassan Sanei. Khoeniha is the owner of *Salam*, long identified as a "hard-line" newspaper but suddenly part of the "reformist" press targeted by "hard-liners." It was its closure which prompted the 1999 student riots, and Khoeniha provided a vocal defense of press freedom after he was arrested. This "reformist" is widely acknowledged to have been the mastermind behind the takeover of the American Embassy, the director of the students who so painstakingly reconstructed documents found shredded there, and the politician who used those documents selectively to smear opponents. The articles which got his paper in trouble smack of the same methods of innuendo, slander, and guilt by association. Khoeniha was certainly not very interested in freedom of expression which he encouraged Khomeini to issue the edict condemning Salman Rushdie to death, nor was he exactly restrained in the practice of judicial terror when he was the country's chief prosecutor. Indeed, it was called a victory for moderation when he was replaced in that office by Mohammad Yazdi, a man now derided as one of the top "hard-liners" but who was then praised for his stance in favor of a deregulated and privatized economy. Mohtashemi, a former minister of the interior, was a chief backer of Hezbollah in Lebanon as well as radical Palestinian groups and has been accused of financing the bombing of Pan Am Flight 103 over Lockerbie, Scotland. He was a constant critic of Rafsanjani and Khamanei, accusing them of betraying Khomeini's ideals and selling out to "American lackeys." In 1997, however, he was out praising Khatami extravagantly and calling for the reformers to take control of the police and judiciary—in order "to slap on the face" those who opposed Khatami. Sanei heads the 15th Khordad Foundation, which offered the multi-million dollar reward for the murder of Salman Rushdie. Despite the pledges of the Khatami government to put the Rushdie matter to rest, Sanei has confirmed that the offer of a reward still stands and has reportedly even offered to increase it. Within the government itself, about half of Khatami's cabinet is composed of such former "radicals" from the MRM and its allies. Other members are mostly long-time political hacks whose presence in the administration does not suggest the imminence of fundamental change.

As for Khatami himself, he and his objectives remain enigmatic. There is much to suggest that he has a genuine commitment to liberal values. Yet at no time has Khatami dared to question the basic dogmas of the Islamic Republic, and there is a worrying ambiguity in his famous slogan that the people "must believe" they control their destiny: Believing and actually having are two different things. His behavior has been equally ambiguous. He appeared genuinely alarmed by the explosion of discontent in July 1999 and seemed to buckle to the demands of the opposition. He has praised highly such unsavory figures as Mohammad-Ali Rajai, whom he actually managed to call "a model statesman," and Asad-Allah Lajevardi, the "Butcher of Evin." When the elderly Abbas Amir Entezam, a minister in the Bazargan administration who had finally been freed after seventeen years of detention as a political prisoner, criticized Khatami for making such comments about Lajevardi, a notorious torturer and murderer, he was promptly arrested and sent back to jail. While Khatami has highlighted many problems and controversies in the society, it cannot be said that he has done much as yet to resolve them. In terms of human rights issues and movement towards a "civil society," the situation has, if anything, deteriorated. Significantly, Khatami refused to meet with Mary Robinson, the UN commissioner on human rights, when she visited Iran in March 1999 and it became clear the issue of human rights was to be discussed. Even Khatami's much vaunted liberalization of the press has primarily had the effect of only making it much easier for the judiciary officials to identify critics and those who are lukewarm in their support for *velayat-e faqih* and proceed to arrest and imprison them. Despite Khatami's repeated speeches calling for freedom of the press, that judicial campaign has continued unabated, even after the removal of Yazdi, the "hard-liner" supposedly responsible for it. Khatami's own Ministry of Culture has supported and initiated such actions, including the arrest and trial of the only woman editor, Jaleh Oskui, so treated. As Masha-Allah Shamsolvaezin, the editor of *Neshat* who was sentenced in November 1999 to three years in prison, wryly put it, the problem in Khatami's Iran has become not so much freedom of expression as freedom *after* expression.

The most charitable view of all this is that Khatami is a genuine re-former who wants to work carefully within the system, who favors a gradualist approach, who avoids confrontation at all costs, and who has shrewdly given his opponents enough rope to hang themselves by ap-pearing reactionary, despotic, and violent. A more cynical view is that he is merely a cat's paw for an unrepentant regime that has used him and his election to allow the disaffected Iranian populace to blow off steam, to stall for time for the economy to improve, to blunt the appeal of the Mojahedin among young people and women, and to conclude economic deals with European governments by again providing them with the excuse of helping a "reformist." In any case, now that Khatami has a clear vote of support in the parliamentary elections and the eco-nomic gift of the highest oil prices in a decade, he is widely expected to start acting instead of talking about change. Otherwise, many will have to conclude that whatever his intentions, he is fundamentally weak and lacks the courage to deal with an absolutely ruthless opposition.

At the same time, any movement towards real change will raise the question of the reaction of Khamenei and the powerful institutions he controls. On the surface, Khamanei remains an extremely powerful fig-ure, shielded from any direct criticism. He has the right to dismiss Kha-tami if he wishes. His authority over the judiciary, the military, the Revolutionary Guards, the Basij, and other groups means he controls all the agencies of state coercion. There are, however, persistent rumors that his health is failing. In his speeches, he appears utterly isolated from reality, unable to rise above the use of worn-out and empty slogans and paranoid denunciation of foreign plots which make him sound like the "Uncle Napoleon" character in a famous Iranian comic novel. His tacit support of Nateq Nouri and most of his subsequent prouncements have left him identified, rightly or wrongly, with the "hard-line" faction. His occasional attempts to emulate Khomeini in giving support to both sides have simply left him looking weak and indecisive. The growing evidence implicating him in the assassination of dissidents abroad and at home has badly tarnished his image, as has the unmistakable impression that he is attempting to cover up his actions with a barrage of vehement anti-American and anti-Israeli rhetoric. It is particularly interesting that Aya-tollah Montazeri, whom Khamenei once said should be tried for treason, has recently been freed from house arrest, is again openly receiving vis-itors, and has become increasingly vocal in his statements in support of reform. Indeed, it was a speech of his on 14 November 1997, criticizing Khamenei for meddling and obstructionism and suggesting limitations on the authority of the Faqih, which led to the rapid escalation of the political conflict in Iran. He was immediately denounced by ayatollahs such as Yazdi and Meshkini, rioters attacked his home and offices in Qom, and the head of the Basij vowed to fight any plots against *velayat-e faqih*. However, a number of other senior ayatollahs have supported Montazeri, and there seems to be a definite effort underway to rehabilitate his reputation and raise his profile in public affairs. At least in theory, the Assembly of Experts could seek to remove Khamenei in favor of a new candidate such as Montazeri, but such a daring move might precipitate action by the paramilitary groups as well as bring the ideological foundation of the Islamic Republic into question.

Finally, there is the still unsettled question of just how far in the direction of genuine change Khatami and the reformists are willing to go or can go without provoking a violent conservative response. One of his ministers admitted that the government wanted to "let in a breeze" but not a storm. What then does it really mean to call for civil society, freedom of expression, and dialogue of civilizations? Judging from responses of spokesmen for the recently elected reformists, this does not extend far beyond legalizing satellite dish antennas or relaxing dress codes for women, permitting debate "within bounds" and jailing those who step outside them, shielding Iranian culture from criticism while heaping scorn on its adversaries, and denouncing "global arrogance" and interventionism while reserving Iran's own right to act abroad in support of the "oppressed."

The issues and expectations being raised at home and abroad go far beyond that. Is compliance with norms of "Islamic" behavior ultimately a matter of personal conscience, or does it remain a subject for state coercion? Does political sovereignty belong to the people, or is it restricted to the will of clerics? Is the principle of *velayat-e faqih* as it now exists beyond debate or change? Can there be political parties and truly free elections in which anyone, including those who question the system or even the Mojahedin, can compete? Will Iran engage in rational and responsible discourse with the United States and Israel, or will it continue to use them as scapegoats, objects of propaganda, and pretexts for adventurism? As Iran faces the 21st century, resolution of these difficult questions seems as remote as ever.

Notable People in the History of Iran

Abbas Mirza (1789–1833). Crown prince under Fath-Ali Shah; responsible for conduct of two wars with Russia; sought to reform and modernize the Iranian military.

Shah Abbas the Great (r. 1587–1629). Safavid monarch when the empire was at its zenith; established contacts with European powers; embellished Isfahan as the capital.

Abou Moslem Khorasani (d. 755). Iranian client of the Abbasid family; organized revolt in eastern Iran that established the Abbasid caliphate; later murdered by the caliph Mansour; various rebels attempted to avenge his death; became a figure of legendary significance in Iranian popular literature.

Abu'l-Hasan Ali b. Bouyeh, Emad-al-Dowleh (r. 932–949). Founder of an important independent principality in western Iran during period of disintegration of Abbasid caliphate.

Amir Kabir Mirza Taqi Khan (1807–1852). Most outstanding reformist minister in 19th century Iran; sought to improve or modernize the military, bureaucracy, economy, and educational system; overthrown and murdered as the result of political intrigues.

Ardashir Papakan (r. 224–240). Defeated Artabanus V, the last Parthian king; founder of Sasanian Empire.

Mohammad-Baqer Behbahani (d. 1792). Osuli Shi'ite religious scholar who decisively defeated the Akhbari sect and established the principle of the authority of the *mojtaheds*.

Cyrus the Great (600–530 B.C.). Founder of the Persian (Achaemenid) Empire; regarded as one of the most illustrious rulers of antiquity for his extensive conquests and benevolent rule.

Darius the Great (r. 522–486 B.C.). Third Achaemenid king; architect of the Achaemenid imperial system; sent the expedition to attack the Greeks at Marathon.

Shah Esmail (r. 1501–1524). Founder of the Safavid dynasty; head of the Safavid religious order and leader of the *qizilbash* forces; reunited Iran after the disintegration of the Turko-Mongol states; established Twelver Shi'ism as the official religion of the empire.

Abu'l-Qasem Ferdowsi (920–1020). Author of the *Shahnameh* (Book of Kings), a great epic poem that preserved the legends and much of the history of pre-Islamic Iran and symbolized for many the Iranian national spirit.

Abou Hamed Mohammad Ghazzali (1058–1111). Distinguished Iranian religious scholar, famous for his critique of philosophy and his reconciliation of Sufism and Sunni orthodoxy.

Hafez (d. 1389). The supreme master of Persian lyric poetry (the *ghazal*), usually on mystical or Sufi themes; his collection of poems (*Divan*) is often consulted for guidance in the way of divination or fortune-telling.

Hulegu (r. 1256–1265). Mongol conqueror of Iran and founder of Ilkhanid dynasty; killed the Abbasid caliph and destroyed Ismaili fortresses in Iran.

Karim Khan Zand (r. 1750–1779). Tribal chief from southern Iran who ruled most of the country after the death of Nader Shah; renowned for his clemency and just rule.

Ayatollah Rouhollah Khomeini (1902–1989). Most important Shi'ite religious figure of the 20th century; relentless opponent of the Pahlavi government from 1963 onward; popularized the idea of rule by a supreme Shi'ite jurist; architect of the Islamic Revolution and the guiding personality of the Islamic Republic.

Khosrow I Anushirvan (r. ca. 528–579). Suppressed the Mazdakites; reformed administrative structure of the Sasanian Empire; fought a major war with Rome and extended Iranian influence throughout the region; legendary for his attention to justice and good government.

Mahmoud of Ghazna (r. 998–1030). Turkish sultan who broke with the Samanids and became governor of Khorasan; fought numerous campaigns in India, gaining fame as a destroyer of Hindu temples; lavishly patronized literature, art, and the sciences.

Mazdak (fl. 485–523). Radical religious reformer in late Sasanian Iran; advocated redistribution of wealth and holding women, children, and material goods as common property of the community.

Mithridates I (r. 161–138 B.C.). Founder of the Parthian Empire; captured Seleucia (Ctesiphon).

Mohammad-Reza Shah Pahlavi (1919–1980). Second and last shah of the Pahlavi dynasty; restored to power after overthrow of Mosaddeq; launched ambitious social reforms in the "White Revolution" and led a drive for higher oil prices in a bid to make Iran a major power in the Middle East; forced out of the country during the Islamic Revolution.

Mirza Hosayn Khan Moshir-al-Dowleh (1828–1881). Qajar diplomat in Bombay, Tbilisi, and Istanbul; appointed prime minister in 1871 and was responsible for encouraging Naser-al-Din Shah to visit Europe and begin a new period of reform; dismissed after cancellation of Reuter Concession in 1873 but held various other posts down to the time of his death.

Mohammad Mosaddeq (1882–1967). Prime minister who led the movement for the nationalization of the Anglo-Iranian Oil Company in 1951; overthrown by an American- and British-backed coup in 1953; the greatest political hero of the liberal and secular nationalists in Iran.

Nader Shah Afshar (r. 1736–1747). General who took over the Safavid Empire and became the new shah; ambitious ruler who tried to unify the country, expand its borders, promote trade, and reconcile Shi'ism and Sunnism.

Nasr II b. Ahmad (r. 914–943). One of the greatest Samanid princes; assisted by the famous ministers Jayhani and Balami; reign marked by spread of Ismaili Shi'ism and revival of Persian literature.

Nezam-al-Molk (1018–1092). Most famous vizier during the Seljuk period; advisor to Alp Arslan and Malekshah; author of a classic Persian treatise on the art of government.

Reza Shah Pahlavi (1878–1944). Officer in the Cossack Brigade and leader of the 1921 coup that led to the overthrow of the Qajar monarchy; as shah, he promoted Iranian nationalism and numerous social and economic reforms; forced to abdicate by British and Soviet forces in 1941.

Jalal-al-Din Roumi (1207–1273). Persian poet who lived most of his life in Seljuk Anatolia; author of the *Masnavi*, perhaps the greatest of all Sufi poems; founder of the Mevlevi Sufi order.

Mosleh-al-Din Sadi (1193–1292). Popular Persian poet, author of the *Boustan* (Garden) and *Golestan* (Flower Garden), which present in prose and verse short, simple, didactic stories on various moral and ethical topics.

Shapur I (r. 240–271). Enlarged Sasanian Empire; captured the Roman emperor Valerian.

Ali Shariati (1933–1977). Influential lecturer and writer who helped lay the foundations for the revival of militant Shi'ism in Iranian politics;

especially popular with young people, students, and religious-oriented socialists.

Zoroaster (fl. ca. 1100 B.C.?). Ancient Iranian prophet and religious reformer; introduced worship of Ahura Mazda.

Glossary

ahura: one of two types of divinities in ancient Iranian religion (*see also daeva*); in Zoroastrianism, these divinities were consolidated in the form of the supreme god, Ahura Mazda.

anjoman: an informal club or group as well as a professional society or association; numerous political organizations of this type were formed in the late 19th and early 20th centuries and were deeply involved in the events of the Constitutional Era.

Avesta: the name given to the collected scriptures of the Zoroastrian religion, originally said to include twenty-one "books." The extant Avesta consists of six texts and a group of fragments, which include hymns, liturgical material, laws, etc.

Ayatollah (sign of God): a term which since the 1930s has supplanted *mojtahed* as the honorary title of a high-ranking Shi'ite religious authority in Iran.

b.: a conventional abbreviation for the Arabic word *ebn* (son [of]) used in traditional name patterns which included the genealogy of an individual.

chador: the large, formless cloth, usually black, customarily worn by women when they go out in public, draped over and around them to cover all but part of the face. It is regarded by some as a patent symbol of the segregation and oppression of women, by others as a benign or desirable feature of authentic Islamic and Iranian culture.

daeva: a category of deities, mostly personifications of heavenly bodies and natural forces, in the ancient Indo-Iranian religion; veneration of the *daevas* was emphatically rejected by Zoroaster, who regarded them as demons.

dehqan: a social class in Sasanian and early Islamic times that held small landed estates and provided military service; the *dehqans* also came to perform important administrative duties and helped preserve the cultural traditions of pre-Islamic Iran. In later periods, the term usually means simply peasant.

faqih, Faqih: one who has mastered the sources and methods of jurisprudence (*feqh*) needed to determine the *sharia* (Islamic religious law). Ayatollah Khomeini developed the idea that one supremely qualified jurist could exercise legitimate authority in an Islamic state; the constitution of the Islamic Republic of Iran established the office of Faqih in accordance with this theory and invested it with the greatest power of any governmental institution. *See also velayat-e faqih.*

fatva: the written opinion of an Islamic religious scholar given in response to a formal request by a Muslim layman for an answer to a question concerning a religious matter or practice about which the petitioner is uncertain.

foqaha: plural of *faqih*.

gholam (plural: *ghelman* or *gholaman*): literally, young man or page; usually applied in Iran to slaves or men of slave origin used for military purposes or as a royal bodyguard (the idea being that the lack of other tribal or ethnic ties in the society would make them more loyal to the ruler).

gholat: an "extremist" form of Shi'ite Islam characterized by one or more beliefs regarded by most Muslims as heretical and beyond acceptability (e.g., reincarnation or transmigration of souls, attribution of divine qualities to human leaders, etc.).

Hojjat-ol-Eslam: honorary title for a rank in the Shi'ite clerical hierarchy below that of ayatollah but higher than a simple *molla* or *akhound*.

Imam (Emam): an Arabic word with several technical meanings; used in Twelver Shi'ism to denote the twelve individuals regarded as the successive legitimate, sinless, and infallible leaders of the religious community.

Ismaili Shi'ism: one of the three major divisions of Shi'ism, along with the Zaydi and Twelver forms, differing on the individuals recognized as Imams and in many doctrinal matters as well. Ismailis established the Fatimid caliphate in North Africa and Egypt and were particularly active in Iran from the 9th to 13th centuries. The Nezaris, an offshoot of the Fatimid Ismailis, had several strongholds in mountain castles in medieval Iran (the so-called Assassins) and followed various leaders down to Agha Khan Mahallati, who transferred the Ismaili imamate to India in 1843.

madhhab (Arabic word, pronounced *mazhab* in Persian): one of the formal "schools" of law in Islam; the rite or system followed by an individual believer.

Majles: a consultative assembly or legislative body; recognized in the constitutions of 20th century Iran as the national parliament but generally constrained in the exercise of true legislative autonomy by either royal power or review by outside bodies to assure conformity with Islamic laws and values.

marzban: title of the military governor of a province during the Sasanian period.

Mazdayasnian: Mazda worshippers; another name for Zoroastrians.

mojtahed: an Islamic religious scholar who has competence to practice *ejtehad*, or independent judgment on religious matters. The *mojtaheds* were particularly important for providing religious leadership to Twelver Shi'ites during the occultation of the Hidden Imam and played an influential role in Iranian affairs from the Safavid period onward.

molla: a Persianized form of the Arabic word *mawla* (master), used as a term of respect (or sometimes scorn) for someone who has completed the minimal amount of formal study to be considered a religious scholar. In Iran, the differentiation of such individuals from lay believers is indicated by a distinctive dress and other indications of social status which make the *molla*s the equivalent of a clergy or spiritual class (*rouhaniyyat*).

The term is more or less equivalent to *akhound*, although the latter is even more likely to be used in a pejorative sense.

qanat: a type of irrigation system widely used in traditional Iran; it consists of a subterranean canal joining vertical shafts and carrying water by gravity feed from a remote source at a higher elevation to the point of use.

qizilbash: Turkoman tribesmen who professed an extreme (*gholat*) form of Shi'ism, particularly those who became fanatical supporters of the sheikhs of the Safavid religious order; they formed one of the main components of the Safavid military institution. It was originally a pejorative term used by their opponents, meaning "red-heads," to refer to the distinctive twelve-pleated red hat they wore in commemoration of the twelve Imams and their allegiance to the Safavids.

shah, shahanshah: king, king of kings; the typical title of pre-Islamic Iranian rulers. It was revived by some medieval Perso-Islamic dynasties and was routinely used from the Safavid period onward. The *Shahnameh*, or "Book of Kings," is the collection of semi-legendary stories about the pre-Islamic shahs which make up the Iranian national epic.

Shi'ism: a general term used to denote several sectarian divisions in the Islamic religion, the most common feature of which is that their adherents attribute special political and/or religious authority to descendants of the Prophet Mohammad. *See also gholat*; Imam; Ismaili Shi'ism; Twelver Shi'ism.

taarof: politeness, deference, civility, *savoir faire*; usually used to denote an elaborate and formalized system of discourse in social interaction which depends heavily on the relative social status of those involved in the exchange.

taqiyya: prudence or caution; an Islamic legal concept which allows normal religious obligations to be suspended or even violated in cases of danger or duress. Both it and its opposite (a zeal for martyrdom) have been deeply ingrained among Shi'ites, who suffered frequent persecution as a religious minority; many routinely practice such dissimulation even in the absence of any obvious threat.

Twelver (or Imami) **Shi'ism**: the variety of Shi'ism prevalent in Iran since the 16th century. It recognizes a sequence of twelve legitimate Imams, beginning with the Prophet Mohammad's cousin and son-in-law,

Ali b. Abi Taleb, and ending with the messianic figure of the Twelfth or Hidden Imam, who went into a complete concealment (*ghaybat*, occultation) in 941, but who is still alive and will someday reappear to complete the triumph of Shi'ism in the world.

velayat-e faqih: a concept developed in the writings of Ayatollah Khomeini, holding that legitimate political authority may be held by a meritorious Shi'ite religious scholar. The doctrine has been incorporated into the constitution of the Islamic Republic of Iran and constitutes the foundation of its political theory.

Bibliographic Essay

The literature relevant to the history of Iran is vast. This survey is confined to works in English and to books that are likely to be of the most interest and use to general readers. Articles that have appeared in journals, though often of fundamental importance for their subjects, have not been included. The many translations of original sources that have been published have also been omitted. For more extensive listings of such materials, readers may refer to one of the specialized bibliographical works that are readily available: J. D. Pearson, *A Bibliography of Pre-Islamic Persia* (London: Mansell, 1975); *Index Islamicus* (various publishers; now on CD-ROM; London: Bowker-Saur, 1998); Shoko Okazaki, *Bibliography on Qajar Persia* (Osaka: Osaka University of Foreign Studies, 1985); Arnold Wilson, *A Bibliography of Persia* (Oxford: Clarendon Press, 1930); L. P. Elwell-Sutton, *A Guide to Iranian Area Study* (Ann Arbor: ACLS, 1952); G. Handley-Taylor, *Bibliography of Iran* (Chicago: St. James Press, 1969); Hafez F. Farman [sic], *Iran: A Selected and Annotated Bibliography* (New York: Greenwood Press, 1968); Sirus Ghani, *Iran and the West: A Critical Bibliography* (New York: K. Paul, 1987); *A Selective Bibliography of Islam and Iran, 1950–1987* (Tehran: Ministry of Guidance and Islamic Culture, 1989).

Two comprehensive reference works are of the utmost value for all fields of Iranian history: the *Cambridge History of Iran* (7 vols.; Cambridge: Cambridge University Press, 1968–1991) and Ehsan Yarshater, ed., *Encyclopaedia Iranica* (by various publishers and in course of publication; it is in 9 vols. up to the letter "F"). The latter can sometimes be supplemented by the *Encyclopaedia of Islam* (Leiden: Brill, 1960–in progress). For a general survey of history, Percy Sykes, *A History of Persia* (3rd ed.; London: Macmillan, 1951), is still useful. Recent periods are covered in Peter Avery, *Modern Iran* (New York: Praeger, 1965). Art history is treated exhaustively in Arthur Upham Pope, *A Survey of Persian Art from Prehistoric Times to the Present* (16 vols., 3rd ed.; Tehran: Shahbanu Farah Foundation, 1977). For literary history, see Jan Rypka et al., *History of Persian Literature* (Dordrecht: D. Reidel, 1968); Ehsan Yarshater, ed., *Persian Literature* (Albany: Bibliotheca Persica, 1988); and the classic work of E. G. Browne, *A Literary History of Persia* (4 vols.; Cambridge: Cambridge University Press, 1925–1928).

Several good surveys deal with Achaemenid or pre-Islamic Iran, including Richard N. Frye, *The Heritage of Persia* (New York: New American Library, 1963); R. Ghirshman, *Iran: From the Earliest Times to the Islamic Conquest* (New York: Penguin, 1954); Josef Wiesehofer, *Ancient Persia* (London: I. B. Tauris, 1996); M. A. Dandamaev, *The Culture and Institutions of Ancient Iran* (Cambridge: Cambridge University Press, 1989); idem, *A Political History of the Achaemenid Empire* (Leiden: Brill, 1989); A. T. Olmstead, *History of the Persian Empire: Achaemenid Period* (Chicago: University of Chicago Press, 1948), is seriously dated in several respects but still worth reading. On Zoroastrianism and Iranian religion, Mary Boyce, *A History of Zoroastrianism* (Leiden: Brill, 1975), and R. C. Zaehner, *Dawn and Twilight of Zoroastrianism* (London: Weidenfeld and Nicolson, 1961), are particularly interesting and informative.

Most works dealing with the period from the Islamic conquest to the Mongols do not focus specifically on Iran but treat it as part of a larger or more general history. A notable exception is the concise, readable, and up-to-date survey by David Morgan, *Medieval Persia, 1040–1797* (New York: Longman, 1988). Fundamental for an understanding of the socioeconomic history of this period and beyond is A. K. S. Lambton, *Landlord and Peasant in Persia: A Study of Land Tenure and Land Revenue Administration* (London: Oxford University Press, 1969). A refreshingly different approach to the history of this period may be found in Peter Christensen, *The Decline of Iranshahr: Irrigation and Environments in the History of the Middle East, 500 B.C. to A.D. 1500* (Copenhagen: Museum Tusculanum Press, 1993). See also V. V. Barthold, *Turkestan down to the Mongol Invasion*

(3rd ed.; London: Luzac, 1968); Elton L. Daniel, *The Political and Social History of Khurasan under Abbasid Rule, 747–820* (Minneapolis: Bibliotheca Islamica, 1979); Roy Mottahedeh, *Loyalty and Leadership in an Early Islamic Society* (Princeton: Princeton University Press, 1980), a social history of the Buyids; R. N. Frye, *The Golden Age of Persia: The Arabs in the East* (London: Weidenfeld and Nicolson, 1975); idem, *Bukhara: The Medieval Achievement* (Norman: University of Oklahoma Press, 1965); idem, *The Heritage of Central Asia from Antiquity to the Turkish Expansion* (Princeton: Markus Weiner, 1996). For religious developments and Shi'ism in general, see Wilferd Madelung, *Religious Trends in Early Islamic Iran* (Albany: Bibliotheca Persica, 1988); Heinz Halm, *Shiism* (Edinburgh: Edinburgh University Press, 1991); M. Momen, *An Introduction to Shi'i Islam* (New Haven: Yale University Press, 1985). An attempt to shed new light on the problem of conversion to Islam may be found in Richard Bulliet, *Conversion to Islam in the Medieval Period: An Essay in Quantitative History* (Cambridge, Mass.: Harvard University Press, 1979). The same author explored the social dynamics of a Muslim city in Iran in *The Patricians of Nishapur: A Study in Medieval Islamic Social History* (Cambridge, Mass.: Harvard University Press, 1972).

On the period from the Mongols to the Qajars, see David Morgan, *The Mongols* (Oxford: Blackwells, 1986); M. G. S. Hodgson, *The Order of Assassins* (Leiden: Brill, 1955); H. Hookham, *Tamburlaine the Conqueror* (London: Hodder and Stoughton, 1962); Beatrice Manz, *The Rise and Rule of Tamerlane* (Cambridge: Cambridge University Press, 1989); John Woods, *The Aqquyunlu: Clan, Confederation, Empire* (Minneapolis: Bibliotheca Islamica, 1976); Roger Savory, *Iran under the Safavids* (Cambridge: Cambridge University Press, 1980); Michel Mazzaoui, *The Origins of the Safavids* (Wiesbaden: F. Steiner, 1972); Laurence Lockhart, *The Fall of the Safavid Dynasty and the Afghan Occupation of Persia* (Cambridge: Cambridge University Press, 1958); idem, *Nadir Shah: A Critical Study* (London: Luzac, 1938); John R. Perry, *Karim Khan Zand: A History of Iran, 1774–1779* (Chicago: University of Chicago Press, 1979).

For a general history of the early Qajar period, Robert Grant Watson, *A History of Persia* (London: Smith, Elder, 1866), remains well worth reading. There is now a thorough biographical study of an important Qajar ruler in Abbas Amanat, *Pivot of the Universe: Nasir al-Din Shah Qajar and the Iranian Monarchy, 1831–1896* (Berkeley: University of California Press, 1997). George Curzon, *Persia and the Persian Question* (2 vols.; repr. London: Frank Cass, 1966), even if rather biased and self-serving, remains a mine of information on the Qajar period. The framework of Qajar foreign policy and contacts with the European powers may be found in Edward Ingram, *Britain's Persian Connection, 1798–1828* (Oxford: Clarendon Press, 1992); Rose Greaves, *Persia and the Defence of India, 1884–1892* (London: Athlone Press, 1959); and F. Kazemzadeh, *Russia and Britain in Persia, 1864–1914* (New Haven: Yale University Press, 1968). Questions of popular dissent, rebellion, and relations of state and religion are treated in Hamid Algar, *Religion and State in Iran, 1785–1906* (Berkeley: University of California Press, 1969); Nikki Keddie, *Religion and Rebellion in Iran: The Tobacco Protest of 1891–1892* (London: Cass, 1966); Mangol Bayat, *Mysticism and Dissent: Socioreligious Thought in Qajar Iran* (Syracuse, N.Y.: Syracuse University Press, 1982); Abbas Amanat, *Resurrection and Renewal: The Making of the Babi Movement in Iran, 1844–1850* (Ithaca: Cornell University Press, 1989); and Denis MacEoin, *The Sources for Early Babi Doctrine and History* (Leiden: Brill, 1992). On Qajar administration, society, economy, intellectual developments, and reform, see Shaul Bakhash, *Iran: Monarchy, Bureaucracy and Reform under the Qajars* (London: Ithaca Press, 1978); Charles Issawi, ed., *The Economic History of Iran, 1800–1914* (Chicago: University of Chicago Press, 1971); A. Reza Sheikholeslami, *The Structure of Central Authority in Qajar Iran, 1871–1896* (Atlanta: Scholars Press, 1997); Guity Nashat, *The Origins of Modern Reform in Iran, 1870–80* (Urbana: University of Illinois Press, 1982); and Hamid Algar, *Mirza Malkum Khan* (Berkeley: University of California Press, 1973). A wonderful sampling of Qajar art and art history may be found in Layla S. Diba, ed., *Royal Persian Paintings: The Qajar Era* (London: I. B. Tauris, 1998).

On the constitutional period, see Janet Afary, *The Iranian Constitutional Revolution, 1906–1911* (New York: Columbia University Press, 1996); Mangol Bayat, *Iran's First Revolution: Shi'ism and the Constitutional Revolution of 1905–1909* (New York: Oxford University Press, 1991); and E. G. Browne, *The Persian Revolution of 1905–1909* (London: Cambridge University Press, 1910); and R. McDaniel, *The Shuster Mission and the Persian Constitutional Revolution* (Minneapolis: Bibliotheca Islamica, 1974). W. Morgan Shuster tells the gripping story of his involvement in Iran in *The Strangling of Persia* (New York: Century, 1912).

The most thorough, albeit uneven, survey of 20th century history is Ervand Abrahamian, *Iran Between Two Revolutions* (Princeton: Princeton University Press, 1982). George Lenczowski, ed., *Iran under the Pahlavis* (Stanford: Hoover Institute, 1978), is a rather laudatory collection of essays, concentrating on the late Pahlavi period. The best book currently available in English on the events after World War I is Cyrus Ghani, *Iran and the Rise of Reza Shah: From Qajar Collapse to Pahlavi Rule* (London: I. B. Tauris, 1998); see also Stephanie Cronin, *The Army and the Creation of the Pahlavi State in Iran, 1910–1926* (London: Tauris Academic Studies, 1997). On the reform policies of Reza Shah, see Amin Banani, *The Modernization of Iran, 1921–1941* (Stanford: Stanford University Press, 1961). Also of interest for the early Pahlavi period are Hassan Arfa, *Under Five Shahs* (London: John Murray, 1964), and Donald Wilbur, *Riza Shah Pahlavi, 1878–1944* (Hicksville, N.Y.: Exposition Press, 1975).

On the Cold War and Mossadeq periods, see Bruce Kuniholm, *The Origins of the Cold War in the Middle East* (Princeton: Princeton University Press, 1980); George Lenczowski, *Russia and the West in Iran, 1918–48* (Ithaca: Cornell University Press, 1949); James F. Goode, *The United States and Iran: In the Shadow of Musaddiq* (New York: St. Martin's, 1997); and James A. Bill and William Roger Louis, *Musaddiq, Iranian Nationalism, and Oil* (Austin: University of Texas Press, 1988). Farhad Diba, *Mohammad Mossadegh: A Political Biography* (London: Croom Helm, 1986), is mostly interesting as an example of Mosaddeq hagiography; an account by an architect of his overthrow, Kermit Roosevelt, *Countercoup: The Struggle for the Control of Iran* (New York: McGraw-Hill, 1979), at least has the merit of being entertaining reading.

For the Mohammad-Reza Shah period, one might start with his own memoirs: *Mission for My Country* (London: Hutchinson, 1961) and *Answer to History* (New York: Stein and Day, 1980). They might well be contrasted with Asadollah Alam, *The Shah and I: The Confidential Diary of Iran's Royal Court, 1969–1977* (New York: St. Martin's, 1992). Critical accounts include Fred Halliday, *Iran: Dictatorship and Development* (New York: Penguin Books, 1979), and Robert Graham, *Iran: The Illusion of Power* (New York: St. Martin's, 1979). A fine study of women's issues during this and other periods is Parvin Paidar, *Women and the Political Process in Twentieth-Century Iran* (Cambridge: Cambridge University Press, 1995).

For the ideology of dissent in the Pahlavi period and the role of the clergy, see Shahrough Akhavi, *Religion and Politics in Contemporary Iran: Clergy-State Relations in the Pahlavi Period* (Albany: State University of New York Press, 1980); Said Arjomand, *The Shadow of God and the Hidden Imam* (Chicago: University of Chicago Press, 1984); Nikki R. Keddie, ed., *Religion and Politics in Iran: Shi'ism from Quietism to Revolution* (New Haven: Yale University Press, 1983); Michael Fisher, *Iran: From Religious Dispute to Revolution* (Cambridge, Mass.: Harvard University Press, 1980); Hamid Algar, trans., *Islam and Revolution: Writings and Declarations of*

Imam Khomeini (Berkeley: Mizan Press, 1981); M. R. Ghanoonparvar, *In a Persian Mirror: Images of the West and Westerners in Iranian Fiction* (Austin: University of Texas Press, 1993); and Ali Gheissari, *Iranian Intellectuals in the 20th Century* (Austin: University of Texas Press, 1998).

The Islamic Revolution in Iran will undoubtedly be a central topic of historical debate for years to come. Current accounts vary widely in interpretation and detail; a representative sampling includes Jahangir Amuzegar, *The Dynamics of the Iranian Revolution: The Pahlavis' Triumph and Tragedy* (Albany: State University of New York Press, 1991); Said Amir Arjomand, *The Turban for the Crown: The Islamic Revolution in Iran* (New York: Oxford University Press, 1988); Misagh Parsa, *Social Origins of the Iranian Revolution* (New Brunswick, N.J.: Rutgers University Press, 1989); Ferydoun Hoveyda, *The Fall of the Shah* (London: Weidenfeld and Nicolson, 1979); Hossein Bashiriyeh, *The State and Revolution in Iran* (London: Croom Helm, 1984); and Abbas Milani, *Persian Sphinx: Amir Abbas Hoveyda and the Riddle of the Iranian Revolution* (Washington, D.C.: Mage, 2000).

On U.S.-Iranian relations in particular, see Gary Sick, *All Fall Down: America's Tragic Encounter with Iran* (New York: Random House, 1985); Robert E. Huyser, *Mission to Tehran* (New York: Harper and Row, 1986); Michael Ledeen and William Lewis, *Debacle: The American Failure in Iran* (New York: Random House, 1981); and Barry Rubin, *Paved with Good Intentions: The American Experience in Iran* (Oxford: Oxford University Press, 1982).

For the early years of the Islamic Republic, an excellent study is Shaul Bakhash, *The Reign of the Ayatollahs: Iran and the Islamic Revolution* (London: I. B. Tauris, 1985). Other titles dealing with various aspects of the republican period that can be recommended include Ervand Abrahamian, *Khomeinism: Essays on the Islamic Republic* (Berkeley: University of California Press, 1993); Saeed Rahnema and Sohrab Behdad, *Iran after the Revolution: Crisis of an Islamic State* (London: I. B. Tauris, 1995); Cheryl Benard and Zalmay Khalilzad, *The Government of God: Iran's Islamic Republic* (New York: Columbia University Press, 1984); Anoushiravan Ehteshami, *After Khomeini: The Iranian Second Republic* (London: Routledge, 1995); Jahangir Amuzegar, *Iran's Economy under the Islamic Republic* (London: I. B. Tauris, 1993); Tareq Ismael, *Iraq and Iran: Roots of Conflict* (Syracuse, N.Y.: Syracuse University Press, 1982); Dilip Hiro, *The Longest War: The Iran-Iraq Military Conflict* (London: Routledge, 1991); idem, *Iran under the Ayatollahs* (London: Routledge, 1985); Robin Wright, *In the Name of God: The Khomeini Decade* (New York: Simon and Schuster, 1989); Ruhollah K. Ramazani, *Revolutionary Iran: Challenge and Response in the Middle East* (Baltimore: Johns Hopkins University Press, 1986); Barry Rosen, ed., *Iran since the Revolution* (New York: Columbia University Press, 1985); Antony Cordesman and Ahmed Hashim, *Iran: Dilemmas of Dual Containment* (Boulder: Westview, 1997); Shireen Hunter, *Iran and the World: Continuity in a Revolutionary Decade* (Bloomington: Indiana University Press, 1990); and Asghar Schirazi, *The Constitution of Iran: Politics and State in the Islamic Republic* (London: I.B. Tauris, 1998).

Index

About the Author

Elton L. Daniel is Professor of History at the University of Hawaii at Manoa and serves as Associate Editor of the *Encyclopedia Iranica* at Columbia University. He has conducted research in Iran, Turkey, Syria, Egypt, France, and the United Kingdom and has traveled extensively throughout the Middle East. He has published books and articles on the history of early Islamic Iran, 19th-century Persian travel literature, and a revised translation of Ghazzali's *Alchemy of Happiness*.